THE SPIRIT OF CORNWALL
A Star Original

The Spirit of Cornwall

Denys Val Baker

A STAR BOOK

published by
the Paperback Division of
W. H. ALLEN & Co. Ltd

A Star Book
Published in 1980
by the Paperback Division of
W. H. Allen & Co. Ltd
A Howard and Wyndham Company
44 Hill Street, London W1X 8LB

Printed in Great Britain by
Richard Clay (The Chaucer Press) Ltd
Bungay, Suffolk

ISBN 0 352 307498

Contents

v

Introduction

Cornwall, or the Kingdom of Kernow as it is sometimes known among a growing band of Cornish Nationalists, has probably inspired more books than any other English county, and quite as many as Wales and Scotland. Here perhaps lies an explanation: Cornwall strikes even the most superficial observer as something rather more than a mere county — it is a place apart, a country of its own. From this angle Cornwall becomes that much easier to interpret and explain; yet when all is said and done, a great deal remains that is elusive and mysterious, lost among those dim memories of past ages which permeate the windswept desolation of Bodmin Moor or the craggy haunted cliffs of Land's End. It is a strange, powerful and literally physical force.

What then is the secret, the spirit of Cornwall? This book is an attempt to provide a fresh answer to that deceptively simple question. Ever since nearly forty years ago when I came to live in Cornwall, I have been fascinated not merely by the place itself, but in particular by the tremendous amount of creative work going on within its boundaries. After living in various parts of the county — in a castle at Portquin, a converted cowshed on the side of Trencrom Hill, a haunted cottage at Sennen Cove, an old vicarage at St Hilary, a beach house at St Ives, a creekside house on the River Fowey, and now an old mill house in the Penberth Valley — I have come to realise the strong if often subterranean link between Cornwall and its creativity. As a Welshman and a fellow Celt, and as a writer, I have of course been particularly sensitised to the whole subject; but you need be neither a Celt nor an artist to be aware of the strange and compelling powers embedded in Cornwall's granite body. Ask almost any holidaymaker why he has come to Cornwall — more importantly why he comes back again and again as is so often the case — and you will get the same vague answer. And I fear, I am able to provide no more myself in this book. After all, if Cornwall could be explained, it would cease to be Cornwall.

Nevertheless, I believe that a major clue to the meaning of the spirit of Cornwall lies in its creativity. When some three decades back I founded the regional literary magazine, *The Cornish Review,* I did so because of my growing awareness of certain unusual qualities about Cornwall which attracted so many creative artists. During its lifetime *The Cornish Review* published works of art and literature remarkable both for their variety and high standard, which went far beyond the normal level to be found in any other English county. For this book I have drawn heavily upon extracts and quotations from the *Review* because I could indeed hardly wish for better evidence. I have also endeavoured to take back the reader into the past as well, showing how many great artists from a wide range of fields have been just as influenced by Cornwall in other centuries. The names sound like a roll-call of fame — Tennyson, Hardy, Dickens, Turner, Du Maurier, Betjeman, Hepworth, Rowse — although I have also quoted from many lesser known artists because fame has little to do with the matter. What intrigues me is *why* does Cornwall effect creative people so profoundly? What alchemy is present that so stirs the creative spirit?

In the hope that answers to these questions may help to a fuller understanding of one of the most fascinating parts of the United Kingdom, I present this personal interpretation of the 'spirit of Cornwall'.

Denys Val Baker

Chapter One

The Mysterious Place

*Whenever I cross the River Tamar, journeying East or West, I am
surprised afresh that one of the world's least penetrable frontiers
should be made evident by so small a width of water.*

W. GORE ALLEN

Although officially included in the country known as England,
Cornwall can hardly be said to be part of that country. Down
through the centuries Cornwall has remained notably and
stubbornly different, a mysterious place of its own. It would
surely be difficult to conjure up much romantic excitement
about, say, 'going to Essex' or 'going to Bedfordshire' — yet to
this day there remains an intangible yet very real romanticism
about 'going to Cornwall'. It is going west, towards the sun,
into the strange land of Lyonesse, into another world.

Of course, it is not really surprising that there should exist a
sharp difference between the Cornish and their nearest
neighbours, for the simple fact is that with their Celtic
background the Cornish have far less in common with the
English than they have, for example, with their cousins in
Wales, Scotland or Ireland. What is even more interesting is
that this similarity goes beyond character and human
personality and extends even into the very structure of the land

1

itself. If you want to find cliffs like the Cornish cliffs, moorlands like the Cornish moorlands, hills as lonely and bleak as the Cornish hills, then you will find them not in Bucks or Berks, Surrey or Suffolk — but in the Western Isles of Scotland, among the mountainous regions of Snowdonia, on the Atlantic-washed shores of Ireland. And just as those regions are famous for their romantic historical associations, so Cornwall, too, is impregnated with great legends: King Arthur and his Knights, Tristan and Iseult, the lost land of Lyonesse. Perhaps it is not irrelevant that it was from Cornwall there sprang the last rebellion on English soil, the Western Rising of 1549.

Cornwall, in the face of all the mass centralisation of our modern society, has managed to remain a place apart. There are some people who believe that if only the Cornish language had been preserved for everyday use, then the county might have attained an independence to compare with that of Wales, Scotland and Ireland. Impressive efforts are now being made to spread a knowledge of the old Cornish language, and there is a thriving nationalist party, *Mebyon Kernow*. But surely this is rather to miss the whole point: Cornwall does not need to create differences to emphasise its apartness from the rest of England. It *is* apart, solidly and unmistakably, and in the fullest geographical sense. Even its position of being the most westerly of all English counties at once puts it, quite literally, 'out on a limb'. No other English county has such a long coastline — in no other English county are even the most inland areas so close to the sea. Surrounded and impregnated by the sea in this unique way, Cornwall inevitably becomes apart, different from the rest of England. After all we have only to remember the fabulous legend of Lyonesse — that vast area of forest land between Cornwall and the Isles of Scilly which was, as John Norden wrote in his *Speculi Britanniae Pars* in 1584, 'swallowed up by the devouring sea'. This derives from something more firm than fantasy: there are in

2

fact numerous records of submarine forests all around the Cornish coast. For instance, a diarist noted in 1777 that in South East Cornwall 'between Ramehead and Looe there is to be seen on a clear day in the bottom of the sea, a league from the shore, a whole wood of timber on its side, uncorrupted.' A submarine forest *does* lie off Looe, in Milandreath Bay, and when heavy seas strip away the sand, tree trunks become visible, reddish and decayed.

Here we come close to the true identification of Cornwall. It combines romance and reality, myth and matter, fantasy and fact in an extraordinarily forceful way. The reasons that most people are so strongly affected by Cornwall is that they have in front of their very eyes all the physical evidence for the mystery and magic that at once so enthrals and troubles them. It is one thing to read as romantic fiction old stories about the Cornish giants of Trencrom and St Michael's Mount, who used to toss rocks at one another with the same ease as a child might throw a pebble, but then climb to the top of Trencrom Hill, look around the ground positively studded with huge boulders lying just as they might have done if thrown from a distance, and you might begin to wonder. An interesting comment on this subject was once made by the folklore writer and historian, A.F.C. Hillstead:

Let us consider the tales of the Cornish giants. To the foreigner they are no more than fairy tales for nought else than entertainment. To the student, however, they offer romance tempered with reality. There are too many stories of Cornish giants not to have a significance greater than mere fiction. Indeed, we may well ask why so many? I seek no further than symbolism for the answer. Cornwall is a land of extremes. Its people are both fair and dark and one sees many of immense stature. In its sheltered valleys there is a vegetation so luxurious that we are reminded of the semi-tropical regions. On the other hand winter brings to the bleak uplands winds like whetted knives. There are sandy bays lapped by the mildest of seas and mighty granite bastions whose feet are forever snarled and fretted by the suck

3

and surge of Atlantic waves. Therefore is it not natural that these opposing features should have been symbolised by giants? Giants who spread devastation in the manner of a tidal wave and yet were known to have moments when they played like normal boys and girls.

It is not difficult to find examples of the way in which Cornwall can provide proof to support its myths. Who, for instance, standing beside the waters of the strange and lonely Dozmary Pool on Bodmin Moor, would have much problem in imagining an arm rising through the waters of the lake to clutch the jewelled hilt of the magic sword, Excalibur? Some years ago I lived in a small castle on the cliffs of Portquin, on the North coast of Cornwall, and it was there that I learned how the entire local fishing fleet once sank around the jagged rocky coast, and that the anguished cries of the drowning men could often be heard above the sound of the waves. Was it entirely my imagination that sometimes, as the sun lowered in the sky and a grey seething swell came booming in, I did indeed hear forlorn voices? Who can say? Does it really matter? The cliffs, the rocks, the majestic seas — against such a background disasters of dramatic proportions are entirely conceivable. A mist of the distant past hovers over Cornwall and anything can happen.

Even then, from a geographical standpoint, Cornwall provides evidence to justify the theme of this book. Although much of the mystery and brooding sense of the past must often be perceived by instinct nevertheless we can see in the very landscape itself, and more especially from the sea-washed coastline, something of that which so intrigues the visitor. It has been said, for instance, that the cliffs from Treryn Dinas to Land's End, most of them now under National Trust ownership, are the most beautiful in Great Britain. As beautiful as the cliffs themselves are some of the rock formations at their feet, rocks that sometimes seem almost sentient in their attitudes, hence the nicknames, the 'Armed Knight', the 'Shark's Fin', 'Dr Syntax'. There is a sense of grim unrelenting battle about this stretch of Land's End coastline. Even on a hot cloudless day in June the sea never gives the impression of being quite at peace. The waves lapping around the salt-flecked rocks, splashing the seagulls and cormorants, have an angry irritable flick to them, the rocks and the cliffs themselves carry that same sense of inward seething and strength. They are alien to 20th century civilisation; they belong to an immense and imponderable past.

From Mousehole you can walk all the way to Land's End: over the cliffs, dropping down into picturesque Lamorna Cove and then up and down again into tiny Penberth and over the cliffs again past Logan Rock down to Porthcurno, home of Cornwall's whitest sands and the cable station to America: Then on past the unique Minack Theatre, incredibly hewn out of the sheer granite sides of the cliff; past St Levan Church and through the tiny fishing village of Porthgwarra, where the way to the sea leads through a hole in the cliff; round Gwennap Head and the coastguard hut perched looking far out to the Atlantic and the distant Wolf Lighthouse; along a twisting rambling coastline with sheer drops down to angry looking rocks and stones until, after rounding Nanjizel Bay, the walker comes in sight of the Enys Dodman rock and then Longships Lighthouse standing sentinel a mile and a half out to sea over Land's End itself.

Northwards after Sennen Cove, with its beautiful white sandy beach, the coast meanders out to the Cape, past the dreadful Brissons rocks, responsible for the wrecks of so many unfortunate ships; on past Kenidjack with its ruined castle and then a number of narrow valleys and coves which once led to prosperous tin and copper mines: Botallack, Wheal Bal and Levant, where a collapse of the shaft running out under the sea bed claimed the lives of dozens of Cornish miners. All along this rugged and lonely coastline, one frequently sees the gaunt skeleton frame of defunct mineheads, stripped long ago of their wood for fuel.

Further along towards the St Ives end of the peninsular is Gurnard's Head, which offers some of the finest rock climbing in Britain and is regularly used by various climbing clubs. Honeysuckle grows in profusion on the cliffs at Gurnard's Head in the spring though as like as not the blossom will be whisked away by the wind. From Gurnard's Head past Zennor towards Clodgy Point and the sudden sandy stretches of St Ives, the coastline is as beautiful as on the southern side, but somehow more remote and brooding. One is haunted by an almost indescribable feeling of solitude. Drive along the road that climbs out of St Ives and turns westward to Zennor and you may understand what I mean. The meeting of the two smooth expanses of land and sea creates an even larger and more disturbing vastness, in which a tree on the land is as rare a sight as a ship on the sea.

So much for a fragmentary stretch of Cornish coastline. The descriptions could be extended all the way up the striking North Coast, with its incredible variety of stupendous cliffs interspersed with vast stretches of sands like Gwithian, where a whole church was found buried. Further up the coast at Harlyn Bay, close to the fishing port of Padstow, those interested in archaeology will find the fascination of a prehistoric cemetery and a museum of relics dating back to 300B.C. Two thousand tons of sand were removed to reveal 150 skeletons, many well preserved. In and around the graves were found implements made from flint, bone, shell and slate, and there were stone spindle whorls for spinning and querns for grinding corn as well as pottery and bronze ornaments. The existence of Harlyn Bay is merely further factual proof to underline the brooding and mystical sense of the past which haunts the northern Cornish coastline. It did not escape Alfred Lord Tennyson when, during a walking tour round Cornwall, he noted the 'glorious grass green monsters of waves' and how 'when the long wave broke all down the thundering shores of

Bude and Boss, there came a day as still as heaven'.

This same vivid imagery is to be found in the poems of another great author of the Victorian era, Thomas Hardy, writing after returning to the Cornwall he had known as a younger man, and to the place, Boscastle, where he had met his first wife, Emma:

> O the opal and the sapphire of that wandering western sea,
> And the woman riding high above with bright hair flapping free
> The woman whom I love so, and who loyally loved me.
> The pale mews plained below us and the waves seemed far away
> In a nether sky, engrossed in saying their ceaseless babbling say,
> As we laughed light-heartedly aloft on that clear sunned March day.
> A little cloud then cloaked us, and there flew an irised rain,
> And the Atlantic dyed its levels with a dull misfeatured stain,
> And then the sun burst out again and purples prinked the main.

Equally colourful passages would be needed to do justice to many parts of Cornwall's South Coast, especially desolate, fearsome areas like the Lizard, and the nearby Manacles rocks on which so many fine ships have foundered. Or the awesome and bleak headland known as Dodman Head, which guards the entrance to St Austell Bay, with the old fishing port of Mevagissey to one side, Fowey and its estuary on the other, and in the background the man-made but haunting images of china clay tips rising up like white mountains.

But Cornwall is not merely coastline; its interior — though hardly any part of it is more than a few miles from the sea — may often be as remarkable as all those hundreds of miles of wandering beaches and coves and harbours and cliffs, and anyone who has, for example, wandered among the ancient no-man's-lands of the tin mines around St Day and Redruth would surely agree. Then there are those St Austell clay-pits to which I have referred, whose imagery features so strikingly in the poems of one of Cornwall's leading poets, Jack Clemo:

My Destiny is drawn
Sharp as the prongs
Of a clay-tip against the dawn,
Unsoftened by the lark's song.

Two gleaming fingers on the white snout
Grotesque above the clotted cone
Of carnal doubt;
They are Dogma's radiant bone.

Bodmin Moor is another notable symbol of weirdness of the Cornish interior. Here is the Cornish Everest, Brown Willy, 1,375 feet high and neighbouring Rough Tor, only 63 feet lower. From their pinnacles you can, on a clear day, glimpse the Bristol Channel on one side and the English Channel on the other. It is like being on the roof of Cornwall, surrounded by silence and a strange sense of desolation, and also by stones 'shaped like giant furniture with monstrous chairs and twisted tables', as Daphne du Maurier described them.

The tors themselves, Cornwall's nearest approach to actual mountains, are largely moorland, here and there rising to granite peaks. Like all of Bodmin Moor they are pervaded with a haunting sense of the past — a somewhat murky past, too, for on the summit of Rough Tor it is rumoured that black masses used to be held, and there are ruins of two small buildings believed to have been part of a chapel. According to an old history of the area, the erection of religious edifices on such sites was due to the notion that the raging of a storm was really a conflict between the forces of the Devil and the Heavenly Host and that sacred buildings, especially those housing holy relics and crosses, kept evil spirits away.

It is hardly surprising that Bodmin Moor, stretching as it does twelve miles north to south and eleven miles east to west, encapsulates the county's atmosphere of mystery. Wherever you go across this comparatively vast and largely unpopulated area you are likely to come upon strange relics of the past:

Hawk's Tork, a Bronze Age monument stretching 180 feet, or the Cheeswring, a colony of fantastic rocks, and King Doniert's Throne. As at Land's End, the latter is another area which has appropriated its own dramatic name for rocks — Lord's Waste, Black Rock, Maiden Tork, Hard Head etc. Everywhere there are fields and place names reminding one of the original Celtic population. High up on the moor in the centre of the biggest parish in Cornwall is Altarnum, better known as the 'Cathedral of the Moor', the church of St Nonna's. Its church tower, which stands 130-foot high, is the tallest in Cornwall. Close by the church is a holy well reputed to have healing powers over the insane. Richard Carew, in his *Survey Of Cornwall*, described the old practice of plunging a frantic person into the water then taking him to the church for masses to be said: 'If his wits returned St Nun had the thanks, but if there appeared some small amendment he was 'bowsenned again and again, while there remained in him any hope of life or recovery'.

It has been said of Bodmin Moor that nowhere else on earth are there landscapes more austerely beautiful, more wonderful in their changes of mood and colour, more splendid in outline. Dozmary Pool, for instance, in its placid moods when it becomes a mirror reflecting the forms of moor and cloud has a charm so powerful, yet so elusive, that it can really only be conveyed visually — a combination of elements: water, sky, earth. Indeed the importance of many Cornish landscapes is essentially their pictorial value, breadth and space, sky and cloud, wide surfaces and simple forms. Or to put it another way, Bodmin Moor shares with the china-clay country a certain starkness, an almost brutally present structure — the suggestion of petrified waves, crested at the tors, otherwise in deep wide undulations. This is the view of the painter Lionel Miskin, who has drawn attention to the deep recessions of ochre and golden grass to be found in winter-time, and of greens in the spring that only lightly cover a sculpture you

9

know to be as black as iron or bronze (for, ploughed or cut for peat, this blackness is laid bare in a geometric pattern that is as dark as that of the clay country a few miles further west is white). Even the cattle on the Moor tend to be black, Miskin points out, and he has described working both on the high land of the moor and in the valley running down to Golitha Falls, looking out on extraordinary shapes of clouds building up as if for a powerful storm, and seeing the shapes of rocks or hills appearing and disappearing in the clouds, the sun glinting on their surfaces like sculpture.

Indeed Cornwall is very much a sculptor's country, being after all, literally made of granite. It is evident not only in the terraced landscape of the little fishing towns and the geological nature of the rock, but the submarine cargo of shells, skulls, fish and plants, evoking a vision back of the fundamental shape of nature. This was certainly the view of my old friend Sven Berlin, a sculptor who lived for many years on the island of St Ives. A colourful figure with his huge frame and bearded face crowned with an old seaman's hat, working every day in his yard hewing away at huge lumps of alabaster and blue stone. I can remember him telling me of the excitement he felt when the Cornish sea 'got into' a shape he was carving, how it charged through the whole of the stone and as if by magic transformed it into an ocean with rocks and tides, shells and caves — a sea dragon.

In order to capture something of the mystery of Cornwall, I turn naturally to the perceptions of poets and artists — yet the impact is as vivid and lasting upon people from many walks of life. Fishermen, tin miners, farm workers, archaeologists, tinkers, tailors, soldiers, sailors, all who come upon this strange leg of land are affected, often profoundly. Sir George P. Christopher, chairman of the Hain Steamship Company of Hayle, once stopped his car on the top of a Cornish moor and feasted his eyes on a vista of great rough humps of granite, their rugged grandeur commanding a spirit of reverence. Let

10

anyone stand in Zennor Churchtown and look up at the rocky hills lying behind the road to St Ives, he remarked, and his heart must be as hard as the granite itself if he is not moved to see something more than a mere profusion of the wastage of nature; and in doing so, to breathe a benediction upon it all for the sense of strength it seems to be giving... let anyone stand on top of Trencrom Hill and look down on all sides upon the quiet land beneath and between the hill and the distant sea; on the great stones all around; at the sheltering rock bastions of Tregonning, Goldolphin, Carn Brea, Trink and Trendrine. Or stand on Gwithian Head looking inland to Trencrom itself, which with the lesser Worvas Hill stands sentinel over the clustering habitations of Lelant, Carbis Bay and St Ives — all these breathe into a Cornishman something of their own calm, their timelessness and the solid front with which they have faced the ages since they were formed.

Rocks and stones, hills and valleys bearing the imprint of men who long ago buried their dead beneath great chambered tombs and worshipped earth goddesses are to be found everywhere in Cornwall. Nowhere in England except Cornwall will you find these symbols of eastern ritual — a fact commented on by Daphne du Maurier, in her recent nostalgic book, *Vanishing Cornwall*:

Great slabs of granite, weather-potted, worn, with another mighty slab, tip-tilted, to form a roof; these were the burial places of priests, perhaps of queens. Set in the high places, amidst scrub and gorse, the treasures they once contained long rifled by barbarians and the bones scattered, they stand as memorials to a forgotten way of life and a once-living cult. Sometimes today the setting is incongruous — a small field, perhaps, with a line of bungalows near by. Yet age has not destroyed their majestic beauty, nor plough and tractor tumbled the foundations. The stones, like the natural granite cast up from the earth by nature, defy the centuries... the mocking course of history with all its triumphs and defeats is blotted out. Here in the lichened stone is the essence of memory itself. Whether it was priest or chieftain, queen or priestess who lay here once, prepared with solemn

11

rites for the passage to the underworld, belief in immortality was theirs, Man's answer, from the beginning, to the challenge of death.

These were the first tombs of Cornwall; but scattered throughout the length and breadth of the peninsula are other stones and other chambers, barrows and trenches, mounds and circles, so that it might be said that death, like the sea, is ever present. Later generations, with the guilt engendered by Puritan or Methodist upbringing, thought all standing or leaning stones were persons frozen by the merciless hand of God for dancing on a Sunday... they sensed that the place held magic, and whatever dwelt there under a brooding sky should be placated. Instinct, infallible, bade them place a hand upon the mound or stone, and spit. If the stone had a hole in it, like the Men-an-Tor, near Lanyon, the wisest thing to do was to crawl through it nine times against the sun. To crawl against the sun 'backened' disease.

The underworld that promised immortality held its treasures, too, so that Cornishmen from the beginning have always dug for wealth... tinners, copper-seekers, quarriers, slate-breakers, clay-workers, farmers; an earthy people with an earthy knowledge. Those who desire to understand the Cornish and their country must ever use their imagination and travel back in time.

In Cornwall it is indeed easy with the use of one's imagination to travel back in time, perhaps never more so than looking out from Land's End to those distant romantic Scilly Isles (of which there are more than 200, though only seven inhabited). The sea between them, which has been described as a clear and marvellous blue in summer but in winter a seething mass of treachery, is so shallow that the slightest elevation of the sea bed would make all the tiny islets disappear to form a single, many-pinnacled granite island. Similarly the ocean stretching from the Scillies to Land's End is not very deep, and the slightest uplift of the ocean floor would produce dry land — hence, surely, the inspiration for the famous legend of Lyonesse, recounted in *Curious Cornwall* by B. Travail.

For legend has it that such a land once existed: a land of great fertility, inhabited by a beautiful race of people who built many splendid cities — does not the dreaded Seven Stones reef mark the site of one of

12

them? — and some 140 equally marvellous churches whose bells from time to time may be heard beneath the sea, gently tolling with the rocking waves. One single night, some 900 years ago, the whole of Lyonesse was overcome by a vast inundation from the sea, which flooded over all but its highest peaks, catching the sleeping people unawares and engulfing the cities and churches in rapid succession. It is said that only one living creature survived this disaster — a man named Trevelyan, of Basil, near Launceston, who was able to flee before the rising wall of water on his swift white horse and reach dry land safely at Perranuthnoe... And so Lyonesse disappeared, engulfed by a wide stretch of glittering sea that separated the newly created cliffs of the Land's End and the just-born Scilly Isles barely visible on the far horizon. Mount's Bay fishermen at one time — perhaps still — would tell you that on clear nights near the Seven Stones the roofs of houses were visible beneath the water, while there is other more down-to-earth collaboration, both historical and geological, of the drowning of Lyonesse. The Saxon Chronicle even states that 'the Lionesse was destroyed on November 11, 1099' — but then who wants proof? We must all be permitted to dream.

Whether we are on Bodmin Moor, at Land's End, among the bejewelled Scilly Isles — we are not only permitted, but encouraged to dream. Cornwall is a dreamer's world, complete, on occasions, with the authentic nightmare. In this granite land we are continually made to feel aware not merely of an immediate past, but of a huge and endless remote past stretching into infinity. Thus still to this day, all over Cornwall, there stand some 400 old Celtic crosses, derivatives of the Bronze Age menhirs, or standing-stones. These crosses had various purposes — to mark holy places, in memory of the dead, as boundary-stones or guide-posts. Carved out of very old, grey granite, crude and simple, often surprisingly large (with shafts up to 20 feet), they speak across centuries. Put your hands on their rough surfaces — or for that matter put your hands on the great granite surface of some of the stones on top of Trencrom, or Castle Dinas, or Chysauster — and it will be difficult not to imagine a tremble of ancient communication. There are indeed, as Shakespeare said, 'sermons in stones'. He was looking not at the hard seemingly immobile and unanswering exterior, but at something which was beyond even the magic of his own muse to express except in that one terse phrase, which embodies the whole volume of inner hidden things which man, consciously or unconsciously, envisages when he looks at these emblems of 'the rock whence ye were hewn'.

Cornwall is a world of stark rock-like shapes looming out of bogs and moors, of weird cloud formations racing across storm bound skies — a world of shadow and substance, marvel and miracle. On Bodmin Moor, on Carn Brea at Redruth, on Trencrom Hill and a dozen other pinnacles where bonfires are ritualistically lit every Midsummer Night's Eve, it is literally impossible to feel one is in any normal, ordinary sort of background. And the same goes, too, of course, for the sea washed cliffs of Bedruthan Steps, of Hell's Mouth, Hayle, or Lamorna or Treen or Porthgwarra; of the Lizard, Kynance, Mullion; of almost anywhere along the endless coastline. It is all summed up for us, I think, superbly in the words of the novelist, Ruth Manning Sanders, recalling long walks out on the Land's End cliffs in the twilight of a wintry afternoon, when nothing was to be seen but the huge dim shapes of the silently withdrawing cliffs and the rhythmically winking eye of the Longships Lighthouse:

It is then that the drowned sailors of the past can be heard hailing their names above the moaning of the waters. It is then that the sense of the primordial, the strange and the savage, the unknown, the very long ago, fills the dusk with something that is akin to dread. It is then that the place becomes haunted: A giant heaves grey limbs from his granite bed, a witch sits in that stone chair on the cliff...

Chapter Two

The Ancient People

The thing about the Cornish is that they are not nice: exciting and attractive but not nice.

ROSALIE GLYNN GRYLLS

If Cornwall is an extraordinary place, a country rather than a county, then it would be surprising if the Cornish people were not out of the ordinary as well. They are in fact rather like their land, an old and knowing race, reticent to strangers, living as much in the past as the present; lacking in much direct creative inspiration of their own, yet with a 'reaction to a sensitised soil' as Rosalie Glynn Grylls, a Cornish born critic and biographer, summed up her native character.

The thing about the Cornish, she says, is that they are not nice; exciting and attractive but not nice. The impulsiveness that goes as far as magnanimity does not sustain generosity; the devotion, loyal as far as fanaticism, has no fidelity; the forthcomingness keeps more back than reticence — like an iceberg under water, if there was not anything less like an iceberg than a Celt. The essence of Celtic truth is that it is faithful to mood, fickle to fact. It does not lie; truth and falsehood are not involved in simply giving the stranger the answer he wants. That is a matter of convention, a behaviour pattern that has proved itself best to save time or keep counsel.

What is more remarkable than Cornish truth is Cornish imagination; its paucity and impotence. Where are the poets and artists and composers of first rank? The Cornish are not great artists; their quick response to stimulus is not imagination, not the creative spirit in action. Seeing piskies on the downs or knockers in the mines has little to do with imagination; rather it is a simple reaction to the sensitised soil. The capacity to make that final effort for delivery which clothes the word with flesh is ultimately lacking. In Cornwall the men of science have come nearest to having it: Humphry Davy, John Couch Adams, Jonathan Couch, inventors like Richard Trevithick or Henry Trangrouse. They have been able to take the leap across the gulf and bring light. And this is part of the Cornish paradox. No other people gambol so much in a Celtic twilight, that awful hour in the real Celtic heyday, which presaged the darkness. Where does it go, then, all the colour? The warm tones of manner, the light and shade of speech? The colour goes into the personality. One might say it is almost enough for the Cornish to be Cornish; but not quite, for they have a full measure of Celtic discontent. The energy that makes for colourfulness goes into the business of living — always a hard one in Cornwall; the fervour into congregational worship — into a personal relationship with omnipotence, not into embellishing its dwelling place; the enterprise into seeking fortunes further afield. A forgotten large part of the population of Cornwall is overseas — pioneers in a great trek to minefields and ranches that has, characteristically, seldom been recorded, for with all their ability at dressing the window the Cornish are not good at selling their wares. They always send back gifts generously and come home when they can (often to die), but it is a small proportion over which to erect perpetual angels of nostalgia. The granite in those that go away is more typical of the backbone of the country than the lichen that remains.

The Cornishman is at his best outside Cornwall, in Rosalie Glynn Grylls' opinion, even if he has to go back to replenish the fire of his spirit; he is at his worst at home. Not in his unpleasantness to his own people, which is something neither to be liked nor disliked but accepted (after all, wit must be kept in circulation, emotions exercised), but in his pleasantness to the stranger. The sins of the miners and the fishermen that Wesley came to save seem almost wholesome beside the charm-mongering which the tourists temptingly encourage. However, sooner or later the foreigner will be frightened away, either by some sudden turning upon him with that Celtic unpredictability that can run from a sudden storm off the Lizard to the prickling of the porcupine, or he will be repelled by the Cornishman's withdrawal. Deeper and deeper will the treasure be hidden until the Cornish disappear after it themselves and the foreigner is left encompassed by a silence from which his own emptiness can strike no echo. 'And in the moment when he shivers, the Little People walking over his grave will be avenged'.

I have lived in Cornwall now for more than 35 years, half a lifetime, yet to this day I and my family remain, indeed, 'furriners'. It is important to any understanding of the Cornish people to grasp the fact, and indeed the significance of the fact. That 'they are not nice' as Rosalie Glynn Gryll noted with devastating accuracy, is in a way putting it kindly. Many non-Cornish visitors have been stung to express more violent reactions. D.H. Lawrence, who spent a year during the Great War living in a remote cottage at Tregarthern, near Zennor, at first declared he could feel free in Cornwall because he was somehow in the world as it was in that flicker of pre-Christian civilisation when humanity was really young. Yet before long he decided that the people were inertly selfish, like insects gone cold, living only for money, mean and afraid. A poet who also spent some time in Zennor, John Heath-Stubbs put it even more dramatically:

This is a hideous and wicked country,
Sloping to hateful sunsets and the end of time.
Hollow with mine shafts, naked with granite, fanatic
With Sorrow, abortions of the past
Hop through these bogs: Black faced, the villagers
Remember burnings by the hewn stones.

Once when climbing to a hill above St Ives a man said to a little boy, 'This was where the Druids worshipped their idol gods'. When the boy asked, 'How long ago?' the man replied vaguely, 'About a hundred years ago, I s'pose'. In reality it must have been twenty times longer — the fact being that past and present, moments and centuries, are all entangled and interwoven in Cornwall. Eternity is contained in a hundred years. And this has been reflected not only in the landscape but in the people. George Meredith, another novelist visitor, observed once of the Cornish that the past was continuously at their elbow:

The past of their lives has lost neither face nor voice behind the shroud, nor are the passions of the flesh, nor is the animate soul wanting to it. Other races forfeit infancy, forfeit youth and manhood, with their progression to the wisdom age may bestow. The Cornish have each stage always alive, quick at a word, a scent, a sound, to conjure up scenes in spirit and in flame.

The Cornish people are a very old people, like all Celts, and this sense of the past continues to dominate them so that though superficially they may seem to change with the times, in reality they remain as they always were — just as Cornwall, the mysterious place, remains very much as it always has been. Dour and difficult as they may be, they are also, in common with the Welsh and the Irish and the Scottish, permeated with a romanticism, but totally removed from the pragmatism of the English. Somewhere in the back of the Cornishman's consciousness there lurk memories of King Arthur and the Knights of the Round Table, of the search for the Holy Grail, of that eternal story of romance, Tristan and Iseult.

Looking briefly at the history of the Cornish people, archaeological records show that neolithic man occupied parts of the country at least 7000 years ago. Later there were influxes of Mediterranean people and an Iberian presence has been recorded in 1800 B.C. Soon after came the Irish, followed later by people from Germany and Norway and eventually in the 9th century B.C. a large influx of the Celts from France (hence the close links to this day with Brittany). By the late Iron Age the Cornish were predominately a Celtic people, speaking the musical Celtic tongue and organised in large tribal groups with a well developed social hierachy. For a time there was a Roman occupation but after their withdrawal from what they regarded as a barbarian country, the development was as of a Celtic people, and continued into the Middle Ages.

Originally the Cornish language was in everyday usage for more than 1000 years, reaching its peak in the Middle Ages, but as Cornwall itself came more and more under English rule and domination, so the use of the native tongue began to die away. The last recorded instance of Cornish being spoken is that of a lady called Dolly Pentreath of Mousehole, near Penzance, who died in 1777. Rather late in the day Cornish scholars like Henry Jenner and A.S.D. Smith and R. Martin Nance managed to encourage a revival of interest in the old language and today there are regular classes in most parts of Cornwall. Nevertheless a dead language can never be totally resurrected and thus we come to the important difference between the Cornish of today and their Celtic cousins: in Ireland and Wales, in particular, and even in many parts of Scotland, the native tongue has never ceased to be actively spoken; it has remained alive, whereas in Cornwall there has been that disastrous break. Even the contemporary Mebyon Kernow Nationalist Movement, sincere as it is, lacks much validity beside the nationalist movements of the other Celtic countries, which have always existed, and have not had to be artificially revived. So we have yet another explanation for the sometimes unreasonable surliness of the Cornish people: resentment at a defeat suffered by a people who subconsciously cannot help remembering having once been members of a unique race with its own language and national identity.

In trying to present a portrait of the Cornish people, as in trying to sketch an outline of the Cornwall and the landscape itself, I am continually haunted by a sense of verbal inadequacy. I have lived surrounded by Cornish people for over a quarter of a century, yet I remain constantly baffled by the elusive nature of my quarry. It is for this reason that I think it helps to quote a variety of other opinions. In the days when I edited the *Cornish Review* I extracted from my colleague, W. Gore Allen, editor of the *Devon County Journal*, a fascinating essay entitled 'A Frontier in Dumnonia', in which he wondered aloud why, whenever he crossed the River Tamar, journeying either East or West, he was surprised afresh that one of the world's least penetrable frontiers should be made evident by so small a width of water. And he went on to give his interpretation of the Cornish:

The Cornishman is a man of faith, a man naturally addicted to prayer and praise, who feels himself always to be either potential saint or actual sinner. His religious nature is not, as cynics might suggest, merely an outcome of his aptness in self dramatisation: it springs from a very real awareness of another world; wholly spiritual and prone to impinge, in and out of season, upon the world of sense. He is self-intoxicated only when he is not God-intoxicated. It is his natural destiny to be looking inwards and his occasional cultivation of a ruthless egoism is but a failure to discover the divinity in his own nature. He is bound to worship; and therefore be grows evil in proportion to the extent to which the proper object of his worship becomes prostituted or mislaid.

The Cornishman, in Gore Allen's opinion, is constantly sustained by a feeling of being separate, almost a chosen people. He is also very sympathetic. Take him a proposal, take him a trouble, above all take him an injustice suffered and

20

everything he is and has is yours. But at his worst he will be bored stiff with you in half an hour and within a week he will have forgotten your existence. He puts much into life, and expects much from it; he looks to everyone else to move at his swift pace. Cornwall is harder to know and its people too greatly individualistic for any sort of orderly dissection as one might apply to any other English county. Undoubtedly many outsiders will be scandalised by the narrowness in Cornish life, yet at the same time entranced by a questioning spirit, thrusting towards a kind of universality.

When he considered the facts of social structure Gore Allen pointed out that Cornish society appears to have achieved a broad equality, with no class-ridden culture, employment or economy. This is an aspect which has always seemed to me of special relevance to any study of the Cornish people, for there is no doubt that, whatever their own faults, they are unusually receptive to the existence of eccentrics and oddities of all kinds. There are, one would imagine, two reasons for this. In the first place the Cornish themselves are a race of eccentrics and individualistic types, which must perhaps breed a certain fellow sympathy. And the second explanation is the simple one that, particularly in the last sixty or seventy years, Cornwall has literally been invaded by very large numbers both of visitors and people (like myself) who have put down their roots in a chosen new country. Naturally enough, these include a high proportion of strong-minded individualists, whose ideas and ways of life have inevitably had a favourable affect upon the Cornishman's insularity.

A good example of what I mean has been provided by the large scale development of artists's colonies in many parts of Cornwall, and most notably in the Western peninsula around St Ives, Newlyn, Mousehole, Lamorna, etc. This is dealt with in more detail in a later chapter, but it is worth recalling here that at the turn of the century, when many London painters came to settle in the little fishing port of St Ives, there was

21

considerable local antagonism among the fishermen and their families, much of it derived from the strong Wesleyan influences which have conditioned many generations of Cornishmen. When, for instance, the well known painter Louis Grier appeared on the wharf at St Ives and set up his easel and prepared to paint a picture *on a Sunday* it was soon made clear to him that if he once dared to appear again on that holy day he and his easel were likely to find themselves in the harbour!

'Them artists' to quote another favourite phrase used by the St Ives folk to describe their strange new visitors, must initially have seemed very much like beings from outer space — yet familiarity bred tolerance, and today the artists and the fishermen, the guest-house owners and the visitors all seem to live in reasonable harmony. So to this extent a certain sophistication and even cosmopolitan attitude has crept into Cornish life — certainly in holiday resorts and most towns, and this I think is bound to exert a certain 'thawing' upon the Cornish reserve.

And yet, as I have said before, to understand the Cornish, indeed to be able to live in any harmony with them, this reserve, these inner mysteries, simply have to be accepted and made the best of. It certainly is not to anyone's advantage to cross swords with Cornishmen for they are very quick to take offence — a fact put succinctly into perspective for me once by a friend who said, 'If a Cornishman can't find anyone else to quarrel with then he'll quarrel with his neighbour'. He knew what he was talking about: he came from Newlyn, a fishing port a mile or so of coastal road away from nearby Mousehole, a smaller fishing port. To this day Mousehole men will talk scathingly of 'them Newlyn skate', and Newlyn men take an equally caustic view of their Mousehole brethren. Yet in all likelihood both clans would close ranks against Penzance, 2 miles away. As for St Ives, 10 miles across the Penwith hills and facing the Bristol Channel — its folk are totally beyond the pale!

Frank Baines, whose childhood was spent in the Lizard area, has spotlighted the extraordinary sense of energy and competitiveness which he found in everyday Cornish life. There was tremendous rivalry between the three ports which made up his local parish, based on a fundamental difference both in fishing technique and social structure. Porthallow thrived on pilchards, Porthoustock exploited crabs and lobsters, Coverack long-lined for plaice and sole. According to Porthallow and Porthoustock, Coverack was the Home of Sin, a sort of original Sodom and Gomorrah, its men nothing but poachers and smugglers, its women whores. In fact, as Frank Baines explained:

Coverack lay isolated like a rajah's whimsy in a wilderness. Its men were dour, reputedly stole from other fishermen's pots, spent their time boozing and sent their daughters up to Churchtown farms as dairy maids, over-dressed and painted — the equivalent in local eyes to living on immoral earnings. There is no doubt that Coverack was one of those outlaw settlements where people are fundamentally different from, and live in a state of suppressed hostility to their neighbours. Cornwall has always been exposed to seaborne invasion and you can see how it used to be even now when you watch the crew of Breton fishermen in Newlyn Harbour eating their communal stew out of a bucket and glaring with hard hungry eyes at the good burghers. The slightest disturbance of internal stability and these people would be out of their boats and taking over. They are nothing but pirates. I think the difference between the Coverack people and their antagonism to Churchtown people lay in this: That they were invaders who settled in this God-forsaken spot and continued to assert a smouldering freedom against ecclesiastical overlordship and administrative dependence of a later day. Of course this was resented by Churchtown who paid them back with every conceivable slander, segregation of social activities and even a ban on inter-marriage. Woe betide the Churchtown boy who walked out with a Coverack girl. He would have to take her without the consent of his parents and flee the parish.

Robert Louis Stevenson was one of many outsiders who

confessed themselves baffled at this internal bickering among the Cornish. He felt unable to understand how a division of races older and more original than that of Babel formed this close esoteric family, kept apart from neighbouring Englishmen. Not even a Red Indian seemed more foreign in his eyes. This, he considered, was one of the lessons of travel — some of the strangest races dwelt next door to you at home.

'It do take years with we to treat a stranger like one of our own. We've been reared to look upon all up-alongs as natural foes' said one of Mrs. Havelock Ellis's *My Cornish Neighbours*, quoted in one of many perceptive books about the Cornish written by an outsider. Certainly as I have already said it does not do to cross a Cornishman. There was a story in the *West Briton* about a Chacewater man being asked, at the time his sister lay dead, whether he was going to the funeral, and answering coolly, 'I don't think I shall because I've got some oats that should be saved immediately'. This trend of hostile indifference is commonly found in local Cornish communities; it often derives from brooding over some quite petty slight or injury received years and years previously. A similar sort of disagreement led to a man, who had quarrelled with his local clergyman, leaving instructions that he must not be buried in the local parish churchyard, but in a space on a nearby hill. On the enclosing wall he had two tablets fixed: 'custom is the idol of fools' and 'virtue only consecrates the ground'. Five thousand people attended the interment!

To some extent this apparent hostility of the Cornish derives from their unwillingness to offend with a negative reply. Hence the development of local sayings such as 'I do believe', 'I spose', 'They do say', and so on. It would be useful to say a word here about Cornish dialect. Although the Cornish language itself has died out, and is only spoken on an academic level, there are still strong elements of local dialects, which help to add to the sense of local character. Some of the Cornish sayings are very much to the point, often based on past

24

incidents. Thus, 'like Tom Rowe's mouth' meaning exactly right, derives from the story of a Cornishman at a feast finding the meat rather tough and carefully cutting it into pieces which would fit his mouth. 'A brown voice' means a deep or masculine voice, and 'a blue voice' means a voice of feminine timbre. 'As bad as John Stone' is a phrase still sometimes used in Newlyn, referring to a local comic character with zany humour. 'Going to coming, like the old woman's butter' may be said of something that takes a long time. 'Not behind the door' means somebody cheeky. 'Nothing but muck and stink' means anything worthless. 'Sour as a wig' means looking cross. And 'take the paint off her and she i'nt no more 'andsome than a frying pan of arseholes' is a forthright expression about a lady who is less than desirable. 'The body of a cow on the legs of a sparrow' describes a plump woman with thin legs, and 'turning round like a cat in the pan' means somebody in the middle of a squabble. 'You must scat'n abroad' means you must break it open, 'I'm scat' means I have no money, and 'it doan't seem fitty' means it doesn't seem right. Of course one could go on for ever with these rather delightful echoes of old dialects, but let me finish with one prize sample given by Claude Berry in his excellent book *Portrait of Cornwall*. He recalls his days as a young reporter and remembers when he covered a parish council meeting where the chairman rebuked a persistent and loquacious member in these words:

What do 'ee mane by it? You keep us here till nine o'clock at night and then cast the town drains in our teeth. You keep us here ploughin' the sands, and then at nine o'clock at night, you drag in that everlastin' red herrin' and expect us to swalla it. You rake up a motion that was carried *non com* at the last mittin' and away you go into the public drains, causin' unnecessary friction. I tell 'ee, 'twon't do, my friend. 'Tes too bare-faced to hold water!

Perhaps a further clue to the Cornish character lies, as well as in surviving dialect, in the immense variety of old customs, many of them still widely practised. Some are simple enough — like the ceremony still annually performed on All Hallows Eve at St Ives, when 'Allan' apples are distributed among the children. Piskies and ghosties and ghoulies and things that go bump in the night are still strong superstitions among the Cornish, and ancient beliefs such as that death can be retarded by keeping the room locked, or that the howling of a dog, if repeated for three nights, means the house against which it howled will soon be in mourning, still persist. Another old saying, 'never carry a corpse to church by a new road' sums up perfectly the impressionable nature of the Cornish. Always they are on the look-out for Lady Luck. If miners come upon a snail in their path they will carefully put crumbs beside it from their food parcel thereby ensuring good luck for the day. Because of the danger of their occupation miners, like fishermen, are particularly superstitious. They will not for instance whistle underground, as this is supposed to be disliked by the 'knackers', i.e. 'the Little People', who, so legend has it, can often be heard tap-tapping in the galleries underground. (Needless to say the wise miner always works in the direction of that sound, and invariably find the mineral vein a rich one!) All this emphasis on the Little People must never be taken too lightly. 'Where have you been son? Mind you don't get pisky-led' was a common saying of an anxious parent.

A people so dominated by superstition are equally faithful to other old customs, like festivals and games, and in the chapter on drama I describe two of the most famous, Helston Furry Dance and the Padstow Hobby Horse. Other ancient pastimes still prevail in the county, like the annual hurling game at St Columb when hundreds of local men chase a silver ball from one boundary end to another. Richard Carew in his *Survey of Cornwall,* published as long ago as 1602, gave this description of hurling:

The ball in this game may be compared to an infernal spirit; for

26

whosoever catch it fareth straightways like a madman, struggling and fighting with those about to hold him; and no sooner is the ball gone from him but he resigneth his fury to the next receiver and himself becometh peaceable as before.

No wonder the shopkeepers of St Columb board up their windows the night before the annual event!

Then there is Cornish wrestling, still practised to this day with elaborate rules and customs, and another example of the enduringly tough nature of the Cornish character (after all it was a Cornishman, Bob Fitzsimmons of Helston, who was the last Englishman to be world heavyweight champion of the world). Attempts to stop the wrestling have been made in the past, most notably by the Wesleyan Methodist preachers, but the spirit of the flesh has prevailed and 'wrastling' as it used to be called is still worth watching, with its special techniques: the 'foreheep', the 'flying mare', the 'fair back' and so on. According to historian Claude Berry, Cornish wrestling goes right back to pre-Roman days, and there are records of how during the Hundred Years' War the Cornish contingent marched into battle under a banner into which was woven the figures of two wrestlers in a hitch; while during King Henry VIII's time there was a Royal Command for the Cornish wrestlers to be sent to a great sporting tourney at Calais. At Feast Days today in Cornwall you may still see exhibitions of this ancient sport which, like so many other of the county's customs, does in its way reveal some of the basic and often hidden traits of the Cornish character.

Of course, like other parts of England, Cornwall has succumbed to the familiar twentieth century invasion of peoples from other parts of the country — particularly romantic-minded middle-class people who, after a lifetime of holidays spent in Cornwall, come happily down for their retirement (Cornwall probably has one of the highest percentages of old people of any English county). Nevertheless, the dividing line does remain, however finely drawn. This is not surprising if one thinks about the sort of life the Cornish people have lived in the past. Constantly invaded, plundered, pirated, etc. — no wonder they have grown up suspicious and wary of outsider's intentions! (And with good reason, indeed, as we see the gradual erosion of all that lovely coastline, and the steady exploitation of resources by outside firms).

I have said little so far about the Cornishman's normal occupations, but these, too, have played their part in moulding the national character. It is not for nothing that the Cornish have been associated with tin mining, with farming, with fishing — three of the most ancient and earth bound (or sea bound) vocations in the world, and three of the toughest jobs, too. It is significant that each of these occupations are essentially individualistic ones where men are dependent on their own resources (in the old days tin miners even had their own parliament and stannary courts). The Cornish are a tough, strong race, despite much earlier inter-breeding, and like all Celts, they are not going to quietly fade away.

There is another reason for this tenacity, reflected to this day, and that is their religious zeal. Once a Catholic country — the natural environment, many people may feel, for a Celtic nation — the Cornish became diverted into Methodism by the great John Wesley. It is not a change which I personally feel has been of great benefit, but it exists, unmistakably, and nothing has remained stronger or more potent in local Cornish life than the local religious life of each community. In many ways this had been a good thing for local life, and certainly any Feast Day in Cornwall is an event of great joy and zest, probably quite unlike anything elsewhere in Britain. After all, Cornwall can look back on a long tradition of marvellous spine thrilling preachers, like Billy Bray and Wesley himself. Again we come across that eternal paradox which makes up the Cornish character: though not themselves highly creative, they respond with immense emotion and fervour to creative people. The 'proper' preacher in Cornwall is a man with fire in his

28

belly and romance in his soul, a man of theatre and melodrama. What could be more natural than that a people who have grown up in a world of melodrama — wild elements, a savage sea, a haunted land, a sense of total mysticism and mystery — should be forever coloured by these experiences? And always, forever and ever, there is this Celtic background, summed up by the historian F.E. Halliday at the end of his *History of Cornwall*:

The tourist traffic is only a seasonal one, a sort of human late-summer monsoon between solstice and autumnal equinox — a season that rarely compares with the earlier one of daffodil, bluebell and gorse — and when the last tents have been taken down on the beaches the primeval magic and mystery reassert themselves along the deserted coast and desolate downs. For in spite of all progress, of railway, motor car, and even aeroplane, Cornwall remains all but an island, un-English, a foreign country, seaward and southward looking 'towards Namancos and Bayona's hold' and beyond Spain to the Mediterranean, the ultimate source of her ancient culture. And in spite of foreign invasion that culture has not been altogether lost in the Celtic kingdom of lost causes and lost industries — for although their numbers continue to shrink there are still thirty times ten thousand Cornishmen, independent, clannish, parochial even, proud of their separate history symbolised by quoit, saint, huer's hut and sky-fingering mine-chimney. When therefore the visitor from the East crosses the Saltash Bridge he must remember he enters a country scarcely penetrated by the English until a few centuries ago, peopled by men whose origins are different from his, who not long since spoke a strange language. And as he travels back westward, back in geological time, he also travels back in the history of man...

A hundred years ago Cornwall's hills were loud with miners but grass and bracken have covered their trackways and workings, and along the coast from Pendeen to Botallack stretch ruined mine buildings, massive as some deserted Roman city, plunging sheer into the sea. Yet these are but recent monuments to the passing of man's achievement, and centuries before the miners came, centuries before the Saints and the Romans, the land was peopled, perhaps more thickly than any other part of Britain, by the builders of hilltop citadels and promontory forts, of megalithic monuments, stone circles, menhirs and the chambered tombs of Land's End. And westward still beyond Land's End, beyond the legendary Lyonesse of King Arthur, lie the Fortunate Isles, among whose sunken shores it may be that relics of even earlier men have perished.

Yes, the Cornish are a very ancient race!

Chapter Three

The Painter's Paradise

Can you imagine the excitement which a line gives you when you draw it across a surface? It is like walking through the country from St Ives to Zennor...

BEN NICHOLSON

Painting is now so popular in Cornwall as to be almost a local industry in itself. Certainly, with the possible exception of London, there can be nowhere else in the British Isles where so many professional artists live and work. St Ives, Newlyn, Mousehole, Lamorna Cove, the Lizard, Falmouth, Fowey, Mevagissey, Polperro, Looe, Tintagel, Boscastle, Port Isaac, Padstow, Wadebridge — in almost every corner of the county, working in converted fish cellars, in wide windowed lofts, in old fashioned wooden studios and in bright new concrete ones built to specification, artists of varied outlooks and techniques have not only made homes but in many cases reputations. The result has been the creation of something quite unique in British life, usually more associated with the Mediterranean — genuine cosmopolitan and colourful art colonies, buzzing with creative life.

Like most other visitors the artists have always been

immediately impressed by their first contact with Cornwall, its light and scenery, its atmosphere and old traditions. The famous nineteenth century engraver Thomas Rowlandson once made a journey round the coast out of which he produced several scores of vivid black and white etchings of the craggy cliffs, wild moorland and huddled fishing ports. Three years after the Duke of Wellington had won the Battle of Waterloo that great landscape painter, J.M.W. Turner, a revolutionary in the art movement of his time, visited St Ives and was absolutely enchanted by the light and conditions. Near the end of the nineteenth century two more famous painters, Whistler and Sickert, both spent a winter in St Ives with extremely productive results. It was about this time that Cornish art colony life began with the arrival in neighbouring Newlyn of Walter Langley, T.C. Gotch, Frank Bramley, Stanhope Forbes and other young painters filled with the then startling new ideas of painting all their pictures direct from Nature. Many of these painters had been influenced by the realist outlook of some of the French painters such as Millet, Courbet and Bastien-Lepage; some, like Stanhope Forbes, had already experimented with painting members of a primitive peasant community in Brittany. Cornwall has many historical and geographical similarities with Brittany, as well as the same warm climate, and it is easy to imagine how the young painters travelled eagerly down to this new world of picturesque fishing villages, unspoiled by industrialism, where they could find not only cheap living but plenty of colourful models among the fishing community and all the vivid background they could possibly require for their open air paintings.

In an article published in the *Cornish Magazine* in 1898 Stanhope Forbes, who came to be regarded as the father of the Newlyn Movement, has left us a charming picture of those early days of the 1880's when artists first descended in large numbers on the simple fishing folk:

These were the days of unflinching realism, of the cult of Bastien-Lepage. It was part of our artistic creed to paint our pictures direct from Nature, and not merely to rely upon sketches and studies which we could afterwards amplify in the comfort of a studio. Artists are common enough objects by the seaside; but it was scarcely so usual to see the painter not merely engaged upon a small sketch or panel, but with a large canvas securely fastened to some convenient boulder, absorbed in the very work with which he hoped to win fame in the ensuing spring; perhaps even the model posing in full view of the entire populace, the portrait being executed with a publicity calculated to un-nerve even our practised brother of the pavement.

These singular goings on of the newcomers at first provoked much comment from the inhabitants, but by degrees they grew familiar with such strange doings, and scarce heeded the work which progressed before their eyes. Even the small folk grew tired of gazing, and at that dread moment when the school doors opened and let loose upon their chosen victims the arch tormentors of our race, a few moments of misery would ensue, and the harassed painter, with a sigh of relief, would find himself alone, once more free to continue his labours undisturbed.

Nothing, too, could exceed the good nature with which the local folk came to regard behaviour which might well have been thought intrusive... I scarcely ever remember asking permission to set up my easel without it being freely accorded.

Stanhope Forbes was writing about Newlyn where he and his fellow 'revolutionaries' set out to produce a series of huge canvases of life in a fishing village; portraits of the fishermen in their blue jerseys and white duck frocks and sea-going boots, their wives in black shawls and aprons, the children playing in the cobbled streets — and also quite melodramatic scenes, such as a mourning feast, or a wedding breakfast, or the crew of the lifeboat setting out on a mercy mission. At that time this kind of painting was much frowned upon by the critics in this country, and when the Newlyn School, as the early group was known, began to show at the Royal Academy their work was violently attacked as 'immoral'. However the critics changed their minds, as is so often the case, and there was soon a wide

33

demand for the storytelling interiors of Stanhope Forbes, the enormous exterior canvases of Norman Garstin (often painted under terrible outside weather conditions, as in the case of his famous *The Rain it Raineth Every Day)*, and the work of a wide number of artists such as Gotch, Langley, Edwin Harris, Bramley, Fred Hall, Sherwood Hunter, Chevalier Taylor, and Ralph Todd. Stanhope Forbes and his wife Elizabeth, also well known as a painter, opened a busy and successful art school, and soon the public interest in the activities at Newlyn led to the opening of the Newlyn Art Gallery, financed by the generosity of a London newspaper proprietor, J. Passmore Edwards. Here were hung many paintings which have since been acquired by the Tate and other galleries all over the world. Although the activities of the Newlyn School were to dwindle for a time the present day Newlyn-Orion gallery, under the enthusiastic guidance of John Halkes, is more active and enterprising than for a long time.

As Stanhope Forbes and his friends were settling in Newlyn, so other painters were being attracted to St Ives, on the other coast, where, among other things, the light was even more translucently clear. In time many of the Newlyn painters lent their support to the developments at St Ives, which gradually came to replace Newlyn as the hub of artistic activities, with the settling in the towns of such eminent painters as Julius Olsson, Algernon Talmage, T. Millie Dow, Louis Grier, Lowell Dyer, Anders Zorn, Noble Barlow and Alfred East. At that time, of course, St Ives was still principally a busy fishing port, and the increasing activities of the painters were viewed with some suspicion. There are many stories related which illustrate this antagonism, much of which was probably associated with the dogmatic religious attitudes of the local people of those days. Perhaps the general attitude was best summed up by a story which Algernon Talmage was fond of telling, of how a fish-cart was being driven up Skidden Hill and the horse jibbed. After exhausting an extensive vocabulary of abuse the driver, walking in the road, exclaimed, as if with his last breath, 'You — you bloody *artist!*'.

Over the years St Ives has not only nurtured the large and strongly traditional St Ives Society of Artists but also provided the setting for the avant garde Penwith Society of Artists who, with substantial backing from the Arts Council, have established a large gallery as well as several workshops and artist's studios in Back Road West, in the old quarters of St Ives.

Since those early days, of course, the art colonies of Cornwall have spread enormously, though still centred mainly in the western tip, around Newlyn and St Ives. As the movement has enlarged, so the aims of the artists have widened and developed enormously, in parallel to the movements in the world of art generally. In the past few decades, for instance, what might have seemed once the daring ideas of the Stanhope Forbes group has been far outstripped by modern movements such as surrealism, abstract art and so forth — with numerous distinguished practitioners, such as Ben Nicholson, Barbara Hepworth, Peter Lanyon, Patrick Heron, Gabo, Bryan Wynter. Today the Penwith Gallery at St Ives, and the Newlyn Orion Gallery at Newlyn, are two of the most important art galleries in Britain, and house a continuous stream of outstanding exhibitions.

Perhaps even more interesting than the physical existence of the art colonies has been the increasingly articulate explanation, by the artists themselves, of just what has drawn them to Cornwall, rather than any other part of Britain. The explanation is a mixture of material and mystical, factual and fantastical, all equally important. The climate, the brilliant light, the Mediterranean blue of the seas, the fascinating formations of rocks and cliffs, hills and valleys, sand and pebble stones — these are some of the more obvious attractions. So, too, the comparative freedom and easiness of life in a small but surprisingly cosmopolitan town such as St

Ives or Polperro, as compared to most English provincial towns; the congenial atmosphere of working and living among large groups of fellow artists; the facilities of numerous art galleries and showrooms, dozens of art societies and clubs; and last but by no means least a sympathetic local population and press, conditioned by several decades of growing up alongside art colonies, so that what might seem an oddity if dumped in some other part of Britain has come to be taken for granted in Cornwall.

Yes, *but*... surely there is something else? Something less easily explained and put into words, yet with perhaps just as strong an influence on artists as the magnetic pull granite often exerts on ship's compasses? There is, indeed, and how better to attempt to capture this unknown quantity than by asking the artists themselves. Jack Pender, a native of Mousehole and a leading member of the Penwith and Newlyn Society of Artists:

Oh, yes, there's a spiritual something here. I have met different people who have reacted to it in different ways: those who come for a week and have stayed years, and those who couldn't stand it and cleared out quickly. Through the war, art training and later teaching, I was out of Cornwall for twenty years... this thing gradually grew on me, I experienced it when I came home on leave or holiday... it became an obsession. I *had* to get back. Even when out of Cornwall I found myself painting pictures of Cornwall, subjects I had remembered. The whole thing became very intense. For me the Cornish landscape means a lot. I've been to other places where it's been lush and soft but I haven't felt altogether happy in it. The openness of the landscape appeals to me, this sense of being on the top, exposed, and yet, in a way, it makes you vulnerable, but in the present state of international art, environment and place seem to have less importance.

Another Cornish-born painter, Margo Maeckleberghe, of Penzance, when asked why Cornwall attracts painters:

I've thought about this a lot. This crystal-clear light, I think is the explanation. It gives everything a new meaning, form and structure of the landscape is defined and enlarged by it. The atmosphere is so very stimulating, savage, strong, primitive, beautiful... it's all these and much more besides. Words are really inadequate. The most important part, to me, is this mysterious x, an artist must *feel* about a place to paint it and be true to his art. Light, atmosphere, shimmering of pale, bleached grasses, surging half seen rocks, mist, rain, storm and sun on moors and headlands and, of course, skies, skies and skies... this is part of what I try to paint. The coasts, seas moors, skies and rocks of Cornwall offer inexhaustible painting material... the peculiar clarity of light which throws this landscape of West Penwish into sharp perspective. It's a land of great antiquity, primeval and sometimes savage. Why, the skies, even on a hot day, hold threats of storm clouds and the clouds, by their shadows, give form to the landscape below... and the light shining through can give exciting effects. Turner, the greatest British painter, I think, spent most of his life painting the effects of wind, rain and storm. There are, of course, many ways a painting can begin. It can be an idea which ties up suddenly with something seen, more often it's a logical development of a previous painting. It's not the beginning, it's often the end or the middle, when the difficulties are greatest.

I draw and sketch a lot... literally hundreds. It might be a movement of a wave over submerged rocks or a thrusting granite headland. Drawing lays bare the bones of the landscape for me, it's like a map into a strange country, it helps to build an image, but it can never be the complete image. One constantly rejects, selects, searches again... an interesting stone from the beach, a lichen twig, a piece of seaweed... they can all help to start the chain reaction for the beginning of a painting...

Margo Maeckleberghe is one of the most exciting painters now working in Cornwall precisely because her work reflects the strange intangible way in which Cornwall, the land, the place, does in fact influence, indeed enter into the artist. In her landscapes the Cornish imagery is so vital and striking that it almost seems to come alive before your eyes — a line of thought enhanced by her most recent series of Atlanta paintings, in which slices of Cornish landscape and coastline

37

merge mysteriously into the shape of a reclining woman. Interestingly, another woman painter, Misomé Peile of St Ives, underlined a similar point when she once confessed that she gave up drawing for three years to learn to think and feel only the painted surface. Hundreds of action-drawings of the wilderness of Carbis Bay, close to her studio, enabled her to break through to the fusion of sky, land and water under the brilliant hillside light — now she sees the human form 'in all landscape and in the heavens'.

And on the subject of the Cornish landscape, this is what Dick Gilbert, also Cornish born, has to say:

It works on me. Take just this one valley where I live. If I stayed here a hundred years I shouldn't have exhausted its painting possibilities. You get this feeling of place. The Cornish landscape exhibits a constantly changing occurrence, it has a large visual depth or distance, in other words you can see a lot of land relative to the sky, whereas in other counties the land is frequently at a distance, but the visual depth is small... in Cornwall there's more land in the visual experience.

With Dick Gilbert one is turning to the field of abstract art. It is not without significance that so many abstract artists have been drawn to Cornwall (and rather amusing that because the landscape is so impressive not even the abstract artists have been able to keep it out of their work). I recall some interesting remarks on this point by the late Charles Marriott, one time art critic of *The Times*, in suggesting that West Cornwall was in particular a draughtsman's country. He felt strongly that seen from a height such as Trencrom or Carn Galve the landscape ran to a decorative pattern, a sort of *cloisonné* effect of little green fields inset in a network of gorse-clad hedges, and he had the notion that even in their abstractions, painters such as Ben Nicholson got nearer to the peculiar magic of West Cornwall than did the painters of earlier years.

Ben Nicholson, who came to live in Cornwall in 1939 and spent the next 20 years in his adopted county, has expounded further on the abstract artist's outlook. He sees painting and religious experience as the same thing, a search for the understanding and realisation of infinity — an idea which is complete with no beginning, no end, and therefore giving to all things for all time. The structure of Cornwall, he confessed, suited him ideally:

I want to be so free that I even would not need to use free colour. I dislike the idea that a picture is something precious, the painter something special. There is an artist in everybody. That was the reason why I welcomed the technique of collage. One discovers new things. One does not paint only in one medium, it does away with the precious quality of easel picture. Art is work and play for me. And work and play are as necessary for me as breathing.

Yesterday I began to paint the garden gate. As soon as my hand touches a brush, my imagination begins to work. When I finished I went up to my studio and made a picture. Can you imagine the excitement which a line gives you when you draw it across a surface? It is like walking through the country from St Ives to Zennor...

Another abstract painter John Wells of Newlyn, had this to say:

So all around the morning air and the sea's blue light with points of diamond and the gorse incandescent beyond the trees; countless rocks, ragged or round and of every colour; birds resting or flying and the sense of a multitude of creatures living out their minute lives. All this is part of one's life and I was desperately eager to express it; not just what I see, but what I feel about it and beyond it... but how can one paint the warmth of the sun, the sound of the sea, the journey of a beetle across a rock, or thoughts of one's own whence and whither? That is one argument for abstraction. One absorbs all these feelings and ideas; if one is lucky they undergo an alchemistic transformation into gold and *that* is the creative work.

It is hardly surprising that sculptors, in particular, have been most profoundly influenced — one might even say uplifted — by Cornwall. This is especially so today; but there was one Cornish sculptor, Nevill Northey Burnard, who made his mark in the early nineteenth century and whose work was marvellously commemorated in a poem by Charles Causley, painting a vivid picture of the sculptor working away at the moorstone until at last he 'quietly lifted out his prize of rock'. Every sculptor who comes to Cornwall is confronted with this exciting chance of lifting out his 'prize of rock' — more so, surely than in any other part of Britain. For, and it cannot be too strongly emphasised, Cornwall is essentially a land of granite, a land whose agelessness is somehow symbolised by that very stone.

Barbara Hepworth, once married to Ben Nicholson, became the most famous sculptor to be associated with Cornwall, and her tantalising and inimitable and often beautiful pieces of polished stone now adorn galleries all over the world. For the last thirty years of her life Barbara Hepworth lived and worked at her Trewyn studio (now arranged as a memorial museum open to the public) and though her work might be termed abstract it is literally possible to see and feel the Cornish influence in shape and form.

To anyone who studies Barbara Hepworth's work it is obvious that in Cornwall she found her correct setting. From her garden she could look out across St Ives and its bay to distant hills; and all around her was the Cornish scene, in all its mystery, with an impact so continual that it was bound to infiltrate into her own carvings. A London critic, Michael Williams, in reviewing an earlier exhibition of her work at the Lefèvre Gallery suggested that she had come under the influence of Cornwall because 'that landscape, perhaps more than any other, must call up a deep emotional response from one so much of whose life is concerned with digging deep into the heart of her materials and searching out basic forms.'

While Ben Nicholson directed the attention of younger artists to the abstract qualities implied in the Cornish landscape, Barbara Hepworth opened a similar pathway into an understanding of the qualities of a sculptors' materials, especially seen against the background of a world peculiarly dominated by ancient stones. Rosewood, alabaster, mahogany, Portland stone and blue limestone were all used by Miss Hepworth to produce her now familiar shapes and forms. She appeared obsessed with the beauty and significance of natural formations of these stones and woods; but at the same time she had a profound ability to capture the lineaments of the human form, and at many of her exhibitions visitors were surprised at the imposing array of drawings in oil and pencil of the human figure. There was, for instance, a most fascinating series of drawings of figures present at a hospital operation. Even in her drawings, however, one was always conscious that they were mainly roughouts for eventual interpretation in wood or stone. There is something remote and impersonal — indeed purely abstract — about Hepworth figures which suits very much the mood of our scientifically obsessed civilization. In Cornwall her art flowered, perhaps more fully than it might have done anywhere else in Britain.

Sven Berlin was another sculptor who always declared that it was Cornwall which helped to release and develop his ability to create living things in stone, the stone being an entity in itself with a centre of vitality and tension that could be made to exist in space. I once asked Sven Berlin to put into words some of his thoughts about his reaction to the Cornwall around him and feel he captured something important in these words:

The open coliseum of each little cove of sand or rock may be the theatre for any natural, supernatural or unnatural agent. The unending presence of the sea breathing ceaselessly over the shoulder of each hill, the rock charged with a thousand sunsets or carved by a hundred years of rain, the little trees loaded with berries growing away from the prevailing wind, offering crimson to green, the mind's incessant vertigo at the cliff edge, and the slow constructional flight of the seagull — these things in some way act as the charming of magicians and open up the deeper rooms of experience in man, making him aware of his being part of the natural universe, at the

41

head of a great unseen procession of gods and devils, spectres and dragons, of being a channel for unknown and undefined forces; of facing the mystery of life, awakening powers of perception which search beyond the frontiers of normal events.

That extract was used in Berlin's book about Alfred Wallis, the old St Ives fisherman turned primitive painter who, at the age of 70, began painting in house paints on old pieces of cardboard, a flood of child-like efforts which today are on the walls of numerous art galleries and treasured in many private collections. At first sight many of Wallis's paintings do, indeed, seem like the sort of pictures pinned up on classroom walls in infant schools — but on closer inspection one begins to have second thoughts, particularly in his last terrifying Death Ship paintings. The fact is that this gnarled, turned-in, suspicious, pernickety old Cornishman was impelled to give creative expression to what was there, in his own land, in a similar way to intuitive outsiders like Berlin.

Wallis is not the only primitive painter of Cornwall. Jack Pender's grandfather, W.J. George, another fisherman, also started painting in his old age, producing hundreds of canvases from the age of 75 until his death at 94. One of these was described by his grandson like this:

Three black boats, brown mizzen sails steadying, white foam creaming their bows, hurrying to Newlyn fish market. Past the granite and white cottage homes of their crews, past the reaching arms of their home harbour, past the protecting island that forms a natural breakwater to the one time busy fishing village of Mousehole. The urgency of their progress is witnessed, felt, recorded.

'Witnessed, felt, recorded' — that is what every painter of any stature who works in Cornwall seems somehow to be compelled to follow. It can be seen in the primitive work of a Wallis or a George, or Mary Jewells of Newlyn, or Bryan Pearce of St Ives — a courageous figure suffering from phynylktenuea, a rare disease that retards mental progress,

42

who nevertheless has produced armfuls of fascinating studies of Cornish towns and landscapes seen through his extraordinarily perceptive eye. In the works of the simple primitive artist the same thing is reflected, although more starkly and directly, that is to be found in the less simple work of abstract painters like Ben Nicholson or John Wells, or in the sculpture of Sven Berlin — or Barbara Hepworth who, as most art critics agree, was deeply under the influence of Cornwall. That landscape, perhaps more than any other, would call up in her a deep emotional response since so much of her life was concerned with digging deep into the heart of her materials and searching out basic forms.

Go into any art gallery in Cornwall — whether the more sophisticated galleries of the Penwith Society at St Ives or the Newlyn Society at Newlyn, or the smaller galleries to be found in Polperro, Looe, Boscastle, Padstow, Newquay, Fowey, Falmouth — and certain interesting factors will emerge. First, by far the greatest percentage of the painters exhibiting will be non-Cornish — artists who have been drawn to Cornwall and have settled here to work. Second, the variety of their work, and that of their Cornish companions, is quite remarkable, ranging from traditional to pop, from figurative to abstract, from landscapes to geometrical formations. Thirdly, and this is the really significant factor, with the possible exception of portraiture, it is almost certain that every single painting or sculpture will somehow reflect that Cornish environment out of which it has been created.

That environment is difficult to pin down directly. Of course, from a superficial point of view there are many obvious aspects of very definite importance in their own way. For instance from the sheerly economical view painter's studios are not to be found growing on trees — in most parts of Britain they would be an unusual feature indeed, but in Cornwall they are in fact, plentiful. St Ives is perhaps something of a special case, but it is worth noting that in this small fishing town alone there are probably upwards of fifty professional artist's studios, all occupied by working artists; some of them, like Porthmeor and the former Piazze Studios set overlooking one of the most beautiful beaches in Britain. Similarly in Newlyn, in Mousehole, Penzance and surrounding areas, artist's studios are to be found in comparative profusion, often tailor built; but equally often converted successfully from former barns, even cowsheds. Where there's a will, there has to be a way. The same can be said for many other areas: Polperro, Fowey, Looe, Falmouth, Truro, Tintagel, Boscastle, Wadebridge. Indeed the artist's studio in Cornwall is almost as commonplace as, say, a pottery in Stoke (though even Cornwall can boast more potteries than any other English county).

In such a background, allied to the multiplicity of art societies and artists' clubs — and even such socially encouraging facts as numerous and attractive pubs where artists can meet for convivial evenings — it is only to be expected that painters feel an empathy, an encouragement to work. Yet when all this is admitted, there remains something further to be said, something that can hardly be put directly, but is most effective when hinted at almost ambiguously, as it once was by one of Cornwall's few native born painters of genius, the late Peter Lanyon. Killed, alas, in a gliding accident in the prime of life, Lanyon had already in his paintings managed to combine the basic linear form of landscape drawing with imaginative abstractions. Some of his most exciting works were among his last, when he started painting out of his experience of gliding, seeing the earth, and Cornwall in particular, from a totally fresh angle.

To conclude this introduction to the painter's world of Cornwall, here is how Peter Lanyon tried once to describe 'The Face of Penwith':

The Cornishman is not double-faced but multiple faced, faults of character which add up to a sort of innocence. He is never still himself except in death, but all the conflicts which lead to a game of hide and seek between native and the so-called "foreigner" are part of a process which constantly surfaces the most diverse and conflicting factors. The Cornishman is fond of private secrets. A solemn intercourse of native with native, often intimate, is mistaken for a gossiping and vicious moralizing. The part of this game which is revealed to the unfortunate "foreigner" is that part which concerns him alone, the rest is none of his business. Prayer is a strong force, and in the greatest days of revivalist services, in Wesleyan chapels, a poetic resolution was achieved. The loss of such inspiring services is as sad for Cornwall as the closing of the mines.

There is a main force which is both centrifugal and centripetal, a complete trust and desire to give absolutely everything and a converse withdrawal, a returning to a protective native envelope. Perhaps these qualities are most often found in insular people, but then after all Cornwall has for centuries been considered almost as an island.

Chapter Four

The Poet's Eye View

The bones of this land are not speechless
So first he should learn their language,
He whose soul, in its time-narrowed passage
Must mirror this place.

FRANCES BELLERBY

Although the fact tends to be less publicised, poets have been drawn to Cornwall just as numerously as painters. When we search back into history and find the great landscape painter Turner touring Cornwall and quickly filling his sketchbook, we can soon match that by discovering that Alfred Lord Tennyson once spent a summer holiday tramping around Cornwall, averaging 10 miles a day and keeping a diary of visits to such spots as King Arthur's Castle at Tintagel. The diary is full of vivid phrases such as 'glorious grass green monsters of waves', and 'when the long wave broke all down the thundering shores of Bude and Boss, there came a day as still as heaven.' Certainly it is not difficult to trace much of the imagery of Tennyson's later epic poems to that summer time wandering along the North Coast — Bude, Boscastle, Tintagel, Camelford, and later on the South Coast, Penzance,

Marazion, St Michael's Mount, Falmouth. Always in sight of the sea...

> After the sunset, down the coast he heard
> Strange music, and he paused and turning — there,
> All down the lonely coast of Lyonesse,
> Each with a beacon star upon his head,
> And with a wild sea-light about his feet,
> He saw them — headland after headland flame
> Far on into the rich heart of the west.

Another great English writer of the 19th century, though best known as a novelist, found unusual poetic stimulation from Cornwall — Thomas Hardy. When only twenty-nine and a struggling young architect, he was invited to St Juliot's Rectory, Boscastle, to make a report on proposed renovations. The rector's sister-in-law, Emma, acted as hostess, and Hardy immediately fell in love with her. Forty years afterwards he sat down and remembered the event in a poem which began:

> When I set out for Lyonesse,
> A hundred miles away,
> The rime was on the spray,
> And starlight lit my lonesomness,
> When I set out for Lyonesse
> A hundred miles away.

And the poem concludes triumphantly

> When I came back from Lyonesse
> With magic in my eyes,
> All marked with mute surmise
> My radiances rare and fathomless,
> When I came back from Lyonesse
> With magic in my eyes!

Thomas Hardy married his Emma, and though the marriage later turned sour, after her death in 1912 his mind turned back to those romantic early days, and he went on a pilgrimage back to Cornwall. Out of that visit, made long after he had given up writing novels, were born some of the most moving and passionate love poems in the English language, almost all of them directly connected with Cornwall. Indeed Cornwall must have sunk deeply into the writer's consciousness, for almost every poem captures an atmosphere peculiar only to this county:

> Beeny did not quiver,
> Juliot grew not grey,
> Thin Vallency's river,
> Held its wonted way,
> Bos seemed not to utter
> Dimmest note of dirge
> Targen mouth a mutter
> To its creamy surge.

Uniquely Cornish places like Beeny Cliff seemed perpetually to draw Hardy's interest. He writes of how 'in chasmal beauty looms that wild weird western shore', and remembers forlornly the woman, his love, who 'now knows nor cares for Beeny, and will laugh there never more'.

Writing of the way in which Cornwall cast its spell upon Thomas Hardy's works, particularly his poetry, the critic Elizabeth Beart once commented that these works could be largely attributed to the especial spiritual quality of Cornwall's hard, silent, indifferent heights, with the lonely buzzard circling above and immense distance all round, with violets hidden in grassy walls and thrift growing out of the very granite. Had it been another county, she wondered, might these works not only have been different but also less good? It was true that the especial quality was always to some extent possessed by all high lonely coasts but not to the extent that Cornwall possessed it. There was a sense that all the things usually considered important had been swept away and were not after all very important. It was something felt in the great expanse of sky, sea and land. More, the sense that something *else* was very important if only one could grasp what. The country with its heightened strenuous bare feeling that drove one inwards to this other important thing engendered the desire for a more spacious, generous and purposive mode of life. There was something in the bareness of Cornwall that stripped one of inessentials, something in the beauty of its contrasts of frail falls of pale ribbon-like water, flowering tide edges and stretches of flowers in deep valleys against the bare silent rock-like structure of its heights that encouraged a desire for more everlasting beauty within civilisation. Something in rocks jutting through bare treeless soil seemed akin to spiritual roots. With such a dark philosophy Thomas Hardy must obviously be numbered among the many artists who had a special regard for Cornwall, the county of his romance, with its quality of sweeping away all that is usual. His lyrics surely owed something to the especial flavour of Cornwall, something that transcended its beauty of form and colour alone.

Tennyson and Hardy are only two of many famous poets of the past who came, saw and were conquered by mysterious Cornwall. It would be possible to produce just as impressive a catalogue, as can be done among painters, to show how in many cases the influence of the county upon the poets was so strong as to draw them back again and again, even sometimes taking up permanent residence, as John Davidson did in Penzance. There have been remarkable Cornish-born poets of the past, men like John Harris, the poet-miner of Camborne, who was working in Dolcoath, Cornwall's deepest tin mine, at the age of only thirteen and wrote:

> The heat, the cold, the sulphur and the slime,
> The grinding masses of the loosened rock,
> The scaling ladders, the incessant grime
> From the dark timbers and the dripping block,
> The lassitude, the mallet's frequent knock,
> The pain of thirst when water was so near,

The aching joints, the blasted hole's rude shock,
Could not dash out the music from his ear,
Or stay the sound of song which ever murmured clear.

The cavern's sides, the vagues of shining spar,
The roof of rock where scarce the candle gleams,
The hollow levels strangely stretching far
Beneath the mountains, full of mineral seams,
Were evermore to him befitting themes,
For meditation and his rustic lay;
While in the darkness his pale visage gleams,
To read rich sonnets on the furrowed clay,
And crabby slabs that jut the ladder's lonely way.

However, it is simpler here to concentrate on examples of a more contemporary nature, and there are plenty enough of these. Sometimes, though seldom, the reaction has been a hostile one. After a tentative visit to Cornwall Walter de la Mare wrote that he did not feel safe again until he had crossed the River Tamar back into Devon; and Dylan Thomas, who spent a few months around Newlyn and Penzance (he and Caitlin were actually married at Penzance Registry Office in 1937) complained that Cornwall remained 'a strange country to me'. Generally though the poet's eye view of Cornwall, with all its fleeting faces, has been a remarkably penetrating one, ranging from the brilliant evocation of visiting poets such as George Barker or John Heath-Stubbs, through the work of what might be called resident 'furriners' such as John Betjeman or the Scottish poet, W.S. Graham, to native poets of the repute of A.L. Rowse, Jack Clemo and Charles Causley. Often, I think, it has been the visitor's unjaundiced and quickly emotional response which has captured most dramatically those usually hidden, or even buried elements of Cornwall. It was, for instance, a 'furriner', John Heath-Stubbs, during a period when he shared a cottage on the cliffs at Gurnard's Head with another poet, David Wright, who wrote that vivid poem quoted earlier beginning, 'This is a hideous and wicked country, sloping to hateful sunsets and the end of time'.

Now a good Cornishman might take exception to the violence of these epithets, yet they do bring to life something which is usually left to sleep — they do remind us that not far below the surface in Cornwall there linger all kinds of strange, weird, sometimes even evil elements. We should not fear to consider such things; who knows, they may be more honest, more real, than other aspects of the more modern Cornwall — aspects paraded bitterly again by the same poet, Heath-Stubbs, in another poem, 'The Last Will and Testament of the Cornish Chough':

> Romantic Cornwall's dead and gone,
> With Stephen Hawker in his tomb;
> The Western Ocean breaks upon
> The Land's End Point in a froth of foam —
> A welter of unappeasable grief:
> The artists caper in St Ives,
> Where, disembarking from his leaf,
> A hermit stepped from the wild waves,
> I, flame-billed Pyrrhocorax,
> Guardian of King Arthur's spirit,
> Croaking my last like Sycorax,
> Denote to those who shall inherit:
> In love of literature I grant
> To that which broods upon this place —
> The vision of the guarded Mount —
> A footnote out of Lycidas;
> To Zennor's fishy-flavoured maid,
> Who in her whirlpool mourns alone,
> By all her men unsatisfied,
> Two polished orbs of Cornish stone;
> To the sad-eyed Phoenician ghosts
> Revisiting, in their essence thin,
> Their ancient bridgeheads on these coasts,
> My dangerous, derelict mines of tin;
> For that notorious Queen of Cornwall,

She who with Tristan held her tryst,
What heirloom could be suitable —
Now that she's turned Methodist?
To the Bardic Gorsedd at Penwith,
And all the Olde Worlde shops,
Appropriately I bequeath
Each moulting feather as it drops;
But the royal soul of Arthur,
Crouched in my body, limb for limb —
I leave it to the British Empire,
Which certainly has need of him.

Perhaps more sympathetic to the Cornish way of life has been W.S. Graham, a Scottish born poet who settled in West Cornwall some 30 years ago, and still lives at Madron just outside Penzance. At one time Graham was hailed as the natural successor to Dylan Thomas and in such books as *The Night Fishermen* he certainly displayed the same amazing ability at adjectival juggling. Possibly this very romantic and lyrical poetic approach, with a vividly unexpected juxtaposition of words achieving the same effect of purpose as abstract painters in their field, does again help us to see Cornwall more clearly for what it really is. These qualities I think come out very clearly in a valedictory poem which Sydney Graham wrote in memory of the famous old St Ives fisherman painter, Alfred Wallis:

World hauled, he's grounded on God's great bank,
Keelheaved to Heaven, waved into boatfilled arms
Falls his homecoming leaving that old sea testament,
Watching the restless land sail rigged alongside
Townful of shallows, gulls on the sailing roofs.
And he's heaved once and for all a high dry packet
Pecked wide by curious years of a ferreting sea,
His poor house blessed by very poverty's religious
Breakwater, his past house hung in foreign galleries.
He's that stone sailor towering out of ther cupboarding sea
To watch the black boats rigged by a question quietly

52

Ghost home and ask right out with jackets of oil
The standing white of the crew 'what hellward harbour
Bows down her seawalls to arriving home at last?'

Falls into home his prayers pray. He's there to lie
Seagreat and small, contrary and rare as sand
Sea sheller. Yes falls to me his keptbeating, painters heart.
An ararat shore, loud limpet stuck to its terror,
Drags home the bible keel from a returning sea
And four black, shouting steerers stationed on movement
Call out arrival over the landgreat houseboat.
The ship of land with birds on seven trees
Calls out farewell like Melville talking down on
Nightfalls devoted barque and the parable whale.
What shipcry falls? The holy families of foam
Fall into wilderness and 'over the jasper sea.'
The gulls wade into silence. What deep seasaint
Whispered this keel out of its elements?

Another visiting poet of great sensitivity, Frances Bellerby,
once wrote in a poem:

> The bones of this land are not speechless.
> So first he should learn their language,
> He whose soul, in its time-narrowed passage,
> Must mirror this place.
>
> Then, speak as he ordered
> In the clear and formal rhythm
> Of soil and rock whose wisdom
> Is the Word.
>
> Made Bone; command the sea-light
> To release the pent, ingenious
> Elements; precise, fastidious,
> Sure, interpret.
>
> By arrangement, by choice. Meanwhile, blind-
> Fold, fingertip, the true veins
> Will hasten eager as fond slaves
> To chart this land.

By way of his own body — prove
The plan of the Bones, the fashion
Also of the changing Flesh, on
His image of Love.

John Betjeman, by contrast, has commemorated a true love
for Cornwall in lighter vein with his nostalgic memories of
childhood holidays along the North Coast at Trebetherick,
Rock and Polzeath. It is fascinating to see how persistently his
muse is prodded by his Cornish experiences:

Where yonder villa hogs the sea
Was open cliff to you and me.
The many-coloured caras fill
The salty marsh to Shilla Mill
And foreground to the hanging wood,
Are 'toilets' where the cattle stood.
The mint and meadowsweet would scent
The brambly lane by which we went;
Now, as we near the ocean roar,
A smell of deep-fry haunts the shore.
In pools beyond the reach of tide
The Senior Service cartons glide
And on the sand the surf line lisps
With wrappings of potato crisps.
The breakers bring with merry noise
Tribute of broken plastic toys
And lichened spears of blackthorn glitter
With harvest of the August litter.
Here in the late October light
See Cornwall, a pathetic sight,
Raddled and put upon and tired
And looking somewhat over-hired,
Remembering in the autumn air
The years when she was young and fair —
Those golden and unpeopled bays,
The shadowy cliffs and sheep-worn ways,
The legions of unsurfed on surf,
The thyme and mushroom-scented turf,

54

The slate-hung farms, the oil-lit chapels,
Thin elms and lemon-coloured apples —
Going and gone beyond recall
Now she is free for One and All.
One day a tidal wave will break
Before the breakfasters awake
And sweep the caras out to sea
The oil the tar and you and me
And leave in windy criss cross motion
A waste of undulating ocean
From which jut out, a second Scilly,
The Isles of Roughtor and Brown Willy.

Sometimes a real foreigner, like the Polish poet Zofia Ilinska who has lived for many years at St Mawes, where she and her husband used to run a large hotel, brings most vividly to life unexpected facets of Cornish life:

We provide the expected Pub; the usual Barber, Baker
and coffin maker
The usual female persons prepared to marry
Bearded men in charge of steamers, hooting in harbours,
Shaggy men in rubber boots magnificent with oars,
Clean-shaven men drying yards of netting,
Several burnt by the wind, mostly fishermen.
We specialise in the smell of seawood;
In the introvert seabirds absorbed in marine vegetation;
In high stepping waders patrolling the estuary,
Endlessly assaulting pallid moluscs.

The same rather unexpected imagery is featured in a poem 'The Tanker And Her Tugs (Death Scene Observed)' where, after describing a huge tanker entering the Carrick Roads on the full tide 'in a convoy of gulls shouting at the sun' the poet goes on to ruminate:

What tossings in broken water before this final
harbour?
What stillnesses and becalmings?
What revellings in foreign ports?

55

What woundings, healings, contritions?
What bouts of terrible chastity, alone with migrating birds in
                                        deserts of water?

What undeclared cargoes?
What inexplicable choices, with the compass faintly shaking?
What ships passed in the night and out of the night — what ships?
And what of those other encounters
With the luminescent organisms that changed your course
Off the Tierra del Fuego and the straits of Juan de Fuca,
With the starfish clinging to the hull
And the diabolical fish rumbling and belching
In the catastrophic sediments?

And now the sun tangles out of your rigging;
And now Three Tugs hasten to offer
What last assistance they may;
Squat vessels — business-like and composed,
They hurry to you without fussing,
Communicating in low voices:
The wife? The doctor? The nurse?
The priest with anointing oils?
The little sailing boats have caught their breath.
Oh the efficiency in these scenes of death!)

Each in their own way, among these visiting poets I have
quoted, has been equally provoked by Cornwall and its
landscape and seascape into a real passion of poetry. Poets are
ultra sensitive souls and so it is hardly surprising that in their
work we find such a vivid reaction. What is perhaps
surprising, and certainly exciting, is the way in which a
geographical background, an apparently dead land mass, can
not only stimulate such creativity — but in the process itself be
somehow transformed from deadness to life. Often this
creative influence inspires touches of poetic magic from quite
ordinary, non-poetic writers:

So we may believe
That on some day when white and piercing rays
Fuse with a water, jade and burning blue,

And foam beats on the milky shore in ecstasy,
A mortal diving deep and faithfully
Shall never die
But live forever
Knowing all
And part of thee
O glorious god, creator and destroyer
Mighty sea.
Or on a night
When white and honeyed moon
Piercing thy deepest hollow,
Leans down and calls
The black and purple waves, to rise in sapphire train
To dance and follow;
Then talking wings, like gray gulls from the granite
So every human sea-enchanted spirit
Flies out forever free in darkest space
Then sinks his rapt and star-transfigured face
To final rest in thee.

Those lines, from a poem 'Sea Magic', are by Dora Russell, ex wife of the late Bertrand Russell, written from her home, Carn Voel at Porthcurno. Although a prolific writer of articles Mrs Russell would probably not claim to be a poet — yet living as she does surrounded by the majestic cliffs of Treen and St Levan, aware constantly of the seething Atlantic waves rolling relentlessly over the long white sands below the Minack, she is literally *forced* into some kind of lyrical expression of her reactions.

When we come to look at the work of Cornish born poets — and today there are a surprising number of extremely talented Cornish poets, some of them internationally known — we may often find an extra dimension in their imagery. Particularly, I think, in the work of that extraordinary man, Jack Clemo, now in is sixties, who has spent his whole life in a small cottage at St Stephen, among the china clay pits. As is possibly well known now, Jack Clemo has suffered much of his life from both blindness and deafness, but, as often fortunately happens, he has reacted to these burdens as to a challenge, and surmounted them magnificently to become one of the major poets of our time. And, of course, essentially, above all, a poet of Cornwall. Fortunately in this instance the poet himself has put on record, in an article 'My Life in the Clay World' which I published in the *Cornish Review*, a penetrating assessment of the affect of Cornwall on his work as a creative artist:

I was well on in my teens before I realised that there was anything symbolic about the scarred and eerie landscape which had resulted from William Cookworthy's love of pottery two hundred years earlier. I had never regarded mid-Cornwall's clay seam from a mundane standpoint, as a mere industrial product, but had simply let its elemental fantasy impress my mind and imagination. All its strong and lonely idiom was in keeping with my spiritual needs, even in childhood. Year after year I watched the clay-land dawns and sunsets, the first golden rays of the sun striking the white peaks, setting the metal prongs and tip-wires glowing and shimmering while the gravel bulk remained in shadow, and then at evening the daylight fading mysteriously from the blurred grey masses and the weird spiked clusters of stacks. At night there was a fairyland touch with the dune-lights, pit-lights and tank-lights twinkling, and the red glare of a furnace occasionally glimpsed through a kiln doorway. So many different features were revealed, some magical, some terrifying, and always free from the over-simplification and sentimentality of the conventional poet's world. As I gradually became aware of the deep metaphysical undertones of this medley of restless contours — the suggestion of a purifying process leading to the 'patterned cup' — I found other parts of Cornwall strangely remote from me as a poet. I saw most of Cornwall's beauty spots before I wrote any mature poems, but even St Michael's Mount did not inspire my muse, and it is only during the past two years that I have been able to reflect the rugged splendour of West Cornwall in my verse. The long obsession with clay images, and the attempt to break their grip when romance made me conscious of fertility, is the central tension of my artistic struggle.

Jack Clemo's poems speak mostly of a particular and indeed

very strange part of Cornwall, the world of the silent rearing white clay heaps which surround his home:

> Sour clay faces slunk from the dream;
> Ascetic contours rasped through summer haze
> Beyond the lithe corn and the poppies' blaze.
> Where the unmined valley
> Closed in on a nudging stream,
> A few stacks loomed tall and obstinate
> Beside the hidden furnace, near a field gate.

And in another poem 'Clay Dams', Clemo uses the local habit of clay damming as a physical image to portray his own religious beliefs:

> Still defiant, still immune,
> My wall of faith surrounds the soft heavings,
> Thus damned and controlled, awaiting a heat
> Subtler than sun or switched current. No bowed bed,
> Or burst joint mars my anomalous structure,
> For it admits no fad-faked chemicals
> That swell the flesh against traditions bounds.

Jack Clemo's poetry is earthy and harsh, even bleak — and very much the work of a Cornishman. The Cornish are, inevitably, less romantic about their county than newcomers. Much that newcomers have to learn — sometimes in painful flashes, as in John Heath-Stubbs' 'This is a hideous and wicked country' — is known *instinctively* by the Cornish-born poet. This is certainly true of Clemo, and of several other of the more articulate younger Cornish poets, like D.M. Thomas, for instance:

> Kerenza is my name. If you betray me,
> expect no pity when the midnight moon steps forth
> and you behold me, or my enantiomorph,
> waiting for you and singing on the shore.
> My eyes, whites black as chert, will lure
> as a ship is tide-drawn to an old wharf
> at the tin-stream's outlet. From Bude to Geevor,

whatever land-child you are lying with,
you will hear a sea-child call you. Faithless wrecker,
you will stumble down the seaward-sloping path,
and there, by tide and rock cut off,
trample through the red-sea-running mirror,

to find all changed. The lights of Perranporth
shining as from the left side of the bay;
kissed, it will be as if you gave
the kiss, a black moon in an orange sky;
a sigh beginning as a laugh
will answer your shriek with, *Give me back the dead.*

Then I will cling to you, your negative,
heart clamped direct to your heart, tears
drilling fires through your breast. Lightning from Ligger
Head will strike the engine-house above
you, and I will whirl you clear
from the rocks to the running storm. For my name is Love.

In this as in much of his other work — which has been published in America as well as here — Thomas captures something of the sea-woven flavour running through most true Cornish imagery. He reacts equally emotionally to inland Cornwall, to places like his native Carn Brea, at Redruth, or to the moors and their ancient stones. 'These holed stones throb as I stride through stones and grass. Rain spits on my face — in a few deft touches something mysterious is suggested. But it is to the sea-washed coast that Thomas, like so many other poets, Cornish and foreign, is drawn as if by a magnet:

Needles flake off into the blue air. Listen.
In the August silence, on the bare cliff path you can fling
a stone and it will not break the silence, but you can hear
the wedges and drills of erosion hammering
in a silence that is uproar, beneath the wrecking Brissons.

The reference to mining shows a Cornishman's awareness. Awareness of a different sort is to be found in the poetry of Dr A.L. Rowse, the doyen of Cornish poets. Although best known

for his historical studies of the Elizabethan age in Cornwall —
not forgetting a memorable autobiography, *A Cornish
Childhood* — Rowse has continued to write delicate and
nostalgic poetry that often recaptures the characteristic beauty
of Cornwall's byways. He brings to life, reflectively, the
quieter corners of Cornwall: the lanes around Gorran School,
the little river at Hemmick winding down to a secret beach:

> Behold the gulled and gorsed rocks,
> Afternoon honey in keen wind sunlight
> Myself on an ultimate stone
> A water world about me
> All movement and wind and sea
> Bobbing seaweed flotsam and spars
> Waves heaving and dipping
> Making uncertain the Napoleonic land
> Little port with deserted fort
> Beyond, ranked and ranged headlands
> Trenarren, Chapel Point, and around to Dodman
> The Gribbin milk-haze in seamist
> White peninsula coves along the flank
> The erect forefinger standing serene
> Over the ebb and flow of tides
> Over the bell-rung flowered sea.

Another internationally known poet from Cornwall, Charles
Causley, is perhaps less dependent on his native county than
many of the others, in that he has achieved his success by a
series of books of lyrical poems, racy and attractive, which
strike home immediately to the reader anywhere. Many of
these poems, like 'Farewell Aggie Weston', commemorate a
six-year period in the Royal Navy when Causley was travelling
abroad. Yet when he wants to he has a capacity for
illuminating our feelings about Cornwall just as effectively as
the others — most notably, of course, in 'A Short Life of Nevill
Northey Burnard' (the Cornish Sculptor.) It is enough simply
to quote the opening verses:

Here lived Burnard who with his finger's bone
Broke syllables of light from the moorstone,
Spat on the genesis of dust and clay,
Rubbed with huge hands the blinded eyes of day,
And through the seasons of the talking sun
Walked, calm as God, the fields of Altarnum.

Here, where St Nonna with a holy reed
Hit the bare granite, made the waters bleed,
Madmen swam to their wits in her tin well,
Young Burnard fasted, watched, learned how to tell
Stone beads under the stream, and at its knock
Quietly lifted out his prize of rock.

There are older Cornish born poets of eminence, too, men
like the playwright Ronald Duncan at Morwenstow, engaged
on writing an epic poem, 'Man', or like Ronald Bottrall, from
Camborne, who was widely published internationally at the
time of Auden and Spender and Isherwood. And even those
originally of Cornish stock like Allen Curnow, a professor at
Auckland University, New Zealand, can never really forget:

Curnow of Anlebra farm at Nancledra, Curnow the sweep,
Curnow of the mercer and councillor, Curnow the barber,
Curnow of Gurnard's Head over by Wikka where deep
In the scoop of the Western swell your grey hulk's harbour

Death, fisher of men, your nets of granite and foam;
Surely you haul us all in, the shoal of our lives,
Mine of a strange sea native, Pacific my home,
And my tribes folk, men of your tetarchate, Saint Ives.

I hear in a winter mist the drowned moan over the moors
And the Zennor Maid sing scorn on the Body and Blood
Green-lashing the moon in her hair and the souls of her wooers,
The beast-girl's image graven in the house of God:

Lithe-tailed Lilith we loved in our sea dreams:
The cross in her sea-glass dangles upside down,
Down, down, deep as the locked Antarctic streams
And the blind isles where the bread of my birth was thrown —

Void as all voyages, for the mast of her mirror
Chases and faces: all constellations glitter
On the surf of her song, the tide's tongue of her terror
Since the gadfly God-word skimmed her curdlipped water.

In Allen Curnow's poem is to be found in abundance all that
strange and particularised imagery which seems to be drawn
out of poets when they come in contact with Cornwall.
Whether Tennyson or Hardy, Graham or Heath-Stubbs,
Clemo or Thomas or Curnow — the accident of being born in
Cornwall is seen to be not so important. What *is* important —
and inexplicable — is the effect of the land (and sea) upon the
human creative worker. This is aptly illustrated in some lines
from 'Minerals of Cornwall, Stones of Cornwall' a long poem,
published in the *Cornish Review,* by Peter Redgrove, teacher
of poetry in the Liberal Arts department at Falmouth Art
School:

Splinters of information, stones of information,
Drab stones in a drab box, specimens of a distant place,
Granite, galena, talc, lava, kaolin, quartz,
Landscape in a box, under the dull sky of Leeds —
One morning was awake, in Cornwall, by the estuary,
In the tangy pearl-light, tangy tin-light,
And the stones were awake, these ounce-chips,
Had begun to think, in the place they came from.

Tissues of the earth, in their right place,
Quartz tinged with the rose, the deep quick,
Scrap of tissue of the slow heart of the earth,
Throbbing the light I look at it with,
Pumps slowly, most slowly, the deep organ of the earth;
And galena too, snow-silvery, its chipped sample
Shines like sun on peaks, it plays and thinks with the mineral
light,
It sends back its good conclusions, it is exposed,
It sends back the light silked and silvered,

And talc, and kaolin, why they are purged, laundered,
As I see the white sand of some seamless beaches
Is laundered and purged like the whole world's mud
Quite cleansed to its very crystal; talc a white matt,
Kaolin, the white wife of Cornwall
Glistening with inclusions, clearly its conclusions
Considered and laid down, the stone-look
Of its thoughts and opinions of flowers
And turf riding and seeding above it in the wind,
Thoughts gathered for millenia as they blossomed in millions
Above its then kaolin-station within the moor,
The place of foaming white streams and smoking blanched
                                                    mountains.

Poets working in Cornwall seem just as influenced by their
environment as the painters. Jack Clemo spelled things out for
us when he reflected upon his life in the clay world, and talked
of 'the deep metaphysical undertones of this medley of restless
contours'. Clemo was referring to the world of the clay pits
which surrounds him, but in Cornwall there are many worlds
to surround the creators, and it would be surprising if they did
not respond with passion and power — mixed, as ever in
Cornwall, with a little sadness.

I see in dreams the lost land of Langarrow
Sleeping under silent sandy waves;
In every house and every roadway narrow
The dry bones stir in their unquiet graves.
On sand-soft pillows in a dry, cold kiss
Skull touches skull as even on that night
They lay without a thought of aught amiss
Until the drifting sand blocked out their light.
The yellowing bones within the taverns cry
For wine to clear their parching throat of sand;
And now those bones forever are as dry
As those dice they rattled in their hand.
Seven churches stood within the walls,
Far-famed their slender towers and stately piers,
Their priests grew fat within the prince's halls,

Their bells are silent now these many years.
The merchants' business now no longer thrives,
The golden sand invades their golden hoards
And chokes the mouths that chattered for men's lives
And bartered bodies over counter boards.
The dry bones rustle fills the sand-sunk town,
Whispering the tales of shame and lust
That brought a rich and powerful kingdom down
And closed its people's eyes with yellow dust.

I cannot do better than close this chapter with the above
lament by Richard G. Jenkin, who as well as being a Cornish
poet is a Bard of the Cornish Gorsedd. Like the painters, poets
give us the colour and the imagery: the rest is up to us. We
would surely be very lacking in imaginative response if, after
reading some of the poetry I have quoted, we did not gain an
impression that perhaps indeed we are dealing with a land, a
place, a world — a county, if we must use such a mundane
word! — very different from most others.

Chapter Five

The Novelist's World

I always feel that I am the original owner of Cornwall, and everyone else is a newcomer

VIRGINIA WOOLF

Surely it is no coincidence that so many of the world's most popular novelists have set their books in Cornwall? Daphne du Maurier, Winston Graham, Howard Spring, Hammond Innes, Virginia Woolf, Compton Mackenzie, Crosbie Garstin, Hugh Walpole — the list could be endless of writers who at some time or other have produced work steeped in the mystery and the strangeness of the county in which they have either made their homes or spent frequent periods. Perhaps it is not without significance that few of these writers are Cornish born: this is, they have mostly been drawn to Cornwall, often from more conventional areas, lured by that same mystic and romantic atmosphere which in turn, so often, they have captured in their novels.

Is this really so very surprising? Who, for instance, driving over lonely Bodmin Moor and suddenly coming upon the forlorn outline of the now famous Jamaica Inn at Bolventor could fail to feel that impact of such a stark, bleak out-of-this-world setting? How well in turn did Daphne du Maurier capitalise upon this atmosphere in her best seller *Jamaica Inn*, deepening the shadows, stressing the unease, heightening the general impression of other worldliness. Consider, for instance, this portrait of the landlord, Joss:

He was a great husk of a man, nearly seven feet high, with a creased black brow and the skin the colour of a gypsy. His thick dark hair fell over his eyes in a fringe and hung about his ears. He looked as if he had the strength of a horse with immense powerful shoulders, long arms that reached almost to his knees, and large fists like hams. His frame was so big that in a sense his head was dwarfed, and sunk between his shoulders, giving that half stooping impression of a giant gorilla, with his black eyebrows and his mat of hair. But for all his long limbs and mighty frame, there was nothing of the ape about his features for his nose was hooked, curving to a mouth that might have been perfect once but now sunken and fallen, and there was still something fine about his great dark eyes, in spite of the lines and pouches and the red blood flecks.

This is writing larger than life and, therefore, eminently suited to a Cornish novel. In other tales Daphne du Maurier has used equally vivid descriptive passages to portray the place as well as people — in *Rebecca, Frenchman's Creek, My Cousin Rachel* there are haunting descriptions of wild cliffs, raging seas, bleak bare lonely spots of a kind that it often seems are only found in Cornwall. In one of her most recent novels, *The House on the Strand* the familiar Cornish legend of land that had disappeared under the sea is given an unfamiliar modern twist by portraying a man who, under the influence of a potent drug, is able to return to the past period when that land was still above the sea.

In a way, here is a perfect example of Cornwall stirring the creative faculties. It is of course possible to make a case for suggesting that Daphne du Maurier *might* have written all her novels, attained the same popularity, if she had spent her whole life living in Tooting or Surbiton. No doubt a writer of such talent would have dug some kind of romance and mystery even out of such mundane settings. But it is still difficult to imagine that Miss du Maurier would have produced *quite* such haunting, disturbing, other worldly atmospheres. Without entering into too many arguments on the point, one is entitled to declare that Tooting is *not* Cornwall — that there *is* some kind of elemental difference between a suburban London street and the cliffs of Land's End, between the glittering West End shops and the equally glittering but much older Dozmary Pool or Looe Bar — between the unseen yet unforgettable Land of Lyonesse, and the very much seen and utterly forgettable building estates of the North Circular Road.

Novelists have been drawn to Cornwall from a long time back. Daniel Defoe visited the county, as did R.L. Stevenson and William Makepeace Thackeray, and, of course, Charles Dickens. It was Dickens, on a walking tour in company with fellow author John Forster, who became excited by the scenery and declared his intention of writing a great novel which would open 'in some terribly iron-bound spot on the Cornish coast'. In the end he did not write the novel, but he never forgot his travels: 'Blessed star of morning, such a trip we had into Cornwall. If you could have followed us into the earthy old churches and into the strange caverns of the gloomy seashore and down into the depths of mines and up to the top of giddy heights where unspeakable green water was roaring.' Forster added this postscript description of how they watched a sunset at Land's End: 'There was something in the sinking of the sun behind the Atlantic that autumn afternoon, as we viewed it together from the top of the rock projecting furthest into the sea, which each in his turn declared to have no parallel in memory.'

After the turn of the century novelists of many kinds came to Cornwall and were inspired into creation, among them Aleister Crowley ('the Great Beast') who wrote vividly of black masses and witchcraft; Walter Besant, who was fascinated by the old legend of Lyonesse; Compton Mackenzie, who wrote his very first novel, *Carnival*, while living at Phillack and at Gunwalloe, on the storm-bound coast of Mount's Bay; Hugh Walpole, who lived for many years at Truro and set his *Rogue Herries* chronicles in the Cathedral cloisters there — and many lesser known but reputable writers, like J.D. Beresford, Margaret Kennedy, and one or two Cornish born novelists, the brothers Joseph and Silas Hocking, and the famous parson-novelist S. Baring Gould, not forgetting J.C. Cobb, whose vividly melodramatic novel about Land's End, *The Watchers on the Longships* remains a best-seller to this day.

Some of these earlier names come as a surprise, like that of R.M. Ballantyne, the author of *Coral Island* and whose first novel, *Deep Down, A Tale of the Cornish Mines*, was written following a period living in Penzance. Then how many people would be aware that Cornwall was much involved in the creation of the classic *The Wind in the Willows?* Its author, Kenneth Graham, was a regular visitor to Fowey, where he stayed with his great friend "Q" (Sir Arthur Quiller Couch), and the two men often went rowing up the delightful River Fowey. In a chapter in *The Wind in the Willows* entitled 'Wayfarers All' there is this picture of a typical Cornish sea port of the nineteenth century, in the words of the Sea Rat:

'And now,' he was softly saying, 'I take to the road again, holding on south-westwards for many a long and dusty day: till at last I reach the little grey sea town I know so well, that clings along one steep side of the harbour. There through dark doorways you look down flights of stone steps, overhung by great pink tufts of valerian and ending in a patch of sparkling blue water. The little boats that lie tethered to the rings and stanchions of the old sea-wall are gaily painted as those I clambered in and out of in my own childhood: the salmon leap on the flood tide, schools of mackerel flash and play past quay-sides and foreshores, and by the windows the great vessels glide, night and day up to their moorings or forth to the open sea. There, sooner or later, the ships of all seafaring nations arrive; and there, at its destined hour the ship of my choice will let go its anchor. I shall take my time, I shall tarry and bide, till at last the right one lies waiting for me,

69

warped out into midstream, loaded low, her bow-sprit pointing down harbour. I shall slip on board, by boat or along hauser; and then one morning I shall wake to the song and tramp of the sailors, the clink of the capstan, and the rattle of the anchor-chain coming merrily in. We shall break out the jib and the foresail, the white houses on the harbour side will glide slowly past us as she gathers steeringway, and the voyage will have begun! As she forges towards the headland she will clothe herself with canvas; and then, once outside, the sounding slap of great green seas as she heels to the wind, pointing south!

There are many other glimpses of Cornwall woven into the fabric of *The Wind in the Willows* — not least in importance being what appears to be a description of my own previous home at The Old Sawmills at Golant, above Fowey:

Leaving the main stream, they now passed into what seemed at first sight like a little land-locked lake. Green turf sloped down to either edge, brown snaky tree roots gleamed below the surface of the quiet water, while ahead of them the silvery shoulder and foamy tumble of a weir, arm in arm with a restless dripping mill wheel, that held up in its turn a grey-gabled mill house, filled the air with a soothing murmur of sound, dull and smothering yet with little clear voices speaking up cheerfully out of it at intervals. It was so very beautiful that the Mole could only hold up both fore paws and gasp, 'O my! O my! O my!'

'Q', Cornish by birth, attained twin eminence — as a Cambridge professor and as Mayor of Fowey (Troy Town in his novels). In a book of essays *From a Cornish Window* 'Q' recollected delightedly how his window looked out from a small library upon a small harbour frequented by ships of all nations — British, Danish, Swedish, Norwegian, Russian, French, German, Italian now and then and American or a Greek — and upon a shore which he loved because it was his native county. Of all views he reckoned that of the harbour the most fascinating and easeful for it combined perpetual change with perpetual repose. It amused like a panorama and soothed like an opiate and once this was realised it was easy to understand why so many thousands of men around this island appeared to spend all their time watching tidal water. Certainly in his novels 'Q' managed to recreate a fascinating aspect of Cornish sea-faring life, and he peopled this thinly disguised Fowey with a rich assortment of local characters.

As, too, did another marvellous writer of Cornish dialect and village life, Charles Lee, who though not a native of Cornwall, is often regarded as one of the most successful re-creators in fictitional form, of Cornish life. He stayed in several parts of Cornwall, including Newlyn and Portloe, during which time in his own words 'as a chiel amang ye takin' notes,' a mixture of reporter, anthropologist and literary artist, he recorded Cornish people's habits, their nuances and tricks of speech, and so gave his tales authentic flavour. These were to re-emerge in such earlier short novels as *Dorinda's Birthday*, and *The Widow Woman*, set in Newlyn about a hundred years ago and capturing the set social patterns of that time, portraying the comfortably bodied and middle wealthy widow, rather like a female spider setting out to capture a new mate. There is a strong comic sense in Charles Lee's work which brings out the best of Cornish life, and never better than in another of his novels, *Our Little Town*, which is really a series of episodes about local life in Porthjulyan which, as one critic pointed out at the time is Portloe so thinly disguised that you might still discover Penticost's and the place where James over-to-Shop dwelt with his wife. In this novel there is a hilarious battle of the Amazons when the women of Porthjulyan attack their menfolk in the citadel of exclusive masculinity, Penticost's cobbler's shop — the women, naturally, getting their way, for in the words of old Uncle Hannibal, one of Mr. Lee's favourite characters, 'When a chap an' a maid do come together chap shut his eyes tight: maid aupens hers a bit wider. How should a chap look to have a chanst?'

But principally Cornwall inspires melodrama rather than farce, and rightly so, for its impact is almost inevitably towards the former. D. H. Lawrence wrote many novels, and although he never set one wholly in Cornwall, in 1916-17 he spent over a year with his German wife Frieda living deep in one of the wildest and most lovely parts of Cornwall. For Lawrence this period at Higher Tregerthen, Zennor, Cornwall was to be merely a passing phase. Yet a writer of his genius would have been incapable of not reacting to such a sensitised place. In his letters he wrote enthusiastically of the magnificent scenery, the seas breaking against the rocks 'like the first craggy breaking of dawn in the world' — a great comfort after all 'this whirlwind of dust and grit and dirty paper of a modern Europe.' He continues:

I do like Cornwall. It is still something like King Arthur and Tristan. It has never taken the Anglo-Saxon civilisation, the Anglo-Saxon sort of Christianity. One can feel free here for that reason — feel the world as it was in that flicker of pre-Christian civilisation when humanity was really young.

Paradoxically Lawrence did not take to the Cornish people, though acknowledging in them a natural gentleness:

I don't like the people here. They ought to be living in the darkness and warmth and passionateness of the blood, sudden, incalculable. Whereas they are like insects gone cold, living only for money, *for dirt*... They are all afraid — that's why they are so mean. But I don't really understand them. Only I know this, I have never in my life come across such inertly selfish people. The Cornish have had a harsh, unprotected life and in order to survive they have had to withdraw into their shells — this often seeming, to an outsider, self-centred.

Lawrence of course, was given to somewhat exaggerated off-the-cuff intuitions — yet he *was* a genius, and there *is* perception in his criticism, as well as his praise. Later on he proposed to Middleton Murry and Katherine Mansfield, with typical enthusiasm, that they and other writers should:

Live here, pitch our camp and unite our forces and become an active

72

power, here, together... It is a most beautiful place, a tiny village nestling under high, shaggy moorhills, a big sweep of lovely sea beyond, such lovely sea, lovelier than the Mediterranean. It is five miles from St Ives and seven miles from Penzance. To Penzance one goes over the moors, high, then down into Mount's Bay, all gorse now, flickering with flowers; and then it will be heather; and then hundreds of foxgloves. It's the best place I have been in.

In the years ahead there were other places to draw Lawrence — France, Italy, Mexico. But probably only in the last did he feel quite as close to the elemental as he did in West Cornwall, and in particular that 'splendid place' on the edge of a few rough stony fields that go to the sea where... 'there is a little grassy terrace outside and at the back the moor tumbles down, great enormous grey boulders and gorse... It would be so splendid if it could come off; such a lovely place; our Rananim.'

Lawrence was never to find his Rananim, but his instincts were on the right lines. Before and since many other artists have been equally tempted by the dramatic background of Cornwall to make it a centre for group-living. In a sense, this is what the artists have done, turning whole areas like St Ives and Newlyn into their own community centres. Writers being much more individualistic, real loners, perhaps one cannot expect quite the same achievement. Yet it is surely significant how many greater writers have been drawn to Cornwall, even if only briefly like Lawrence.

Virginia Woolf, whose literary eminence was achieved at much the same time as Lawrence, was a totally different kind of writer, though in her own way just as much a genius. Yet, she too, was inexplicably affected by Cornwall, and in particular the same corner as Lawrence knew — the area around St Ives Bay, stretching from Godrevy in the East to Zennor and Gurnard's Head in the West. Unlike Lawrence, Virginia Woolf spent many long periods in Cornwall, where her father, critic Leslie Stephen had a house at St Ives. From the window of this house, in Talland Road, young Virginia could look out on a panoramic view of the vast sweep of St Ives Bay in which, pre-eminent, stands out the white lighthouse of Godrevy. Many years later that setting, indeed that lighthouse, was to provide the background for one of Mrs Woolf's most famous novels, *To The Lighthouse*. It is very much an intellectual's book and yet constantly in the descriptive passages, even if put into people's mouths as conversational pieces, the images and influences of Cornwall are forever breaking through. Like every other major writer who has ever visited Cornwall, Virginia Woolf was never able to forget the extraordinary impact of this wild and elemental place:

The romance of Cornwall has once more overcome me. I find that one lapses into a particular mood of absolute enjoyment which takes me back to my childhood. How I wish you were here — as only the Cornish bred see its stupendous merits.

It was as a child, with her sister Vanessa and her brothers Thoby and Adrian that Virginia Woolf whiled away many a languorous summers' day playing on the sands of Porthminster and Porthmeor or climbing the granite rocks to Clodgy Point or up to the little fishermen's chapel on top of the island. There were boat trips with her father across the bay, stopping for some mackerel fishing on the way back — outings which left vivid and useful imprints on the novelist's mind, later reflected, as in the novel *Jacob's Room*:

The mainland, not so very far off — you could see clefts in the cliffs, white cottages, smoke going up — wore an extraordinary look of calm, of sunny peace, as if wisdom and piety had descended upon the dwellers there. Now a cry sounded, as of a man calling pilchards in a main street. It wore an extraordinary look of piety and peace almost as if the end of the world had come and cabbage fields and stone walls, and coastguard stations and above all, the white sands bays, with the waves breaking unseen by anyone, rose to heaven in a kind of ecstacy.

Although later, particularly after her marriage to Leonard Woolf, the novelist spent more of her time in London and

Sussex, she was always avid to return to the mysterious land of her youth, and once there she would write memorable letters:

It is pitiable to think that you are bothering about pictures and no doubt leaving your umbrella on Haverstock Hill while I am watching two seals basking in the sea at Gurnards Head. This is no poetic licence. There they were, with their beautifully split tails and dog-shaped heads rolling over and diving like two naked dark brown old gentlemen. Two minutes before a viper started up under my feet. The smell of the gorse which is all in bloom and precisely like a Cornish picture against a purple sea is like — I don't really know what. We are on the cliffs quite by ourselves, nothing but gorse between us and the sea, and when I have done this letter we are going to take our books and roll up in a hollow over the sea and there watch the spray and the bees and the peacock butterflies.

This was in a letter to her sister the painter, Vanessa Bell: The same ecstatic note is struck in a later letter to the critic Saxon Sydney Turner:

We are between Gurnard's Head and Zennor. I see the nose of the Gurnard from my window. We step out into the June sunshine past mounds of newly sprung gorse, bright yellow and smelling of nuts, over a grey stone wall, so along a track scattered with granite to a cliff beneath which is the sea, of the consistency of innumerable plover eggs where they turn grey-green, semi-transparent. However, when the waves curl over they are more like emeralds, and then the spray at the top is blown back like a mane — an old simile doubtless, but rather a good one. Here we lie roasting though L. pretends to write an article for the *Encyclopedia* about Co-operation. The truth is we can't do anything but watch the sea — especially as the seals may bob up, first looking like logs, then like naked old men with tridents for tails. I'm not sure that the beauty of the country isn't really its granite hills and walls and houses, and not the sea. Of course its very pleasant to come across the sea spread out at the bottom, blue, with purple stains on it, and here a sailing ship, there a red steamer. But last night, walking through Zennor, the granite was — amazing is the only thing to say, I suppose, half-transparent with the green hill behind it, the granite road curving up and up. All the village dogs were waiting outside the

75

church, and the strange Cornish singing inside, so unlike the English. I think a good deal about the Phoenicians and the Druids and how I was a nice little girl here, and ran along the top of the stone walls.

Of course Virginia Woolf's profound feeling for Cornwall can be traced in several of her novels, apart from letters, and in particular in *To The Lighthouse*. There is a passage where she describes one of the main characters, Mrs Ramsay watching the beam of the lighthouse stroking the floor of the bedroom in the night, watching with fascination, hypnotised, 'as if it were stroking with its silver fingers some sealed vessel in her brain whose bursting would flood her with delight... happiness, exquisite happiness, intense happiness'. And in the same novel there is an evocative description of Mrs Ramsay looking out upon the bay and seeing the great plateful of blue water before her:

...the hoary lighthouse, distant, austere, in the midst; and on the right, as far as the eye could see, fading and falling, in soft low pleats, the green sand dunes with the wild flowing grasses on them, which always seemed to be running away into some moon country, uninhabited of men.

Virginia Woolf was awarded the Hawthornden Prize in 1927 for *To The Lighthouse*. At about the same time another novelist who was to be deeply impacted by Cornwall was beginning to establish a reputation — Howard Spring, one-time child of the smoky suburbs of Cardiff and Manchester, who spent the last half of his life around Falmouth. Here, he recollects:

The sea sweeps into a magnificent harbour, and off the harbour ran broad arms of water that felt their way deep into the recesses of the hills; and themselves in many cases throwing off other arms that go in countless ramifications through the countryside. All were subject to the sea, so that the surge and sigh of waters governed by the steadfast laws of the tides drew music through all the hollows of the hills. Great ships went up and anchored deep in the heart of the country; and at every turning one might come upon an inland village with a sweep of shingle beach, a tiny jetty, and a marine flavour. In those days no motor-car or charabanc disturbed the quiet; to get from place to place a boat was used to cross the blue shining fiords, and at such times the novelist often remembered spying old men, telescope to eye, following the fortunes of vessels they had known more intimately. In sunny gardens palms grew to a splendid height, and the intense colours of the sea, seen between their stems, gave to the landscape a sub-tropical illusion. Then there was the blue and green transparent water of the sea and the creeks inviting the body to its cold embrace...

Howard Spring was an extremely professional writer, with years of journalistic training, and so in his novels one finds a great deal of exact reportage, with the most detailed and accurate scene painting, as in this passage from his last novel, *Winds of The Day*:

I stood there alone. Dros-y-Mor has now become an accustomed house to me, but I wish to write of what I saw then. I stood with my back to it and looked upon the creek. This twisted a hundred yards or so from the house, so that I saw little of it. But I saw and felt the quietness: the fields that sloped down to the water, the heron wading along the shore, a tree here and there mirrored in the glass of the water, a swan making for the bank with a flotilla of brown cygnets behind it. The water ended at my feet, arrested by a wall that had been built up of the local stone, and to my right stone steps climbed to this grassy platform on which I stood. It had that day been shorn, and the smell of cut grass was all about me, filling the air which trembled now on the verge of night, with the new moon going down. I turned and looked at the house that had been behind me, long and low and white. The tall trees, bursting into full leaf, rose behind it, sheltering it with great arms, birch and elm and sycamore. The stream that ran through them here met the sea. A ghostly tinkle of water, as it tumbled over one edge of the platform, was in my ears, and there, glimmering now, their gold turning dark, the king-cups grew.

In Spring's most famous novel, *My Son, My Son,* the hero and narrator goes to join a friend staying in Falmouth:

It was the first time I had travelled into the West Country, and once I had crossed the Saltash Bridge, leaving Devonshire behind, and had entered upon the strange, riven countryside of Cornwall, with the railway passing over viaduct after viaduct, carrying us above chasms filled with dusky woods, and through tilted, angular postures, and alongside the great white cones of the clay works that rose against the sky like giants' tents, and giving us here and there glimpses of a distant sea bluer than any I had known, and nearer views of unaccustomed vegetation, eucalyptus and palm and a profusion of hydrangeas; why, then I felt the North fall like a smoky burden from my back and a deep willingness for lotus-eating take possession of me.

Spring, in this quieter, more even approach, still eventually conveys much the same message as Daphne du Maurier — in almost every one of his novels that have a Cornish setting (and few have not, in the later years) he is constantly stressing that magical moment when one 'enters upon the strange riven countryside of Cornwall' — or when 'I felt the North fall like a smoky burden from my back' — in other words, he recognises Cornwall is not as other places, but a world apart.

Another internationally famous novelist to base many of his tales on Cornwall, where he spent more than a decade living at Perranporth, is Winston Graham. Like Daphne du Maurier, Graham has been drawn irresistibly to the past — not surprisingly, for the past of Cornwall is rich in sources of inspiration for serious writers of fiction: religion, piracy, wrecking, mining are all themes with a large appeal. Winston Graham is one of those rare writers who manages to create imaginatively from factual evidence. He is a great believer in using only known facts, and endless research went into his famous 'Poldark' series. Together they form a continuous novel, covering in minute detail the period 1783-1793 — a time of rapid transformation in the economic and spiritual life of a county where the currents of rural and seafaring activities intermingled and were also affected by mining and its affiliated interests. In case this sounds dull stuff let me hasten to say it is quite the reverse. Here is what that perceptive literary critic, Ernest Martin, had to say:

The value of a work of this length and range lies in its imagination and its care for detail. All long chronicles of family life tend to lose their impetus at some points. Mr. Graham has created characters who live on in the mind. Ross and Demelza and Dr Enys, Caroline Penvenen and the Warleggans are all convincing persons with their own identities, and the long account of their lives does not flag. In common with several other counties, Cornwall shares in an existence subjected to the demands of tourism on the one hand and the threat of environmental devastation on the other. Therefore it is not just escapism to project the mind back in time and live again in the calm of the old Cornwall. It must also be a kind of fulfilment.

This influence of Cornwall on Winston Graham's writing can be seen in almost every paragraph, as in these lines from his ghostly story, *Coty's Cove*:

The sandhills were a desert of salt with deep pools and ravines of shadows. Across them and through them she plunged, sometimes waste deep in darkness, sometimes in full light, her shadow like a dog at her feet. She walked as if in a dream. At the cliff she hesitated. The surf was a line of phantom cavalry dividing sand and sea. At the bottom the sand was soft and pale and secret. The lightest of cool airs wafted and she shivered, but it was not cold. The rocks were sharp edged like witches' faces and the shadows were monstrous and misshapen. It was a midsummer's night's dream, all of it a dream, in which she walked lonely and afraid.

Always, it seems, novelists are drawn by the more mysterious elements of Cornwall, those facets which are at once subterranean and yet, in a way, all-pervading. How fortunate, for instance, has been the novelist Ruth Manning-Sanders to spend a large part of her working life living high up on the cliffs at Sennen Cove. Small wonder that, recollecting walking out on to Land's End in the twilight of a wintry afternoon when nothing was to be seen but the huge dim shapes of the silently withdrawing cliffs and the red rhythmically winking eye of the Longships lighthouse, Mrs Manning-Sanders wrote so vividly about 'the drowned sailors of the past can be heard hailing their names above the moaning of the waters'.

In a way it may seem surprising that there have not been more ghost novels about Cornwall. In fact down the centuries there have accumulated a vast collection of basic Cornish ghost stories (many of them collected in a series by Mrs Manning-Sanders). What contemporary novelists have done is not so much repeat familiar old mysteries, but use the same ghostly background, the haunted Cornwall touch, in which to elaborate their more personal themes. It is not difficult to find such backgrounds — even evil ones. Cornwall has evil as well as good buried in its great granite boulders — a factor well understood by Aleister Crowley.

Just as Crowley's Black Masses would not somehow seem surprising in Cornwall, any other eccentricity seems more acceptable in the Cornish setting. It is no accident that Cornwall is an obvious haven for the beatnik, the dropouts, the beautiful people. In Cornwall there is always an underlying sense that anything and perhaps everything can and does happen. To live in such a place, to be made aware physically of the vast and imponderable nature of the universe, may be disturbing, but for a novelist, at least it is stimulating, a challenge. Many a young novelist who has later gone further out into the world, has spent his almost obligatory year or two living in some lonely Cornish cottage. I did so myself, once inhabiting a castle at Portquin, later a cowshed on Trencom, still later Bernard Walke's old vicarage at St Hilary. In each of these places I received impressions and influences whose impact I shall never forget. In particular I remember walking upon the magical face of Trencom by moonlight, when the giants were surely stirring in their uneasy sleep — looking from the winking light of Godrevy on one side to the twinkling night-city of Penzance in the South — and feeling a strange sense of being part of a world quite beyond the confines of London or Birmingham or Manchester.

This sense, I think is conveyed quite often in many quite little known novels about Cornwall. You will certainly find it in the novels of Frank Baker, best known for his best-seller of *Miss Hargreaves,* but author also of several evocative Cornish novels like *Embers,* and *The Downs so Free.* In an article in early issues of *The Cornish Review* Frank Baker wrote perceptively of the effect of Cornwall upon a young writer living in a lonely cottage by Cape Cornwall, in Kenidzhak Valley:

At last I came to the gate and swung it aside. Down came the smell of stock, sensuously opening out to me in the spring flowering of the hillside. The warm moisture of the flower-filled night surged into me and drew me also deep into its living centre. I was an operative part now of all this, I said, as I climbed the last bit of steep path past the almost invisible beds of bulb flowers. I paused by the well, listening to the blackbird singing wildly from the stone hedge at the bottom, an outpouring of ecstatic song which touched the strings of my heart and called out to music there. The wind blew from the west, and it was warm. Into my head came a melody for the four-line Elizabethan lyric I had always wanted to set:

> O Western wind, when wilt thou blow
> That the small rain down can rain?
> Christ, that my love were in my arms,
> And I in my bed again!

Yes, I would compose, I told myself. Later, I would find a cottage, get a piano down, set those lines, and Flecker's *Don Juan;* score Keat's 'Ode to Autumn' for string quartet and oboe which I knew I had it inside me to write. Or should it be the first novel? For this was simmering to come to flame in me. The novel (like all first novels) which should tell an unlistening world all that I had to tell it about Frank Baker and his world. Novel, or song? I was not sure. The usual sweat of indecision was upon me. Caught in excitement between the two choices — music or writing — I went past the well with its trailing periwinkle to the stone steps outside the only door to Edge O'Beyond. Firstly slight anxiety. Would the key be where Maxie had said it was — under a particular stone? I felt; and after a little fumbling, found it. Next slight anxiety: Would I be able to open the door? It had always been tricky, so seldom was it locked; we had had trouble with it on our return from these long summer walks, I remembered. I tried it. After a turn or two, the lock yielded. The door of my newly found freedom opened to me.

Of course it would be possible to go on quoting endlessly from the words of the novelists themselves to show the extreme relevance of Cornwall on their work. What is perhaps most interesting is the variety of that influence. Most novelists, naturally — like the poets and the painters — are irresistibly drawn by the sheer majesty and picturesqueness of the Cornish background. But then there is another side to the coin altogether: the simplicity offered to the creative worker by life far from the madding crowd. One of many writers who emigrated into Cornwall — Colin Wilson, who has lived for many years at Gorran, near Mevagissey — once remarked on this aspect, saying that he found life in Cornwall beautifully slow and the feeling of relative anonymity nice.

'People take you for what you are. They may say "he's a writer" but they wouldn't really care. Nobody is the least bit celebrity-conscious, at least not about writers. It is a good place to bring up children with the personal touch, important I think for a child's sense of security and identity.'

From his home at Gorran Colin Wilson has produced an amazing number of lengthy books, mostly about the occult, in between sorties to America where he conducts university seminars. This is another point about Cornwall's effect upon writers — it does seem to encourage an impressive high level of productivity, even if sometimes as a means of making sure of being able to stay in Cornwall! Leo Walmsley, who once lived not far from Colin Wilson, at Fowey, was one such writer, with a deceptively simple style which makes him very easy reading — it is worth delving into some of his autobiographical books, such as *Paradise Creek* or *Angler's Moon*, to get the flavour of a writer's feelings about being in Cornwall, though it was in fact in a novel, *Love in the Sun* that Walmsley created a portrayal of the simple life in Cornwall that was to be a literary best-seller. This simple story of a man and a girl coming to Fowey and finding a hut on the shores of a creek, renting it for a few bob a week, making their own furniture, growing vegetables, fishing for food, having a baby, being poor but very happy, seemed to appeal strongly to people in this rat race age.

There is something in Cornwall that is very unusual, very much subterranean, and very, very potent. As the novelist Thomas Burke once commented: 'There is little one can say, description conveys nothing, and reflections are meaningless. What it has to give must be received individually...' So much of Cornwall, of what happens in Cornwall, is larger than life. Wrecks, storms, gales, mine disasters, clay mountains and haunted moor — nothing is quite normal; and this is responded to, instinctively, by writers and painters — in particular, as one might expect, by the novelists, with their eye for the sheer drama of it all. Paradoxically, at least among novelists, few Cornish-born writers seem to respond in quite the same way. It is as if perhaps by their blood-link they have been partially immunised. The two novelists, Joseph and Silas K. Hocking are good examples; although in their time they became famous purveyors of popular novels of the day for the masses, their Cornish origin appeared almost irrelevant. Jack Clemo, a distant relative, once wrote of them that, despite the fact that they and he were sons of the same parish, and the possible derivation of his talent from them, he felt that he had lived all his life in a Cornwall they never knew, and could never have attempted to describe. In considering them as Cornish writers, he pointed out certain inhibitions that might have resulted from the early struggle which made the associations of their childhood distasteful to them when they had escaped to a higher social level. In Silas's reminiscences, *My Book of Memory,* there were practically no Cornish scenes, he recorded nothing of those poverty-stricken early years in the dour little cottage on Terras Moor, the narrow flat waste

83

between Meledor and St Stephens. The clayworks, with their powerful symbolism, the idiom of the new, industrial Cornwall, were beginning to scar the hillsides all round when Joseph and Silas left home for college. This fresh land, teeming with craggy and purgatorial images, awaited its interpreter; there was religious mystery in the cross tip-beams pointing skyward; erotic mystery in the sharp white breasts of rock that were cleansed for the kilnbed. But the Hockings saw these features only as signs of a messy industry with which they had no concern. They turned away to the fashionable world which provided them with material for naive tales of Society life and for Silas's book of amusing anecdotes about the celebrities he had met.

To accuse the Hockings of dishonesty to the Cornwall they had known would be easy, but hardly just in Jack Clemo's opinion, for they had known it only with the surface of their minds, that surface which registered normal tastes and reactions. They were rendered impotent as creators and interpreters by the very wholesomeness of their mental texture. Silas in his later years condemned modern novelists of the D.H. Lawrence calibre as 'excessively morbid'; but the key to all original interpretation lies in the abnormality of approach that is usually called morbid. Lawrence evoked more of the essential Cornish character in a dozen pages of *Kangaroo* than the Hockings could do in a score of novels — precisely because he was 'morbid', reacting simply and sensuously with the living flow of his subconscious mind. But the Hockings did not even attempt the superficial yet detailed portrayal of the Cornish background which we find in such novels as Crosbie Garstin's *The Owl's House* and Compton Mackenzie's *Carnival.*

Jack Clemo goes on to draw the interesting conclusion that what was lacking was the true Celtic vision, the vision that should rise instinctively in an imagination which is an off shoot of centuries of semi-tribal blood intimacy under the

Christian symbols:

D.H. Lawrence felt this primitiveness in the Cornish people, yet until recent years no Cornish writer had even hinted at its existence. 'Q' wrote on a far higher intellectual and artistic level than the Hockings, but he was as devoid as they of this elemental mystic awareness, the sense of 'mud and Godhead' in the Cornish texture. Did they leave the county too soon before it had really spoken to them? Or was there an innate fastidiousness that made them recoil to the protection of civilised and cultured life? They certainly lacked the Celtic capacity for obsessions *which might be expected to show itself in Cornish writers no less than Welsh and Irish ones.*

The italics are mine, for I feel that Jack Clemo has put his finger on a crucial point. Why, I do not know, and cannot explain. But there does appear to be this blanketting off of the natural Celtic creativeness among the Cornish. Here and there, of course, there are exceptions: a Cornish poet of high talent, like Clemo himself, or a novelist like Crosbie Garstin with his remarkable Penhale trilogy (*The Owl's House, High Moon* and *The West Wind),* which cries out to be televised; but in general most Cornish writers have remained second class. This becomes evident if we consider the richness of Welsh literature — Dylan Thomas, Vernon Watkins, Alun Lewis, Caradoc Evans, Gwyn Jones, Glyn Jones, Gwyn Thomas, Richard Llewellyn, Rhys Davies. Or the Irish — Frank O'Connor, James Joyce, G.B. Shaw, 'A.E.'., Liam O'Flaherty, W.B. Yeats, Sean O'Faolain, Sean O'Casey. There is just no comparison... and this is a great pity because in seeking to understand the mysterious qualities of Cornwall we would benefit greatly from the interpretations of truly native figures.

Instead we have to look to the eternal 'foreigner' for our evidence. Fortunately, as I hope I have been able to indicate, there are plenty of persuasive exponents. Something about Cornwall and its settings, particularly its sea-washed coastline seems to bring out splendour in writing. I am reminded of the novelist and autobiographical writer, Frank Baines, who spent all his early childhood on the Lizard, and has commemorated those years most brilliantly in *Look Towards The Sea*. In that book there is an unforgettable recollection of a famous Cornish event: the wreck of the *S.S. Mohecan* on the Manacles. Read it, and you capture a large slice of the truly dramatic Cornish life *which is yet almost everyday experience*. Here is how Baines concludes his description:

The end of this story is pure myth. It tells of a strange man at dawn at Helford Passage. Down through Newgan and Manaccan this stranger had been traced from St Keverne during the night. Seaweed was his hair and barnacles his knuckles and his eyes were open and starey and perfectly unblinking. He seemed to have difficulty in closing the lids. He sat with a hand up to shield his face from the light. Over his arm he carried a jacket folded inside out, and had been helping with the wreck, he said. Some noticed that there was gold braid on his cuffs and shoulders, and they took him for a sailor. Tradition had it he was the captain of the *Mohecan*. Did George see him plunge into the sea? Could he have saved himself and escaped in this matter or was it a ghost?

'Or was it a ghost?' In Cornwall the question seems a perfectly normal one; much that is unnatural, and even supernatural, somehow becomes absorbed, and almost natural. Transpose many of the great novels about Cornwall, set them in some conventional realistic setting and probably they would be read as artificial and false. They would certainly lack some kind of underlying power and strength. I do not think many novelists, alive or dead, would deny the incalculable effect that Cornwall has had upon their writing.

Chapter Six

The Stuff of Drama

The guary miracle, in English, a miracle-play, is a kind of interlude, compiled in Cornish out of some scripture history, with that grossness, which accompanied the Romans "vetus comedia". For representing it they raise an earthen ampitheatre in some open field, having the diameter of this inclosed plain some forty or fifty foot. The country people flock from all sides, many miles off, to hear and see it; for they have therein devils and devices to delight as well the eye as the ear...

RICHARD CAREW

In Cornwall the word 'drama' can be said to have a very wide interpretation: after all, drama or perhaps melodrama, has been and still is the very stuff of daily life in many parts of the county. Shipwrecks, mine disasters, landslides and other events are commonplace in a land so exposed to the vagaries of the weather. So in some senses, indeed, why bother to invent drama? However, the Cornish, remember, are a Celtic race and among Celtic people self expression has always played a large part in local life, and here Cornwall has been no exception.

Historically one of the earliest and most famous examples of purely Cornish drama was *Bewnans Meryasek*, sometimes known as the 'Ordinalia', a series of religious plays written in the Cornish language in 1504 and widely performed at that time. The original manuscript consists of no less than eighty-three hand-written folios of text on parchment devoted to various Old Testament events. From the text one realises that the plays are long drawn out affairs indeed, being designed for presentation on three successive days, each play running to some 3000 lines. This must be one of the first examples of 'theatre in the round', now in vogue again, for the 'ordinalia' was usually put on at one of several 'Plain an Gwarry, or playing places, such as the big amphitheatre still in existence at St Just in Penwith, or Perran Round, near Perranporth. In the Middle Ages travel was a difficult business, and since putting on the 'Ordinalia' was a three-day event, people would make a proper holiday of the outing, camping out for several days in the fields around. After each day's play there was invariably an invitation from the stage to continue with drinking, dancing and cockfighting and other revelries.

Among the ampitheatres that have been preserved, Perran Round is well worth a visit. It consists of a turfed embankment surrounded by a shallow fosse; standing within the enclosure one finds it rises in a complete circle save for two entrances cut into the bank. There is a level area 130 feet in diameter, the rampart rising nine feet or so, narrowing at the top, where it is seven feet wide; around the inner side there used to be rows of seats cut into the turf, now mainly replaced by wooden seats. Since the 'Ordinalia' was a religious play, obviously the theatre was designed to suit its ideological requirements, and it is still possible to trace the remains of a shallow trench running into a spoon-shaped pit, supposed to represent Hell.

Cornwall must have been an exciting place to live in when the land echoed to 'the Cornyshe speche' and huge crowds gathered to see such spectacles as the 'Ordinalia' performed in Cornish with a truly enormous cast of 125 characters. Alas, with the coming of the Reformation all entertainment came to be regarded as sinful and the plays fell into disrepute and were

Above, a once-familiar sight along the Cornish coast: wreck of a fishing boat aground on rocks near Land's End (Reg Watkiss); *below,* Levant tin mine and a raging sea, taken from Pendeen Lighthouse (Ander Gunn)

Above, Cape Cornwall against a stormy backcloth; *below*, annual Guise Dance through the streets of St Ives (both Ander Gunn)

Right, the crumbling ruins of Tintagel Castle, a mecca for thousands of tourists fascinated by the legend of King Arthur; *below,* St Michael's Mount, ancient home of Lord and Lady St Levan, a fairy-tale castle joined to the mainland by a causeway cut off at high-tide (both Ray Bishop)

Left, Bernard Leach at work in his pottery at St Ives (Peter Kinnear); *below*, nineteenth-century St Ives fishermen outside a salt cellar (Andrew Lanyon Collection)

From any viewpoint Kynance Cove has its attractions (R. L. Fowkes)

Mevagissey . . . once the scene of huge pilchard catches and still a favourite centre for sea-fishing (R. L. Fowkes)

Above, transferring the catch in St Ives Harbour (Ray Bishop); *below*, a picturesque granite bridge links the ancient harbour towns of East and West Looe (R. L. Fowkes)

Britain's south-west buttress . . . Land's End (R. L. Fowkes)

banned. However during the present century, parallel with the revival of the Cornish language, a group of Cornish scholars were encouraged to produce a shortened version of *Bewnans Meryasek*. Here is an account by Helena Charles of directing a performance during a Celtic Congress at Truro:

We decided that while the only Plain an Gwarry that is in good state of preservation is at St Just, the surroundings of this are uninteresting, and of all possible sites, unquestionably the most attractive was Perran Round. The origins of this circular fortification with a diameter of 50 yards are uncertain. It is probably an Iron Age Camp. There are those who deny that it was a medieval theatre, but the traces of tiers in the bank indicate that performances of some kind took place there, and, whether it was the sixteenth or the twentieth century that discerned its virtues as a theatre is irrelevant.

The play itself was very short, deliberately, owing to the strangeness of the language. It told the story of the clash between Meryasek, who lived at Camborne, 'a little to the west of Carn Brea', and the heathen King Teudar, who tried unsuccessfully to catch and kill the Christian Saint. Meryasek, having blessed his rock, and prayed that his well may be for the healing of insanity and disease, asks a sea-captain who conveniently appears, to take him to Brittany. It has been suggested that the ditch and depression that almost divide half of Perran Round in two, may have been used in early performances of the play to separate Cornwall from Brittany. We decided on this for the final episode. Saint and sailors step across the ditch, and a sailor says:

> Tremenys yu dyogel
> Lemmyn genen au chanel
> ('Now the channel is safely crossed by us')

As the Saint leaves the stage, the seaman sees the off stage rock, bowing down to receive him, and cries out at the miracle.

We planned our programme to correspond as nearly as possible with the festivities of medieval times. After the play the M.C. called the original invitation from this play, for piping and dancing. A recorder band from Camborne County School struck up the Helston Furry, and the Portreath Folk Dance Group and dancers from St Ives led the audience in the Furry and the Helston Country Dance which, till 1914, was always danced immediately after the Furry. Cornish and Breton dancing was followed by traditional and modern songs in Cornish, by a display of wrestling, and finally an impressive rendering in Cornish of 'Land of our Fathers' and 'Shall Trelawney Die?' sung by the Skinners Bottom Male Voice Choir, standing bareheaded and to attention, while outside the Round, St Perran's Cross, the ancient flag of Cornwall fluttered in the breeze. A B.B.C. commentator described the entertainment as 'nationalist'. Be that as it may, Anglo-Saxon it was not, and those who, from ignorance or timidity, refer to the Cornish, the original British people, as 'English', could have learnt their mistake in Perran Round, as surely as those who persist in asserting that Cornish is dead. This play and entertainment were one sign among many that the Cornish language and spirit are far from extinct.

Miss Charles mentioned the Helston Furry Dance. Along with its companion Spring celebration, the Padstow 'Obby' Oss, this forms what one might call Cornwall's most famous annual dramatic event. In recent years the Furry Dance has been regularly featured in newspapers and on television, and it certainly makes a colourful spectacle, with dozens of couples, dolled up in their Sunday best, gravely pirouetting around in their perpetual dance to the strains of the Flora Day tune. Now held on the first Saturday of May, Helston Flora Day attracts tens of thousands of visitors from all over the world: many of them, of course, Cornish exiles drawn back irresistibly by such a communal celebration — but many curious strangers as well, fascinated by this festival rooted so pointedly in the past.

In recent years the Padstow celebrations have gained considerably in fame, and indeed have become altogether a more spontaneous and — more importantly — primitive event. It is impossible even for a 'foreigner' not to be strangely stirred, even *disturbed*. All kinds of intimations and images of past ages are contained in the relentless, lurid — often sexual — motions of the 'Obby 'Oss as it writhes and shakes and shivers its way through the tiny streets. This, one feels, is something that is still linked with Cornwall's own very personal, very primitive past. John Betjeman, the present Poet Laureate, devoted to Cornwall all his life, has given this vivid account:

St Petroc may be neglected in Padstow today. But the Hobby Horse is not. Whether it came in with the Danes who sacked the town in 981 and drove St Petroc's monks to Bodmin or whether it was a pagan rite which St Petroc himself may have witnessed with displeasure the Padstow Hobby Horse is a folk revival almost certainly of pagan origin. Moreover it is genuine and unselfconscious, and not even broadcasting it or the influx of tourists will take the strange and secret character from the ceremonies concerned with it. For this is what happens: On the day before May Day green boughs are put up against the houses. And that night every man and woman in Padstow is awake with excitement. I know someone who was next to a Padstow man in the trenches in the 1914 war. On the night before May Day this Padstow man became so excited he couldn't keep still. The old 'Obby 'oss was mounting in his blood and his mates had to hold him back from jumping over the top and dancing about in No man's Land.

Now imagine a still night, the last of April, the first of May, starlight above the chimney pots. Moon on the harbour. Moonlight shadows of houses on opposite slate walls. At about two o'clock in the morning the song begins. Here are the words:

> With a merry ring and with the joyful spring,
> For summer is a-come unto day
> How happy are those little birds which so merrily do sing
> In the merry morning of May.

Then the men go round to the big houses of the town singing below windows a variety of verses:

> 'Arise up Mr. Brabyn I know you well afine
> You have a shilling in your purse and I wish it were in mine.'

Next on to a house where a young girl lives:

> 'Arise up Miss Lobb, all in your smock of silk
> And all your body under as white as any milk.'

Morning light shines on the water and the green-grey houses. Out of the quay comes the Hobby Horse — it used to be taken for a drink to a pool a mile away from the town. It is a man in a weird mask, painted red and black and white, and he wears a huge hooped skirt made of black tarpaulin which he is meant to lift up, rushing at the ladies to put it over one of their heads. The skirt used to have soot in it. A man dances with the Hobby Horse carrying a club. Suddenly at about 11.30 in the morning, there is a pause. The Hobby Horse bows down to the ground. The attendant lays the club on its head and the day song begins, a dirge like strain:

> Oh, where is St George? Oh, where is he, O?
> He's down in his long boat. All on the salt sea, O'

Then up jumps the Hobby Horse, loud shrieks the girls, louder sings the crowd and wilder grows the dance.

> With a merry rigg and with the joyful spring
> For summer is a-come unto day
> How happy are those little birds which so merrily do sing
> In the merry morning of May'.

This same kind of atmosphere is sometimes captured — often fleetingly and unexpectedly, defying accurate charting — in the numerous Feast Days held all over Cornwall for the town concerned *the* day of the year. For some reason, which I often feel may be significant, most of these appear to take place in West Cornwall: in St Ives, Zennor, Marazion, and St Just. St Just Feast Day is a great occasion in that far-flung corner of the Cornish Empire. As at Helston and Padstow, thousands of people flock for the day and though there are no longer the *Bewnan Meryasek* plays at the St Just round amphitheatre, as there would have been in the good old days, there are all kinds of special events, including a ceremonial football match between St Just and Plymouth Argyle. At night the five St Just pubs, miner's pubs basically, are crowded out and the merry-making goes on into the early hours.

Festivals are not the only public outlet for the Cornishman's love of the theatrical. A carnival in Cornwall is a big affair, to be taken very seriously. Local groups spend months in their preparations of the most intricate and ambitious floats, and the final processions sometimes last for six or seven hours. I remember in younger days driving a car for a large float in the annual Newlyn Carnival, when that affair took in a trip through the neighbouring towns of Mousehole and Penzance. My engine was boiling over by the time the enormous procession finally reached home again. I counted no fewer than sixty-three separate floats in that carnival, and I have attended similar events at St Ives, at Falmouth, at Fowey, with equally impressive statistics. An interesting aspect of Cornwall's carnivals is that they provide an opportunity for many sly (and broad!) digs at authority, or the raising of some long festering grievance about local conditions. Certainly there is more to them than first meets the eye, and to participate is a salutary experience.

Furry Dances, festivals, carnivals, lead us almost automatically to another Cornish theatrical event that goes back many hundreds of years for its origins: *Gorseth Kernow*. The revival of interest in the Cornish language, to which I have referred to in an earlier chapter, has been paralleled by an enthusiastic revival of the old *Gorseths* (modelled in many ways on their more famous counterparts in Brittany and Wales). Appropriately enough the first of the revived *Gorseth Kernows* was held in 1928 at that magnificent memorial of past ages, the Bronze Age Circle of Boscawen-Un — the very spot where it is thought likely that 1000 years earlier the Bards of the whole Isle of Britain had gathered in a similar ceremony. Since then the *Gorseths* have been held all over Cornwall, in spots varying from a dramatic setting by the Zennor moors to the centre of a town, Liskeard, on the busy A38 road (though on the site of a medieval castle). The objects of the *Gorseths* are to give expression to the national spirit of Cornwall: to encourage the study of Cornish history and the Cornish language, to foster Cornish literature, art and music; to link Cornwall with other Celtic countries; and to promote co-operation among those who work for the honour of Cornwall. Many of these aims are pursued all the year round through meetings and rallies, but inevitably the annual *Gorseth* is the *piece de resistance.* There, at an impressive ceremony including crowning of the bards and various rituals spoken in old Cornish, a great deal of ancient drama is rekindled.

But what of the future? G. Pawley White, an immediate Past Grand Bard, has considered this question:

Have the flowing blue robes, the sounds of the Corn Gwlas and the harp and the ceremonies conducted in a once-defunct language any place in modern times? The robes, as do academic robes, certainly play a picturesque and colourful part in the ceremonies, the sounds of horn and harp are more pleasant than many of the sounds which afflict our ears elsewhere, and the language is recognised as an essential part of the Cornish heritage. There will always be a place in the life of the community for the beauty and colour of pageantry and spectacle. The real work of the College of Bards, however, is done not at the open *Gorseth* for everyone to see 'in the eye of the sun', but in the continuing work of the members in the various organisations they serve. Much of their enthusiasm will continue to come from their association with other workers in the *Gorseth,* which, through its Council, can give a lead to public opinion in matters affecting Cornish life. In these days when the importance of nations, governments, industries and organisations is judged by sheer size, the peculiar treasures that minorities can contribute to the Commonwealth tend to be forgotten. It is through such activities as those of the College of Bards that regional individuality may be preserved and fostered, so that we are not all reduced to a dull uniformity. Gorseth Kernow will continue to foster the progress of the culture of Cornwall, to enrich the common life by the development of resources latent in the Cornish people and to encourage peace and friendship amongst all people. Thus in the seventh decade of the twentieth century would it fulfil its watchwords of *Kernow: Cres ha Kerensa* — Cornwall, Peace and Friendship.

I have stressed the theatrical nature of such events as the Furry Dance, the 'Obby 'Oss, Carnivals and Festivals, and the Cornish *Gorseth,* because they are all peculiar to the county of the origin. After all, there is no Devon *Gorseth,* or Berkshire

Gorseth, and the idea is somehow unthinkable; equally the Furry Dance and the 'Obby 'Oss just could not be transferred to any other part of England. So we see that these events belong, dramatically, to the Cornish way of life — and as such they have often a profound effect upon the people living and working in Cornwall.

When we turn to drama, as it is more conventionally understood, that is, drama in the form of professional theatre, we find in the past there has been a paucity of it in the county. Over the years various attempts have been made to bring professional theatre to Cornwall, and there have been repertory companies at Penzance, at Perranporth, at Falmouth, but they have generally failed after a short period. The reason for this is the obvious one that the Cornish prefer their own amateur theatricals: many hundreds, perhaps 1000 or more, will attend some popular performance by the Redruth Operatic Society or the Truro Society or the West Cornwall Theatre Group — whereas I can remember, during a period when I assisted the Avon Players, a professional company based in Falmouth, often playing to houses of twenty or less. However, in more recent years there has been an increase in professional theatre albeit on a small scale, with the founding of the travelling Foots Barn Theatre, a group with the specific intention of serving 'as a focal point for the community in much the same way as the church, the town fair and the pageant of old.' The reason for the Foots Barn success has been simple enough — their enthusiastic company have been ready to take their drama out and about, down to the smallest villages. For instance when they took *Giant* on what has now become a Foots Barn tradition, the annual May tour, the group camped out in tents, collecting audiences by parading through villages and staging their show on village greens, on beaches and on car parks. Since their early days the Foots Barn has added to their theatrical performances such side shows as impromptu clown shows and Punch and Judy shows, even a mime show. Many members are adept at juggling, fire-eating and playing musical instruments, skills which come in useful for special children's performances. Another feature of the Foots Barn approach is that they believe in developing local themes — thus *John Tom,* one of their latest full length plays, is based on the life of a Cornishman born in St Columb in 1799, who became a Messiah and travelled the world. Rather late in the day the South West Arts Association have made a grant to enable Foots Barn to develop, and similar grants are now encouraging one or two other small professional groups, like the Shiva Theatre, as well as annual theatre festivals held at St Ives, Polgooth and other centres.

Perhaps significantly the one sphere in which drama *has* flourished in Cornwall has been the open-air theatre — in particular the Minack, that unique area carved out of the granite cliffs at Porthcurno, just east of Land's End. Here in a setting of true mystery and grandeur an audience would find it difficult not to be intrigued, indeed overwhelmed, by the sheer physical drama of the occasion. On the occasion of a typical Minack performance on a fine summer evening the single road leading down to Porthcurno and approached either via Sennen or Treen is crowded the cars and coaches bringing eager parties of theatre-lovers. Many more people walk along the lanes, or take short cuts across fields, or follow the beautiful coastal paths. Everyone is going in the same direction; everyone sooner or later passes by the tiny stone box-office and follows the winding gravel path that leads inexorably down and down. Now, indeed, the sea stretches towards the infinite horizon, making a unique and perfect backcloth. But all attention is directed nearer at hand to the lovely stretch of greensward bounded by natural granite boulders on the east and west and, even more dramatically, by the man-made balustades and walls, and a great throne along the southern edge. Row by row, the wise ones bearing blankets and other protective clothing against possible squalls, the audience assembles around the semi-circle of tiers of grass seats. There is no curtain, but perhaps a trumpet sounds, or a herald's voice is heard, and the first players appear, decked in richly coloured garments. The play begins...

Nora Ratcliff, the first playwright to be commissioned to write a play for the Minack, has some interesting reminiscences:

The theatre haunted me. Again and again and again we came back to a discussion of the plays to be done and I found myself dissatisfied not with the plays themselves, but with the fact that they didn't fit the theatre. The Minack demanded its own play. Whatever play was put on the Atlantic would be the main factor...

Finally it was agreed that Mrs Ratcliff should write her own version of the *Tristan & Iseult* legend.

Looking back the rest seems to have been comparatively simple. I read up the material with the Minack in mind. Anything that didn't fit automatically dropped out of recollection. My imagination was chiefly caught by the 'theatre' of the scene where Mark hands Iseult down to the Lepers. As I read I saw Iseult moving slowly down from the top gate... a half-mad Mark stared up at her; grey, lichen-like shales of lepers lay on the rocks to the audience's left. Obviously the long wall over to the right became Mark's inner castle; the entrance from the harbour had to be up the steps on the right — and so on. Scene after scene unfolded itself; all that remained was to write it.

Thanks to the kindness of Miss Cade, owner of the Minack, I was able to go down to the Minack and stay there with nothing to do but write... the play couldn't have been written anywhere else but at the Minack: not only so that one could check the staging but so that the sea, the gulls, the changing light could find their way into the imagery of the play itself: tilted wing of a gull, black as a rock's shadow, torn through the rock teeth...

Subsequently Mrs Ratcliff not only produced the play but joined the Chorus and tasted the play from the stage itself:

I shall never regret having done so: the joy of playing on the Minack stage, of feeling a part of the total effect, sensing the attention of the

97

audience (even hearing the screwing-back of thermos flask tops as a new scene opened) was a high reward for wearing a scratchy hessian frock and scrambling down to the dressing tent over rocky paths in the uncertain flicker of storm lanterns.

At one of the early rehearsals with the Minack cast some bright spirit suggested a 'midnight matinee', and the idea grew to resolution. It didn't matter if nobody came. We wanted to play the whole thing in stage lighting — perhaps that was the reason, or perhaps we knew that by the last night we should be so Minack-drunk that to leave the theatre at 10.30 p.m. would be an anti-climax. So the midnight matinee was launched; to start at 11 p.m., less than an hour after the normal performance had ended. It seemed to us as we waited for the first horn-call, that half Cornwall wanted to see a play at midnight; if, as someone said, we were mad, then the entire Penwith peninsula was peopled with lunatics! A black, lava-like stream of audience oozed down the treacherous path; pale blue programmes twinkled under pocket torches: a full moon — perhaps that explained things — glimmered on white head-dresses of the players; fringes of white foam sighed round the Minack Rock. Second horn-call: we each clutched our cheese, our salmon, basket of eggs, and the last performance of *Tristan of Cornwall* started. It was then I knew that for at least fifty people scattered about the shadowy rocks, the Minack Theatre, an immortal love story, and the warmth of friendship engendered by mutual creation, would be inextricably interwoven in a lasting memory. Thank you, Cornwall.

Since then Minack has been the setting for many notable performances — including *King Lear, Othello,* Shaw's *Caesar and Cleopatra,* Christopher Fry's *The Firstborn* and Norman Nicholson's *Prophecy to the Wind* — as well as several more specifically Cornish plays by Nora Ratcliff. Whatever the play, or the performance, it is the setting that dominates and imposes a curious and indeed unique influence. Drama at the Minack is certainly unlike drama anywhere else in Britain. Many of the plays performed at the Minack have also been put on at other open-air theatres in Cornwall — most prominently Perran Round, near Perranporth, Gwennap Pit, at Redruth, and the grounds of Restormel Castle, above Lostwithiel.

Open-air drama seems right for Cornwall and this in a way is further evidence of the importance of the physical background in this county.

Cornish playwrights, alas, are few — the best known being Ronald Duncan, who has written several verse dramas such as *This Way to the Tomb*, though none of his works have been set in Cornwall. However in recent years Donald Rawe of Padstow has emerged as the author of a series of interesting plays based on old Cornish legends, such as *Petroc of Cornwall*. First presented in Bodmin Church by a group Rawe had formed himself, called the Kernow Players, this work, written in blank verse after the fashion of the old miracle plays, made a striking impression. Inspired by this success Rawe has started writing plays — which are suited to open-air theatre like *The Trials of St Piran* and *Geraint last of the Anthurians*. Like the old medieval dramatists Rawe seems to have an instinctive flair for utilising such settings as Perran Round, and seeing one of his plays can be an uncanny experience because in a way it invokes the very ghosts belonging to the period when the old miracle plays were flourishing. The audience sit back on the rim of the massive earthenwork and watch figures appearing on the ramparts — figures once part of a heritage obscured and enriched by legend. To the actors, too, the experience has proved an unusual one. Up there on the ramparts darkness has erased all signs of civilisation and they feel themselves enveloped by hundreds of years of custom and tradition. Unfortunately because they usually deal with such unfashionable periods as the fifth century B.C. Rawe's plays are seldom seen out of Cornwall; but within the county they come to life with passion and colour.

Although Cornwall today has few playwrights, in the past it appears there was quite a vogue for cashing in on the public tending to equate Cornwall with a truly dramatic situation and setting. Drama critic, J.C. Trewin, himself a sturdy Cornishman *Up from the Lizard*, to use the title of his autobiography, once wrote an amusing article 'Pins in the Images', describing how he had made a lifelong hobby of collecting commercial plays about Cornwall — nearly all of them very melodramatic, few memorable. As it seemed to Trewin, 'Melodrama; Cornwall,' the words chimed together. Among the plays he had collected it was noticeable that:

Cliffs, mines and lighthouses were all uncommonly useful; among these we gather, Cornish people made what precarious living they could. Matters had been almost as bad in the eighteenth century. Then you rarely went to Cornwall by normal means; you were wrecked there on a coast that drew vessels to it like needles to a loadstone. Set out for Portugal and you would land — with luck — on a drifting spar at Porthcurno!

Among his collection Mr Trewin refers to two recent plays which their authors obviously felt to be truly atmospherical and full of local colour.

One, set in West Penwith, contained a malignant witch woman, an aged mother-in-law who raised storms; we had also a death by drowning and a fall from a cliff. I felt we had slipped into the Middle Ages and were being shown round, anachronistically, by a student of Synge with no ear for the rhythms. Another piece, even worse, contained a housekeeper who jabbed pins into waxen images and a victim who was throttled in a mine near Land's End. It was this that made me reflect upon neo-Cornish drama as a set of variations on the world gloom; boom, loom, doom, tomb.

Not one of these plays was written by a Cornish writer, of course. However, in the allied field of opera, Cornwall has produced some composers — notably George Lloyd, Inglis Gundry, and Philip Cannon. The first opera to be written in this generation by a Cornishman turned to the old myths of the land: it was 'Iernin' written by George Lloyd with a libretto by his father, William. The Lloyds lived in Zennor and young George grew up with Cornwall in his blood, so it was hardly surprising he should choose as his theme the local legend of the Nine Maidens, that great circle of granite boulders near

100

Land's End — the maidens having been turned into stone for dancing on a Sunday.

Inglis Gundry, a Cornish bard who has devoted most of his life to the study of Cornish music and language, has tapped a rich vein of Cornish lore for his operas. *The Tinners of Cornwall* is, as its title suggests, about the early miners; *The Logan Rock*, actually written for the Minack Theatre, is an attempt to recreate the old Cornish 'drolls' which used to be enacted in earlier times at the open-air round theatres.

Philip Cannon, the third of the Cornish operatists, whose opera *Morvoren* was recently produced in London, wrote of it in an article in *Musical Times:*

Opera has been in my mind ever since I was a boy in Cornwall. The Cornish half of me wanted to reveal in musical terms the fascinating hinterland where truth and legend meet, where the ancient culture and superstitions of Cornwall would appear against their true background of ruggedly beautiful coast line and wilder sea. It was this inner life, the musical inflection of Cornish speech, I felt I could set to music.

Maisie Radford, who wrote the libretto for the opera, has this to say:

The underlying theme the hidden conflict which is the life of opera, was the contrast in the Cornish character: the home-loving, chapel-going life with something wilder and more primitive which comes of being always up against the elements, the sea and the hard life of the sea. With this in mind it seemed that the story of Morvoren, or the Mermaid, offered the perfect theme. There are many legends of mermaids to be found around the Cornish coast, of which the story of the Mermaid of Zennor, associated as it is with the carving of the mermaid on the pew-end in the church, is the best known. The stories usually take roughly the same form: the beautiful unknown maiden who comes to the village, is eventually drawn back to her true home in the sea, taking with her the young man who has fallen in love with her. In *Morvoren*, the first scene is set in a Wesleyan schoolroom during preparations for a Harvest Festival. Morvoren is called upon

101

to lead the singing of a hymn to those at sea. She begins shyly but in the last verse is carried away and sings a different tune above the hymn, changing its whole character. This contrast foreshadows the conflict in the heart of Matthey, the young fisherman, which is to lead to his tragedy.

The preacher, stable and sensible but narrowly determined to shield his flock from strange imaginings; Thirza, the old seaweed gatherer who alone suspects Morvoren's strange origin, the old Huer, who keeps the look-out for the shoals of fish, were all strongly characterised.

Cannon made a careful study in his recitatives of the inflexions of Cornish speech — in particular the rise at the end of a sentence which is common in Celtic voices. The choruses of fishermen going down to the boats and the gossip of women gave ample opportunity to the chorus. The final scene, in which Matthey is drowned and all the warring elements — the storm at sea, the voices of the unseen chorus of mermaids, and the hymn tune by which the preacher tries to rally the frightened villagers — are combined, swelling to a fine climax.

From opera it is a natural step to music, in the drama scale:

To live in Cornwall is to live in the midst of music. Nothing comparable can be heard in the neighbouring counties, yet they too are largely rural, lacking big towns and facilities for large scale entertainment. Why was this tradition of musicality established and how is it faring today? The background can only be briefly suggested; the Celtic blood; the pattern of life associated with mining, frequently leaning to a strong tradition of choral singing; the religous revival, working in a people oppressed by economic and climatic hardship — and having a musical expression similar in its fervour to that of the oppressed negroes in the northern states of the U.S.A. and the isolated rural community life of earlier times.

Joy McMullen, director of the Cornwall Rural Music School, made those comments once when she explained how widespread musicality — not considered a preserve of the comfortable middle classes — has been the special mark of Cornish music-making:

Brass bands and small orchestras sprang up in the smallest village community. Even today you will find villages where one family can supply enough musicians for all festive occasions, religious and secular. Singers formed not only church choirs and male voice choirs but in the town, operatic and choral societies. Talk to any one of these old school vocalists and they will describe how they worked many extra hours in the evenings, so they might make enough money to pay to travel frequently long distances by train, catching the 'Workmen's Special' early in the morning, to have their much-prized individual tuition — perhaps once a week, but more likely once a month, since fees could be anything up to a guinea even fifty years ago. String players, too, will tell you how, as a youngster, one of them would have the violin lesson and run home to his friend's back kitchen, to pass on the latest advance skill — like a saffron bun hot from the oven. Instruments in those days had to be bought outright, and again meant months and years of hard work and saving.

All that happened fifty years ago or more. What goes on today? Musical life still flourishes, but perhaps with a change of emphasis. Probably less children learn the piano, but more take up brass and stringed instruments, and get to a higher standard, with more opportunities to play. Other instruments — mainly orchestral woodwind and brass — are available. For the adult, there are bands, orchestras, choirs and operatic societies. Every sizable town has both a choral and an operatic society, as well as its numerous church and chapel choirs. All this activity represents the work of small, local bodies; of the Brass Band Association; the Local Education Authority, and the Cornwall Rural Music School.

Cornish ways may change, the land remains the same: that narrow, elongated lobster-claw still stretches westward into the sea. Few people have the means or time to travel more than perhaps ten miles for leisure pursuits and this means — in a county this shape — that centres for leisure activities must be scattered over a wide area. The Rural Music School has to provide peripatetic tuition and music-making. It is, like Tudor royalty, a 'movable feast', progressing round the country, complete with its own regalia of timp sticks and music stands. Every July, for instance, the school removes itself from its work-a-day base to the beautiful St Mylor Church, near Flushing. Here it gives a festival of evening concerts of seventeenth and eighteenth-century music, blending choral and instrumental, professional and amateur, in a varied, often unusual programme of music with something to delight every ear. This event comes annually at the end of a hard year's teaching work, in which staff have covered several hundreds of miles. Tuition centres at present cover central Cornwall: Falmouth, Helston, Truro, St Austell and Bodmin. The orchestral meetings draw people from Penzance, up to Bude, and Liskeard, and can really be said to serve the whole county, but tuition cannot yet be offered so widely. The dichotomy of high teaching standards and reasonably low fees is schizophrenic enough; to add heavy expenditure in travelling would be suicidal. In conjunction with the L.E.A. the C.R.M.S. is responsible for string class teaching in Central Cornwall, and this has been a further factor in the school's development.

The music festivals that Mrs McMullen mentions are only a few among many. Every year, in all kinds of remote corners of Cornwall, quite imposing festivals are held — like that at St Endemellion Church in North Cornwall, to which musicians from 'up country' come for a whole week of performances. Another unusual festival is the Porth-en-Alls Music Festival held in a private house at Prussia Cove, Perranuthnoe — the house being built into the side of the cliff, with the front door on the top floor and the lowest floor, three landings below, standing on the rocks on which the sea breaks.

When we arrived, one day before the final concert in Penzance, the orchestra was rehearsing in one room, the choir in another, and the children were running their own orchestra in a third. I mention the children because this festival is very much a family affair. All the houses on the estate were occupied by families, all of whom took part in the music, singing, playing or both. About half were amateurs, some of whom had travelled from as far as Liverpool, but many were natives of Penzance, Newlyn or Mousehole. The other half were professionals, amongst whom was Ilse Wolf, who still love music enough to come to this house for a week to make music with us amateurs just for the enjoyment.

These words are taken from Anthony Gillingham's account in the *Cornish Review* of a week at the Porth-en-Alls Festival, one of the unusual musical experiences to be found in Cornwall in which the setting is, as ever, a vital part of the experience. Since then the Prussia Cove musical gatherings have widened in scope considerably and, under the artistic direction of Sander Vegh, master classes of professional musicians are now held annually, with public performances being given at local centres. Last year enthusiastic crowds attended concerts at Penzance, St Michael's Mount, St Ives, Helston, and Mylor, near Falmouth, and the musicians have also taken part in the St Ives Festival.

And so — instrumental music in the low-beamed sitting room of some Elizabethan Cornish house, choir-singing in the ancient granite hall of a 16th century church, brass band music blaring out in the narrow cobbled street of a china clay village like Bugle up among the 'white mountains' — or simply the dancing lilt of the Helston Furry Dance as it moves round the streets of that old market town — these are all part of a world of drama and music peculiar to Cornwall.

Chapter Seven

The Creative Crafts

*A potter at the wheel is totally involved with his pot until it is finished.
You feel the rhythm, you scarcely dare to admit it in case you break the
flow; you just hang on by your eyebrows letting it flow through your
hands.*

BERNARD LEACH

In an area of such antiquity and timelessness as Cornwall,
where indeed to feel this sense of past one has only to place the
palms of the hands against some smooth worn shape of granite,
it is perhaps only natural that crafts have always flourished.
Craftsmanship has been described as the gradual transfer of
the bodily knowledge of the right usages of material and the
intimate co-operation of small groups of workers. If the
continuity is broken and the workers and their materials split
up then not only is a craft lost but often a whole heritage.
During the last world war there was a very real danger of
craftsmanship dying out but fortunately quite the opposite has
happened and there has generally been a tremendous revival of
interest in the art and craft of making things by hand.

Nowhere has this been more striking than in Cornwall
where there are now about 500 separate crafts in existence.
Some of these, such as the painting of sea shells and the

making of fancy jewellery and decorations, are somewhat superficial and intended mainly for the tourist trade. However the interesting thing about most of the crafts practised in Cornwall is that they are very old and very traditional — the crafts of the blacksmith, the wheelwright, the saddler, the coppersmith, the weaver, the potter. Among exponents of these crafts have been some of the best known members of their profession not only in Cornwall but in Britain: Bernard Leach, the potter, Francis Cargeeg, the coppersmith, Robin Nance, the furniture maker, Percy Mitchell, the boat builder, Jeanne Stanley, the rushmaker, Gladys Haymer, the weaver. Some of these are now dead, but their pioneering work has been carried on by others to an impressive degree.

In Cornwall, too, there has been the important link with the Celtic past, from an era when craftsmanship reigned supreme. When we think, in more general terms, of Inca pottery, Negro wood carvings, Neolithic figurines and so forth, all giving visual significance to the ritual of birth, life and death, we should not forget there were master craftsmen of the Celtic world who bequeathed such treasures as the Battersea shield, the Ardagh chalice and the Tara broach. It was a curious almost instinctive interest in their work growing out of his love for Cornwall and its history, which first encouraged Francis Cargeeg, one of Cornwall's greatest craftsmen of the twentieth century. He became fascinated in the rich legacy of Celtic art, the creativity of a race whose dominion stretched for a thousand years from the Black Sea to the western coast of Ireland, and whose artists and craftsmen gave to Europe a masterly abstract art of curvilinear and geometric ornament:

They excelled particularly in metal-work, and in hammered sheet bronze, which is copper with a little tin added, they found a medium that perfectly suited their instincts and achieved astonishing results in the technique of 'embossing' designs which we now know as 'repousse'. Their designs were drawn by the flow of light on polished metal, which gave an elusive beauty to their oft-times flamboyant and

107

bizarre forms. Thus Celtic metalwork and hammered copper appeared as an ideal medium to interpret the spirit which lived in the scrolls, the spiral and trumpet motifs and the amazing patterns of knot work so beloved by the ancient artist craftsmen.

My interests went hand in hand with a certain artistic urge which sent me to an art school in the evenings and to the open air with easel and water colours whenever possible. In this pilgrimage a dream slowly took shape of devoting myself to the awakening of interest in Celtic art and to restoring the prestige of beaten copper as an art-form. The interest in Celtic art in the antiquarian coteries in Cornwall was almost nil, and the art schools a subject for distinctly 'sniffy' comments; whilst owing to the ease with which copper can be manipulated by the machine, the once lovely art of beaten copper had become degraded to the point of extinction and served but to brighten the ironmongery department and solve the problems of the seaside souvenir hunters. So I left the security of an engineering job up-country, crossed the Tamar into my native land, and set myself the task of literally hammering out a new pattern of life and making a distinct contribution to the Celtic revival of Cornwall.

My tribute has been by hand, hammer and fire to try to make a living reality of a great traditional art. My experience has brought me an acute sense of fellowship with my forerunners, and a satisfaction in sharing in the significant and inevitable revival of the crafts. Significant because it is part of that questing for those basic aesthetic values which, hag-ridden by the analytical spirit of a scientific age, the artist bewilderingly seeks. Inevitable because all they seek has been part of the way of life, labour and thought of artist craftsmen since the dawn-cultures of mankind. Hence the haunting of the studios, the hopeful drawing together of the artist and craftsman, the emergence of the artist craftsman of a new age.

Francis Cargeeg referred to what has been encouragingly evident in recent years: a vast return to, as well as a development of the crafts in Cornwall. The reasons for this are very much the same as apply to the painters and the poets and the writers — craftsmen (and women) too are similarly drawn to this unique world of surging sea, of white washed sands, of craggy cliffs, of desolate moors and haunted interiors. This aspect is very aptly summed up in the work of R.H. Cory who, working from his home at Widemouth, near Bude, has developed a strange and hauntingly beautiful craft in driftwood. What this gifted man does is wander around the coast of North Cornwall — beachcombing in fact — collecting all kinds of driftwood and then working on shaping them. He has found himself increasingly interested in the sources of the wood, the changes which take place owing to action of seawood, the relation of winds, currents and tides to the supplies of the raw material and so on:

The techniques used to develop shapes from driftwood are matters of individual choice, as is the preference for tools. My own methods are essentially simple. I remove all bark, soft and rotted surface and faulty pieces by using files, chisels and a coping saw. There then remains the basic wood, which is obviously different in shape from the original piece. At this stage decision has to be made as to the ultimate shape required, so imagination and artistic sense come into play. The wood is viewed from all angles, regard being given to the grain and pattern and how they follow the curves, and account is taken of hollows and cavities and how best they may be used to enhance the completed model. Many pieces of driftwood contain very attractive colours, which are discovered only when the inequalities and blemishes of the exterior have been removed. Once when working on a piece of walnut root, I was thrilled to find black, orange and purple and an intermingling of colours impregnated into the basic colour of the wood. I discovered that any wood exposed to the action of sea water over a long period underwent two changes; one in colour and the other in texture. Changes in colour are due mainly to the dissolved mineral and chemical salts carried by the rivers into the oceans. Long immersion causes the wood to become infused with the salts.

Cory's is an especially vivid example of a particularly Cornish craft; one sees that the end product is literally alive with the feeling, the haunting presence, of the county of its creation. Where else, as Cory has said, except along the wild exposed sea coast of North Cornwall would he have found an intricately shaped piece of Canadian maple which he was able to carve into the shape of a ballerina? Or a piece of myrtle wood with infused black and orange colours which was eventually turned into a bird shape? Or again, specimens of bog oak, first mistaken for ebony, which he stumbled upon searching the pebble ridges of Millook, with its gigantic and magnificent folded strata cliffs towering majestically into the sky? And then there was an interesting example of nature aping life when Cory found a curved and twisted piece of gorse root, which had been swept into the ocean and returned to the shore, looking like a copy of Zadkin's famous commemorative monument standing in the middle of Rotterdam (i.e. the gorse root suggested the same experience of life, cruelty, torture, suffering, death, as Zadkin deliberately set out to achieve in his original carving).

Another Cornish craft which has grown greatly in popularity in recent years arises directly out of the nature of the county itself — namely the collecting and polishing and shaping of rare mineral stones. Cedric Rogers, one of the chief exponents, has pointed out that like archaeology, stone collecting has a special significance for Cornwall. While there are other areas of Britain, notably Cumberland and Derbyshire, where minerals occur in some quantities, Cornwall is exceptionally rich. There are few places in the world of comparable size where so many different varieties (up to 300) are to be found. In the 19th century, when Cornish mining was at its peak, mineral collecting was a flourishing by-product. Fine crystals were continually being dug out with the rough ore. The miners would set aside the best specimens to sell to dealers, who, in turn, were kept busy supplying minerals to museums and private collections the world over. The output of at least one mine, whose ore was particularly well endowed with crystalline minerals, suffered because so much of it was boot-legged to dealers. The supply of such spectacular material has dropped in recent years, but collecting in Cornwall is still a very active hobby. Its devotees range from professors and their

110

students, for whom mineral collecting is a practical extension of their studies, to amateurs, retired people, residents and weekending holiday makers. To quote Cedric Rogers:

If you haven't been bitten by this particular collecting bug, you may wonder what the appeal is. One is unlikely to find any specimens like the beauties to be seen in museums, but with patience anyone can acquire a modest but attractive collection, with the odd rare specimen cropping up, which makes it especially worthwhile. It is also a *practical* hobby. The outlay is cheap, the bare equipment being a hammer and a magnifying glass; the materials are free; it takes one into the open air and supplies the incentive to exercise for those of otherwise lazy inclinations. On the other hand, it appeals to our romantic side. One's imagination is tickled with wild dreams of treasure hunting — for gold or precious stones. The discovery of crystals of some unfamiliar mineral is as exciting as finding a chest full of pieces-of-eight; anyone who has ever dreamed of being a prospector is already halfway to being a mineral hunter. It is also instructive and a jumping-off ground for more serious study. In Cornwall glamorous minerals abound — gold and silver beryl, topaz, zircon, garnet, turquoise, tourmaline, rhodonite, moonstone, perdot — and then the quartz family, amethyst, citrine, cairngorm, opal, agate, onyx, cornelian, chalcedony, jasper, praze, bloodstone. Cornwall is noted for its fine crystals of glass clear quartz — sometimes referred to as 'Cornish Diamonds' — as well as various other shades from white to black. The crystals are always six-sided, usually prisms ending in six sided pyramids; small and slender or large and stumpy and stained brown with iron oxide.

The first thing that a would-be mineral collector must know apart from what to look for is where to look. The easiest and most natural place for the casual searchers in Cornwall is one of the dozens of beaches. Anyone is a potential hunting ground, though some may produce only a monotonous repetition of the same kind of pebbles, but the beach at Marazion (opposite St Michael's Mount) has a wonderful variety of quartz and other pebbles which may contain the occasional amethyst or citrine. Other beaches may produce pleasant surprises of the same sort. Cliffs will often contain minerals which are easily visible, but hard to extract, since they form veins embedded in the solid rock; but sometimes, with the patient use of a cold chisel and a heavy hammer, you may get some good specimens.

The serious mineral collector will waste no time in seeking out some of the old mine dumps. A drive through Cornwall will quickly reveal where the mine workings are grouped, and a rough rule to follow is that the greater the concentration of mines, the greater is the chance of a varied mineral concentration. The first area to head for in West Cornwall is that at Botallack, just north of St Just. If you find no interesting minerals, which is unlikely, you will be rewarded with some stunning scenery. A little to the north is Geevor tin mine, one of the only two mines at present operating in Cornwall. The second great mining area, even more extensive, is that extending eastward from Camborne to Redruth, Gwennap and beyond St Day; the other working mine, South Crofty, is located in the shadow of Carn Brea. North-east of this is St Agnes, with a smaller, but important concentration of mines, which extends to the east of Perranporth. The largest mining area in East Cornwall centres around Callington, once very active, and a key point for the collector now. Copper was mined here as well as tin, and occasionally silver; and interesting and rare copper minerals may still be found on some dumps.

Elinor Lambert was a craftsman who took the stone collecting habit one degree further. Around Mevagissey she would go out and search the beaches in a spirit of expectancy that was open and awake for a miracle, ready for any event, even — as has sometimes happened — the discovery of a familiar shape, a stone she threw back to the sea one dark night many months ago, slightly changed by the flux of the tides. Back on the floor of her cottage she would spread the stones out and looking at them would imagine past forms of the mighty spirit of forests, broken up and disintegrated, raw material for a new creation:

Now begins the fun. My stone and I get together intimately. I review it from all angles, almost always the figure I am chasing seems to be mysteriously cloaked in a shawl, a hood, or a cowl. My first attempts to emphasise by adding on were crude. Heads and hands had all the appearance of being stuck on; but with persistent self criticism, research and striving after texture and suitable colouring I arrived at a true marriage between my additions and the rock, sometimes

112

modelling an entire torso emerging from a barnacled skirt. The making of one large figure is an elaborate and lengthy process. Additions are modelled on the stone, left to dry and shrink, and finally after several weeks to fall off. Then I start in with adherents (no drill will penetrate the stone) and after a further wait of several weeks pack into the join durable and weather-proof cement paints. The finishing textures are important both for their protective qualities and for their resemblance to the rock surface.

Working on a stone for an hour or so Elinor Lambert often found some chance lighting would bring a vivid sense that here was a character that once lived in history or had been created in literature. In this way she evolved such stone images as Shakespeare's Orphelia, Emily Bronte's Cathy, Socrates, Undine, the patriarchs of the Old Testament and others. Once she resurrected two little saintsof her own town, Saint Meva and Saint Issey, the gull and the stream, who were said to have met here and given Mevagissey its name.

Living for any appreciable time on this strip of England which somehow is not really English one is caught in that strange net of influences of which the natives are unconscious because they are part of its fabric. It is secret, often sinister, and in league with the earth's dynamic centres. I have tried to catch the spirit of this, using a long rectangular stone as a wall and fashioning fishermen leaning on it, as they are in the habit of doing when they can't go to sea. There may be a row of them gossiping on that wall overlooking the harbour, but they are not with each other even in their talk. They are out there with their ships, suspended somewhere between the weather omens and the heaving tide that tugs at the wooden legs propped under the hulls. My fishermen have no faces, they are viewed from behind. You may speak to them and they will answer without turning. They speak to the bowl of the harbour.

Once the method and materials are mastered the scope of my work with stone is unlimited. So without end is it that while one may relax when contemplating the coves and beaches from the cliff top one is almost afraid to descend, to touch, to handle, to chose the individual stones, afraid because they all seem to wait to be chosen for recon-struction. Almost all have potential character, yet few can be brought to being as Stone People. The rest must be washed back with the tide, till their time is come.

Wrought-iron work has always been a feature of Cornish life, where until recently at any rate every village had its own 'smithy. Perhaps the best known exponent was the late Archibald Carne of Truro, whose exquisite traditional pieces won many prizes at important shows. He once recalled his early days, in the late nineties, when he grew up in a world of horses and carts, ploughs and harrows, that was when he first caught the fascination of a village forge, discovering that to watch a half a dozen or more big steaming horses waiting to be shod in the light of the forge fire while the smithy worked merrily and commandingly with red hot bars of iron was a thrill. Schooldays over he became apprenticed and learned the proper use of tools. However at the same time evening classes at Truro Art School in pencil work proved a useful parallel to the apprenticeship in hammerwork. Later, after service in the war, a visit to the new world of India, and contact with all sorts of ideas and philosophies, Archibald Carne found that ordinary smithy work was not enough. He went back to art school and began tentatively copying natural forms of leaves and flowers in ironwork. Like the true and natural craftsman he was he began thinking that design in iron should surely bring out the characteristics of the metal itself, and so he began producing a beautiful range of wrought iron items — fires, log forks, candlesticks, screens, coal containers, mosaics. Especially he began to consider the full possibilities of iron in use and design, a place in a setting of modern architecture and life.

Purpose and programme for a craft were forged at the anvil and brought out at the bench as well as with the pencil and book. Ideas for the piece, from the poker to the elaborate grate, made a contribution to the wider conception of what metal could do and what a smith could and should do with metal. The process was and is one of challenge and response in terms of craft, as in business practice it

114

appears as demand and supply. But both are live factors. The settings of architecture, the problems of furnishing in our time are challenges to an ancient craft, heavy with tradition in working and design. How far can tradition be modified, discarded? How far can new designs or methods be created without loss of quality, the propriety that lies in the sense of metal? This, apart from love of tool work, is the exciting quest which the iron-smith shares with modern members of other crafts. Where the smith like his fellow craftsmen has the main initiative he has the greatest freedom in conception. It is for this I have deliberately studied the designs of tradition to get what inspiration they might give either for development and adaptation or in rejection for the seeking of some new shape and line. But the study and work with the pencil must be tested and proved with the hammer to see again what iron may do and what place it may take in a world of changing styles, always to make the proper piece in its rightful place.

Looking back over a long life as a Cornish craftsman, Archibald Carne concluded that each craftsman within his range could make his contribution to the re-establishment and maintenance of his craft, not only in producing his work but also in continuing the ancient process of recruiting and bringing up in apprenticeship new men, and to co-operate in willingness with local educational authorities — and this has been done at his forge and by many other craftsmen.

Rushwork is another interesting example of an old craft, revived in Cornwall in the 1950's by the late Jeanne Stanley. It all began for her one afternoon when she sat on a stool in a farmyard making a waste-paper basket out of direct rushes from the borders of the River Fal:

A neighbour passing by stopped and said: 'Did 'ee know that be an old, old Cornish job?' And he went on to explain how the old folk used to 'trace' the rushes and make them into maunds for field work — 'tracing' being plaiting or tressing the rushes, 'just like 'ee do trace a little maid's hair'. In the old days the rushworkers would take out pith and rub it in their hands to make the wicks for candles and fish-oil lamps. Farmers used rushes to thatch ricks, and housewives made mats for their blue stone floors.

At that moment rushcraft became alive for me. The only tools I wanted were sack needles, a ruler and sharp scissors. I could make baskets with no tools but my fingers as the American natives did. I had no textbook, but no book can teach as well as practical experience, and I have had plenty of that...the vagaries of Cornish field rushes would fill a huge tome.

After that Miss Stanley searched into the history of Cornish rushwork, discovering that near Devoran, Falmouth, there was once a rush factory; that the Ancient Britons made rush baskets which were so admired by the Romans that they took them back to Italy (to this day Italians make rush trays in which to carry their fruit and vegetables); and that at one time Cornish children used to make their toys out of rushes, tiny baskets being favourites. Using all this knowledge Miss Stanley steadily developed her unusual art, and before her death was awarded the title of *Gwyadores Bronnennow* ('Weaver of Rushes') at the Cornish *Gorseth*.

Weaving in general has enjoyed a notable revival in Cornwall, where there is a flourishing Cornwall Guild of Weavers, whose secretary, Margery Hicks, has kindly supplied me with details of some of her members' activities. For instance, one of the best traditional weavers not only in Cornwall but in England had her workshop at Pontewan, near Mevagissey — Gladys Haymer, renowned for her samples of fine silk, woven on a dobby loom, that have the elegance of eighteenth century French brocade. Studios like hers, and Jennifer Angove's near Crantock, where the weaver can be seen working at the loom, seem immensely attractive to craft-hungry tourists. The Roseland area of Cornwall is the home of several weavers — at Portscatho and at Veryan and at St Mawes. While not far away at Helston, an ex-Army officer, John Madden, built up Tweenstream Weavers and proved that anyone bold enough to enter into open competition with mass production can do so. Over at Praze, a retired engineer harnessed the power of an old water mill to drive his loom, and

116

there are many other fascinating workshops to be found down remote Cornish byways, like the sail-loft workshop of a retired London bank manager near Port Isaac. Finally, mention must be made of that gifted designer, Wyn Evans of Bolingey, whose wall hanging 'nebula', a striking conception woven from aluminium strips on a ground work of fiery starlets, was bought by the Victoria and Albert Museum. Wyn Evans is one of the most exciting craft workers in Cornwall — particularly in her wall hangings such as 'Tresco', in which scimitar shapes of eucalyptus leaves from the gardens of Tresco Abbey on Scilly, are punctuated by dark blobs of bark picked up on St Agnes Beach and held in a shimmering web of muted plum and gold and grey.

It was an embroidery-friend of mine, Erma Harvey James — occupied in a craft close to weaving — who once gave to me one of the most impressive explanations of the effect that Cornwall can have on a craft worker. Her childhood was spent at Hayle, where she was always wandering along the famous 'three miles of golden sands' and she remembers how shells and seaweed and fierce frail wings seen against sand and sun-pierced water formed an unconscious bias towards a particular emphasis, a personal conception of reality, which emerged many years later with the recognition of the remote connection between these images and the texture of thread on linen. The past, she came to realise, was nothing less than a very real source of richness, indeed like buried treasure which having lain in silence and darkness suddenly becomes accessible.

Crafts are very much a normal and natural part of daily life in Cornwall. In many a small fishing port or village, in quite remote country areas, as well as in market towns, the visitor is likely to find some craftsman working away down a side street, whether it be a wrought iron forge at Lelant, a boatmaking yard at Penryn or Mevagissey, or a furniture making workshop like Robin Nance's at St Ives, or (as was the case some years ago) Guido Morris's unusual Latin Press Printing workshop on

117

the Island, overlooking Porthgwidden Beach.

In fact, endless examples can be quoted of Cornish craftsmen at work. To conclude, one cannot do better than consider the phenomenal development of a particular craft which in many ways is perhaps the best known of all in Cornwall — pottery. There are, of course, historical reasons why this ancient craft is associated in particular with the county, for it was in the areas of mid-Cornwall and North Cornwall and North Devon that William Cookworthy first made his original discoveries of ball-clay which led to the development of such a major industry. And with clay being mined in the area it was perhaps only natural that small potteries should start up. In fact raw clay was to be found in various parts of the county a long time ago and can still be dug up in such areas as St Hilary or St Erth, where the old clay-mines remain.

Today, the number of studio potteries at work in Cornwall is quite remarkable — at the last count the figure was nearly 100, and increases every year. It is certainly most unlikely that any other English county has a half or probably even a quarter of that figure. In Stoke-on-Trent, of course, there are many active commercial potteries, but that is really a different industry, and the difference between it and the studio potteries such as those found in Cornwall has been well put by a leading exponent of the latter:

The artist craftsman should be the natural source of contemporary applied design, whether he works in conjunction with industry or prefers, as most of us do, to carry out our ideas in clay, cotton, wood, glass, metal or leather, etc., mainly with our own hands and at our own tempo. The hand is the prime tool and it expresses human feelings intimately; the machine for quantity, cheapness and, at best, a marvellous efficiency, but it turns man into a modern slave unless it is counterbalanced by work which springs from the heart and gives form to the human imagination.

When Bernard Leach wrote those words he could well have

118

been thinking of developments over the past thirty years of the Cornish studio potteries — and indeed the Leach Pottery at St Ives in particular. Founded in 1920, the Pottery still occupies the same premises, at the top of The Stennack. Until 1937 the ware was fired in an old-fashioned wood kiln, but this has since been replaced by oil-burning kilns that produce a wide range of high-fired stoneware 'because it suits the conditions of modern life best and offers a wider field of suggestion and experiment.'

Not surprisingly the Leach Pottery and the distinguished reputation of its founder — and subsequently his sons, David and Michael Leach and his wife Janet — drew many followers. From the beginning a deliberate policy of taking students was adopted, while in addition short courses are held periodically for art students. Altogether more than 1000 students must have passed through the pottery, so that its influence has been considerable. The co-operative side of the venture was always very important to Bernard Leach, who was himself trained in Japan, home of the cooperative pottery movement. He once said:

At the Leach Pottery, by accepting the Cornish motto of 'one for all and all for one' and by making the workshop a *we* job instead of an *I* job, we appear to have solved our main economic problems as hand-workers in a machine age, and to have found out that it is still possible for a varied group of people to find and give real satisfaction because they believe in their work and in each other. To me the most surprising part of the experience is the realisation that — given a reasonable degree of unselfishness — divergence of aesthetic judgement has not wrecked this effort. When it comes to the appraisal of various attempts to put a handle on a jug, for example, right in line and volume and apt for purpose, unity of common assent is far less difficult to obtain than might have been expected.

Bernard Leach believed strongly that the educated craftsman of today is thrown up as a reaction against the over-mechanisation of labour at a certain stage following the

Industrial Revolution, and that this kind of person possesses an insight into the epochs of man's culture and in his or her own workshop passes such influences through the mesh of personality. And he believed equally strongly that Cornwall, a unique place, offers a unique opportunity for craftsmanship to flourish. Today the Leach Pottery is by no means the largest concern of its kind in Cornwall — there are two studio potteries in Newlyn alone (The Celtic Pottery and the Troika Pottery) that perhaps employ more people — but it is true to say that the Leach influence has drawn many potters to Cornwall. This does not mean that copying has been slavish; for instance, stoneware is not all that common, and most of the Cornish potteries produce earthenware pots.

The visitor will not travel far without finding a studio potter at work. Here are just a few of them: The Tintagel Pottery in Sir Richard Grenville's old home at Bossinney; Michael Cardew's stoneware pottery at Wenlock Bridge, near Bodmin Moor; John Nash's pottery at Marazion, overlooking the wide sweep of Mount's Bay, and the nearby looming mass of St Michael's Mount; the Celtic Pottery and The Troika Pottery, both in former fish-cellars at Newlyn; Little Penderleath Pottery up on the moors at Nancledra, between Penzance and St Ives; the Polperro Pottery at the entrance to that famous and picturesque fishing port; the Millstream Pottery overlooking beautiful Fowey Harbour; John Vaisey's Old Forge Pottery at Lelant; John Buchanan's Pottery at Halsetown. Several potters may also be found in the Craft Market, St Ives, one of several similar concerns which have recently developed in Cornwall, adding still further to a pleasant atmosphere of craftsmen at work.

Far from the hustle and bustle of the big cities, in a world where artists are taken for granted and accepted as a natural part of the landscape, the potters of Cornwall have learned to appreciate their good fortune. It is seldom that a potter ever leaves Cornwall; though, contrariwise, not a year goes by without another handful making the trek West, searching for that old barn, that former fish-cellar or some similar building suitable for converting into a pottery. This, indeed, is the trend among all crafts, for the Rural Industries Bureau confirms that more and more such people are moving into Cornwall. Not only is this one invasion that might surely be welcomed, for a change; it is a simple yet impressive proof of the scope of that mysterious net in which Cornwall seems to enmesh all kinds of creative workers.

Chapter Eight

The Savage Sea

The Mohecan struck at about eight o'clock at night in high wind and sea while the passengers were at dinner. She tore out most of her bottom and hung poised on the rocks. Her bow and her stern were over about twenty fathoms. She started pounding straight away, heeled to starboard and began to settle. Almost immediately her lower decks were awash...

FRANK BAINES

The sea *is* Cornwall, to a large degree — like a lover it constantly caresses and embraces every nook and cranny of the strange mass of land which hurls itself out in granite abandon into the face of three oceans — the English Channel in the South, the Atlantic Ocean in the West, and the Irish Sea and Bristol Channel in the North. Just as it is no doubt impossible to understand the true meaning of Scotland without considering the place in its life and and history of those magnificent peaked Highlands, so the stranger to Cornwall, though he must indeed understand as the poet said that 'the bones of this land are not speechless', above all, has to grasp the true significance of the greeny blue waters forever lapping at the sandy edges of England's longest and most romantic stretch of coastline.

When I wrote earlier that it would be difficult to think of a place like Cornwall on the same level as Essex or Surrey, Kent or Berkshire, or Northamptonshire, I was thinking of the sea as well as the land. Many counties, of course, are cut off completely from the sea, but among those that have a coastline like Kent and Sussex, the contrast with somewhere like Cornwall can sometimes be a stunning one. I have lived in both Kent and Sussex, and of course both these counties have their share of savage seas and storms, and equally of placid sunny days and children playing on the sands; but if only in their basic flatness their relationship with the sea seems to lack something of the mystery and grandeur immediately visible in almost any part of Cornwall. Even in its colouring, the sea seems different — certainly around the South Eastern Coast, the sea often seems grey and uninteresting, whereas along the Cornish coast the dancing waves are literally coloured an exotic mixture of green and blue, flecked sometimes with silver. Near to my home at Tresidder we have some of the loveliest coves in Cornwall — Penberth, Porthgwarra, Nanjizel, St Levan. Here the waters are absolutely translucent, the sands bleached a perfect white; it could be somewhere on the Continent, in the Mediterranean, were it not for the restless surging tide, with a rise and fall of twenty feet or so. Down almost every cliff face there are winding steps which take you down into a magical world of caves and rock pools — many of them in coves that are cut off when the tide is in, their treasures available for only an hour or two. It is in areas like this, and over at Botallack and Gurnard's Head on the North Coast, that the intrepid visitor can take advantage of one of the subtle combinations of sea and land: rock climbing. Here is an attempt by a friend of mine, climber Mike Borg Banks, to capture the feeling of such an experience:

Because the tide was low we were able to get right down to the very bottom of the climb at the base of the cliffs. Although the surface of the sea was smooth on this sunny, windless day, great long oily rollers were sweeping in. They pounded themselves into surf on the sands by

Logan Rock and thundered against the outcrop of rocks on which we were standing. The granite that we were to climb rose sheer above for some two hundred and fifty feet before its tooth-like summit made a cruel silhouette against a metallic sky. We uncoiled our nylon climbing rope, and each taking an end tied a bowline around our waist. I was all too well aware that this climb was of a 'severe' standard, and would tax both nerve and strength before the top were attained.

As I approached the first pitch of the climb I felt again that cold pang that I have come to know so well, almost to expect at this stage. In the presence of such an ageless and immutable massif, I experience a deep feeling of inferiority and impotence, as if it were an impertinence to sully those dignified granite walls with climbing boots and festoon them with ropes. But the feeling is transient in the face of the reality of the rock. The eyes and spirit were torn down from the soaring heights to the very material problem of negotiating the first pitch. This was in the form of a crack in the cliff wall sufficiently wide to admit a man's body, and is described in mountaineering jargon as a chimney. I squeezed into this tomblike cavity, made chilly by the morning tide. The granite here was washed hard and smooth by the ceaseless action of the sea, and consequently presented an utter lack of holds. It was a worthy start to a worthy climb, and had to be ascended in the manner traditional to chimneys. A concerted heave, groan, grab and grunt gains a few precious inches, which must at all costs be retained by jamming the knees or elbows until another effort carries the climber up yet a few inches more. I painfully ascended the cold clammy walls until, panting and weary, I emerged on to a sunny ledge; all apathy and apprehension had now vanished.

The granite, being well above the high-water mark, had changed from the cold, slippery texture of the chimney to that rough, fawn rock, mottled with lichen, which besides being a delight to the eye afforded a host of small but safe footholds to the jagged teeth of the tricouni climbing nails set around the edges of our climbing boots. Here the cliffs rose above, lying just a few degrees back from the vertical. A rough, broken line of weakness on the left indicated the only reasonable route. I climbed out round an awkward ascending corner which, although plentifully supplied with holds, tended to throw the climber off balance to the left. Above, the cliffs rose again

124

sheer, the holds being ample for toes and fingers. Careful movements and good technique triumphed, until once again I tied myself to the rock. I was now striking form, and the rough granite cliff unrolled in front of me like a dappled carpet.

It was the mood that makes one relish difficulties, so that the granite that looked so forbidding from below, now appeared to be smiling and encouraging me. I suddenly became conscious that the noise of the surf had mellowed and a gentle breeze was fanning my cheek. Only then was I aware that I had ascended about a hundred and fifty feet, the rollers creaming far below...

The climber has an unusual, even an extraordinary experience of the sea, suspended as he is between it and the land. Another fascinating way of experiencing the sea in Cornwall is from a boat. For many years we have enjoyed voyaging in our old motor fishing vessel *Sanu* around the coast of Cornwall. To this day I have never forgotten our first arrival, when we had bought our boat 'up country' at Southampton and how, after passing the striking Eddystone Lighthouse, a lonely finger of granite sticking out of the sea, forty miles out from Plymouth, at last with an accompanying blaze of mid-day sunshine we emerged from a sea mist — and there was Cornwall spread out in a vast jewelled sweep all around: Looe, Polperro, Fowey, St Austell Bay, the dreaded Dodman Head, Portscatho, St Anthony Head with its black and white lighthouse and the opposite hump of Pendennis Castle. Helford and the vague outline of the Manacles — on the horizon the tall white building of the famous Lizard Lighthouse. It was all wild and beautiful. Later, we were to pass the rugged cliffs around Larmona Cove and Penberth, Land's End and then Cape Cornwall, steering well clear of the Brisons, then taking a bearing on Pendeen Lighthouse and Botallacko's crumbling mine stacks as we headed eastwards up the North Cornish Coast past the lovely cliffs of Gurnard's Head and Zennor, across St Ives Bay, on and on up the wild coast so bereft of shelter save for Hayle and Padstow, both with their awkward sand-bars. On past Trebetherick and

Polzeath, Portquin and Port Isaacs, Boscastle and Tintagel:

> Whence men might see wide east and west in one
> And on one sea waned moon and mounting sun.
> And severed from the sea rock's base, where stand
> Some worn walls yet, they saw the broken strand,
> The beachless cliff that in the sheer sea dips,
> The sleepless shore inexorable to ships,
> And the straight causeway's bare gaunt spine between
> The sea-spanned walls and naked mainland's green.

as it was once put by Algernon Swinburne, one of dozens of great poets who have been inspired to write about the Cornish coastline.

The best way to approach Cornwall is from the sea, sailing from Southern Ireland to the Hayle estuary as the first traders did more than 2000 years ago. Daphne du Maurier once said this and she imagined arriving with the same shock of surprise and relief. After a stormy passage with the prevailing sou'westerly wind veering between the quarter and hard astern, one would encounter the inhospitable rock-bound Cornish claw thrusting into the Atlantic in quest of victims to find the immediate north west of its scaley hump, a welcome haven. Then, as today, the contrast was profound between the forbidding grandeur of the coastline about Land's End, with its hinterland of granite tours, and the sudden emergence of St Ives Bay, an encircling arm protecting the shallows and the yellow sands and the estuary of Hayle.

For the watcher today, crouching among the sand dunes and the tufted grass, looking seaward to where the shallows run, imagination can take a riotous course, picturing line upon line of high-powered flat bottomed craft, brightly coloured, their sails abeam, entering the river with the flood tide. What cries and oaths, what turbulence of Mediterranean chatter interspersed with Irish, as the traders ran their vessels on the sand or anchored them to swing midstream, what speedy loading or unloading of cargo between ship and settlement. What feasting, when the work was done, beside a fire of turf and furze; what interchange of views with dance and conquest! And then the image fades and the dreamer, stiff from crouching in the dunes, sees how the sand has, through the centuries, invaded the coastal countryside north of hayle. Hurricanes, in the long distant past, whipped up the swirling mass into dense clouds which settled on the land below. Whole farmsteads were overwhelmed and now lie buried, while the waste land known as the towans, a mixture of sand and sea-rush — a stiff stemmed reedy grass planted in the old days by the inhabitants to stay the driving sand — stretches through Phillack and Gwithian parishes until the ground rises into the headland of Godrevy Point. Gales and storms have been ever frequent on both north and south Cornish coasts, bringing havoc and disaster with them and a multitude of wrecks, but a hurricane of sand, destroying homes, was the grim fate of these Gwithian farmers.

This vivid picture of just a small section of the Cornish coastline comes from the pen of a writer who in her time, together with her husband the late General Sir Frederick Browning, spent a great deal of time sailing in Cornish waters. If you live in Cornwall then it is more than likely that sooner or later the sea will draw you into its world, either sailing or swimming, or perhaps indulging in the almost exclusively Cornish sport of surfing. I have done all these things: when our family was young we lived in a house facing the great Atlantic rollers on Porthmeor Beach at St Ives, and the great delight each day was for all of us, carrying our slender surf boards, to march out until the sea was up to our necks; then turning and waiting for the right wave, suddenly thrusting the board forward, launching ourselves as into space, kicking wildly with our feet, hoping to be caught up in the relentless momentum of the wave, and carried on in a marvellous flurry of sound and speed until eventually we would be washed up, glowing with exhilaration, on the white sandy beach. Surfing is a sport almost unique, in the British Isles, to Cornwall: there are some excellent surfing beaches all along the North Coast notably at Newquay, Peranporth, Polycath and Bude. Later on, when we had our own boat we were able to explore the

Cornish sea in more detail, venturing into hidden coves and crannies, down great estuaries like the Fal and Fowey, entering busy fishing ports such as Mevagissey and Newlyn, teaming with the fishing folk's life — or across the great Atlantic swell to the magical, mystical humps of the Isles of Scilly (where once, indeed, in the channel between Bryher and Tresco our boat actually sank but was eventually resurrected thanks to the ever watchful Scilly life-boatmen).

The sea is such an integral, all important part of Cornwall that it is often literally impossible to separate the two things, to say where one begins and the other ends. Of course, technically the sea ends where the tide leaves its wriggling line of sea shells and seaweed and strange ridges of sand (which on many huge beaches, like Whitesand Bay, Sennen, change formation every day) — but in fact the *influence* of the sea carries on far beyond that tide line, permeating not merely the immediate surroundings but, I would say, the entire atmosphere of the whole of Cornwall. After all, not only does Cornwall possess the longest coastline in the British Isles, there is also the extremely relevant factor that almost nowhere in the strange, elongated county can you be more than a dozen or so miles from if not the sea, then some estuary or river. Small wonder that, along with their well known propensity for being found tunnelling into the earth down mines all over the world, the other most likely occupation of the Cornish is to be sailing the seven seas. After all, in such a grandiose sea-enclosed world, it is only doing what comes naturally.

First, though, in any consideration of the sea in Cornwall's life, or for that matter Cornwall in the sea's life (for as I say the two are interwoven like perpetual lovers) I think one simply must consider the sheer physical majesty of the ever changing seascape. It is little wonder that this sort of scenery has drawn some of the finest painters of our time: there are records of several visits to Cornwall in the early part of the nineteenth century of the great J.M.W. Turner, including one journey of hundreds of miles during which he made many sketches. He followed the inevitable southern coastal route, Looe, Fowey, Falmouth, Lizard, Penzance and Mount's Bay, and then up the North Coast via St Ives, Newquay, Padstow, Tintagel, Boscastle, Bude. Some of his paintings were comparatively conventional — pictures like 'St Mawes at the Pilchard Season' now in the Tate Gallery, and 'Saltash with the Water Ferry' owned by the Metropolitan Museum, New York. But it was when he came to the truly dramatic and romantic spots on the Cornish coast that the sparks, or rather the paint began to fly. When he produced his painting 'Longships Lighthouse Land's End', it was described by John Ruskin as a picture full of the energy of storm, fiery in haste, and yet flinging back out of its motion the fitful swirls of bounding drift, of tortured vapour tossed up like man's hands, as in defiance of the tempest '...waves defeated by walls of rock and beaten back until the whole surface of the sea becomes one dizzy whirl of rushing, writhing, tortured undirected rage, bounding and crashing and coiling in an anarchy of enormous power'. There is another engraving by Turner entitled 'The Lost Sailor' or 'Storm over the Lizard' showing again an immense wave about to engulf the world. Through films of spray looms a towering cliff; in the distance a rocky headland is surmounted by a small building, probably one of the original Lizard lighthouses; and there is a pathetic glimpse of the body of a lost sailor being tossed ike flotsam among wreckage in the dip of terrifying waves. Some critics accused Turner of painting Cornwall larger than life, increasing the menace of the huge waves, the steepness of cliffs, even the size of the enchanting fairybook St Michael's Mount, but in truth he was only responding, as every creative artist has done, to the ultimate melodrama of the wild coastline.

It is hardly surprising that rough seas, spray-covered cliffs and above all horrendous shipwrecks loom large in the sea mythology of Cornwall. Today more than ever there is quite a literature of books devoted to the history of Cornish shipwrecks, and fascinating reading they are (especially those of the local historian Cyril Noall). Yet often, to be truthful, everything contained in these detailed accounts may well be summed up more vividly, more unforgettably, in a single photograph as, for instance, in the marvellous photographs of the Gibson family of St Mary's, Isles of Scilly, generations of whom have carried on the family tradition of photographing major wrecks in that storm bound area. Not long ago the eminent author John Fowles edited and introduced a remarkable collection of these photographs but even he, craftsman though he is in words, gave the impression of feeling that there was little he could add to the stark impact of those terrifying photographs of lovely old barquentines and majestic three-masted schooners being pounded to pieces by the merciless sea.

Sometimes a writer has managed to capture something of the essence of a Cornish shipwreck — as Frank Baines did, in his fine book *Look Towards the Sea*, where he reconstructed the famous wreck of the Mohecan on the Manacles Rocks, off the Lizard:

The *Mohecan* struck at about eight o'clock at night, in high wind and sea, while the passengers were at dinner. She tore out most of her bottom and hung poised on the rock. Her bow and her stern were over about twenty fathoms. She started pounding straight away, heeled to starboard, and began to settle. Almost immediately her lower decks were awash. But she remained in this position until 10.50 p.m. Her lights failed at 8.10 p.m. Thereafter everything was conducted in the pandemonium of darkness or by light of flares. There seems to have been immediate panic. Her alleys and companionways were crammed with passengers searching for relatives or assembling baggage, while the reverberating clangings resounding through her, terrified everybody. She worked on the rock. Now and then the steel hull burst with a crack and shorn-off rivet heads popped all over the place like bullets. As bow and stern settled into deep water, while amidships she was held in place by the rock, her plates buckled and great rents appeared in her side, as in tissue-paper. The sea poured in, dislocating cabin furniture and fittings; the plumbing and drain pipes came away and the steam pipes burst. The hiss of escaping steam, the shrieks of panic, the roar of wind and sea, unnerved even her officers, and no attempt was made to come to terms with the situation.

Quite soon the third-class cabins and steerage quarters were flooded, and the sea made sounds slopping about deep down with the grinding of her hull, which were like the alimentary disorders of a great beast. At 8.23 p.m. the water reached her fire-boxes and she blew her boilers. The explosion shattered the bulkhead between the up-draught and the first-class dining saloon hung with mirrors where most of the passengers had gathered, splattering them with cinders and red-hot coals, broken glass and fine ash. The coastguards on Manacle Point reported the cloud of sparks and illuminated steam. She made two attempts to get her boats away with forty souls in each, but the stern falls of the first boat jammed and it upended in the air, throwing everybody into the sea. The second boat actually got away, but the P'roustock lifeboat passed it two hours later, floating bottom up. It was this boat that I saw twenty years after in the Porthkerris quarries.

When the lifeboat came up to the *Mohecan*, the captain was in the wing of the bridge with a megaphone in one hand and a bundle of documents in the other, illuminated by a flare. 'This is the *Mohecan,*' he shouted. 'I have five hundred passengers on board. What shall I do? What shall I do?' They told him not to send any more boats away. The upended boat was still hanging down the ship's side by the jammed falls and prevented the lifeboat from coming alongside. The lifeboat put one of its own men on board the *Mohecan* to cut this boat free. He nearly went down with her. Then they put their oil-bags over the bow and went in. As they were making fast the line, George told how he saw the captain throw the megaphone and documents into the sea and jump in after them. While the lifeboat was alongside the passengers threw in their babies and children and the men had to stand up and catch them. Some of them fell into the sea. Then those on deck made a rush to jump into the boat, breaking legs and limbs and injuring the lifeboat crew. A ship's officer, brandishing a revolver, was running up and down deck threatening the panic-stricken passengers and trying to restore order, but nobody took any notice of him, and eventually he threw his gun into the sea and left. Presumably he went and got himself a drink to help drown with. The lifeboat took forty-six souls on board, cast off the line, and made for P'roustock.

All this time wind and sea were increasing and the people on shore began to show more concern for their lifeboat than for the *Mohecan*. The coastguard continued signalling: 'Are you all right, P'roustock? Are you all right? Coverack cannot launch. Keep in touch.' When the boat left the *Mohecan* she went away like a bird. Such as the sea was then, everyone thought that a landing in P'roustock would be impracticable and they would hae to make for Helford. But the coxswain was convinced that the wreck would break up soon and he was determined to make one more trip to her. If they made for Helford this would be impossible. Soon after leaving the wreck he signalled the coastguard: 'Am determined to land P'roustock. Have fifty men.' And the coastguard replied: 'You may attempt to land'. When they came through the Shark's Fin passage, the lifeboat was doing nine knots with gunwale awash and all the crew crowded on to the windward thwarts to keep her from swamping. A woman had started to scream on the bottom boards. Right out on top of the Shark's Fin a man was standing. He was the manager of the quarry. 'Down sail and man your oars. Come in on the sea. We got two hundred men in P'roustock. We'll get you in, don't be afeard'. In order to pass this message he had clambered across the wave-swept rocks, but was cut off by the tide and had to spend nine hours there. He was rescued next morning completely exhausted. They say he never recovered from this experience with the drowning and the dying clutching for the rock at his feet. For ever afterwards he was haunted.

Owing to the danger of the boat swamping, the coxswain had to ease her up before the wind, and they could not weather the Grugan. There was a narrow passage inside the Grugan about ten feet broad, with fifteen feet of water at this tide. George volunteered to adventure it and took over the tiller. She shot through this passage like an arrow. On the quarry pier a crowd of men had collected and they saw her disappear into a smother. 'Dear God, save our lifeboat', prayed the minister, who was one of them. But by the time he had opened his eyes she was out the other side and racing across the cove. They dropped their sails off P'orthkerris pier and manned their oars, turned the boat stern to the beach, and drifted in, keeping head to sea. The whole of church-town was down to P'roustock and they had the best men in the parish. The wire was laid ready at the water's edge with slack payed out. Ten men manned the winch. When the boat struck the beach twenty men a side were to rush into the water and hold her head on by main force regardless, while the hawser was made fast to the ring at the foot of her sternpost and the winch men wound her in. Fifty yards from the beach the boat hove to, waiting for a big sea to come in with. 'Pull starboard'', said the coxswain gently, or 'Pull port'. The crowd on the beach was silent; it was only the breakers' roar you could hear and the sobbing of the women in the boat. George was straining his eyes to sea, watching for that black hummock of water against the faint skyline. One comes every seven. Then: 'Lay to our oars', said the coxswain; and 'Back water — pull'. A great comber was rolling past Porthkerris pier, stretching the whole width of the cove. The men dug the oars into the water, using the short stroke. 'One, two; one, two; one, two'. A hiss went up from the watching people. Then high above the noise of the water the coxswain's singsong voice: 'Long pull; one, two; one, two;' and the boat came swinging in on the crest of the wave. She struck the shingle dead true and plumb in the right place. Fifty men rushed up to their necks into the water and held her there. The hawser was fast before the sea receded: 'Haul away — pull', and she was halfway up the beach. It was a perfect landing under the most difficult conditions.

I have given rather a lot of space to that description in order to emphasise this all important aspect of sea life in Cornwall — melodrama, disaster, stupendous physical impacts. But of course the sea is not always in such angry moods, and Cornwall can provide a smiling face, like any other warring tiger! Though the county has few rivers, those that exist are fascinating ones to explore, particularly the Fal, which provides at its Falmouth entrance what is regarded as one of the world's finest natural harbours, and where the narrowing river, winding its way up to the county's capital town of Truro, is full of interest to the naturalist and bird lover, with winding bends overhung by trees (an unfamiliar sight in a land generally scoured clean of trees by relentless winds). I have often chugged up the Fal, though I have done this more often on its neighbour eastwards, the River Fowey, where we lived five years at an old mill near Golant, about three miles up river. Here all is calm and peaceful, the tide ebbs and flows, dozens of gaily painted boats bob at their moorings, and as our near neighbour, Daphne du Maurier once observed, birds are everywhere:

Oyster catchers — 'sea-pie' to the Cornish — with a quick seeping cry swoop to the mudbanks in a flash of black and white. The smaller redshank and sanderling scurry to probe the slate. Further up river, where a dead branch of a fallen tree, strung about with seaweed, overhangs the water, a heron stalks, prinking his way like some grave professor fearing to lose a galosh, then suddenly stands and broods, his wings humped, his head buried in his feathers. Later the tide slackens the trees darken, the birds are hushed, and there is no sound except the whisper of water past the anchor chain until, if the yachtsman is lucky, he will hear, during the magic moments before true dusk falls, the night-jar call. It is a summons unlike any other, churring, low, strangely compelling, so that on first hearing it you must think of neither bird nor beast but of some forgotten species, a scaly lizard cross-bred with a toad. There is no sweetness here, no nightingale passion, no owl foreboding; the call is primitive, insistent, with a rhythmic rise and fall, coming not from the wooded slopes but from open ground beyond, where amidst foxglove and gorse the night-jar crouches.

The silent reaches of the Fowey and Fal Rivers, and of the Camel on the north coast, are the very opposite to the wild seas of the rocky coastline. Somewhere in between the two extremes stand the long white sandy beaches with which Cornwall abounds — for, as with everything in Cornwall, many of these beaches are often not all that they seem. Thus at Harlyn, on the North Coast, an ancient burial ground was discovered when, fifteen feet below the surface, a slate coffin was found containing a human skeleton. Removal of some 2000 tons of sand disclosed about 150 such burials. Many of the skeletons were in a good state of preservation, buried in a crouched position, heads pointing to magnetic north. Tools were found, including stone spindle whorls for spinning and querns for grinding corn, and there were traces of fire and charcoal and shells. A house and a museum have now been built and can be visited. Archaeologists are now inclined to think that the burials go back as far as 7000 years. Certainly there is a strange atmosphere at Harlyn Bay, especially coming from the sandy beach into the little museum. Jack Clemo, the Cornish poet, captured it thus:

> We question together, our feet still tingling
> From the Atlantic swirl on shingle cleared of graves.
> What deities were worshipped
> Inside the delicate white curve
> Of that girl's skull? Did she tramp inland,
> Perform weird rites on the knoll
> We call Brown Willy, her dark breasts stripped
> In frenzy at full moon?

At Gwithian, further west along the north coast, there is a popular legend of a whole village buried under the sands, 'lost land of Langarrow sleeping under silent sandy waves', and this legend crops up elsewhere around the Cornish coastline. But the beaches have other surprises, too. At Porthcurno, for instance, one of the finest beaches in the whole of Cornwall, the visitor has three surprises in store. First, he will find himself standing on the very sands under which the huge telephone cables run from the nearby Cable and Wireless headquarters down into the sea and way out across the Atlantic to America. Second, over to the west he can see one of the most famous clifftops in Cornwall, the Logan Rock, a huge rock balanced like an upraised finger which was supposed once to have been toppled over for a bet by a naval lieutenant — his employers, the Royal Navy, forced him at his own expense to have the rock put back! Third, and by no means least, a short climb up some cliff steps will bring the visitor to the wonder of the Minack Theatre, about which I have already written. Hewn out of the rocks, it looks far out over the waters of Mount's Bay to the distant winking light of the Lizard Lighthouse.

Lighthouses, of course, have played an important part in the history of Cornwall and the sea. Cornwall has the largest quota of major lighthouses in Britain, and of course some of the most famous — including the Lizard and Land's End, and Bishop Rock, on the Scillies. I suppose pre-eminent among all the eleven major lighthouses is the Lizard, whose familiar three second flash has so often been recognised with relief by ships that have battled their way across the usually turbulent Bay of Biscay and into the English Channel. The late Sir Francis Chichester, for instance, was one of dozens of long distance yachtsmen for whom the friendly Lizard was a first welcome home signal. The Lizard is in fact the oldest lighthouse in Britain, let alone Cornwall. It began when Sir John Killigrew, head of one of Cornwall's oldest and most renowned families, the Killigrews of Falmouth, obtained a patent from James I to erect a lighthouse at a cost of some £500. He hoped — vainly as it happened — to maintain the light by means of voluntary contributions from owners of ships which benefited from the service, which finally began in the year 1619. The benefits were made full use of but the contributions were practically non-existent and in the end that particular 'light that never failed' was extinguished as an economic necessity. However about a century later, Thomas Fonnerau built a four tower lighthouse with coal-burning lights at the Lizard and this operated well into the 19th century. The present elongated structure was then set up and has remained ever since dominating a large area of the south western coast of England.

Although the lighthouse has retained much the same appearance for so long, there have been marked changes on the technological side. Today the lighthouse is fully electric with the most powerful beam in the British Isles — no less than

136

4,000,000 candlepower! This and the fact that the lighthouse is 250 feet above the sea level enables the beam to cover an effective distance of nearly 22 miles — a fact we have appreciated on more than one occasion when returning on our old MFV *Sanu* from some cross-channel excursion — though not on the very first occasion when being very tired I became mesmerised with the light and sailed dangerously close, developing hallucinations that I could see people moving around on the shore *in the dark!* Fortunately I had the sense in the end to turn out seawards before we impaled ourselves on one of those awful jagged rocks that poke out of the sea in front of Lizard Point.

Cornwall's other oldest lighthouse is at the other extreme from the Lizard in more senses than one — at Pendeen on the grim Northern coast, close by a dark and ugly mining village. Although the inland district is dull, the coastline itself is extremely beautiful, stretching from Cape Cornwall to Gurnard's Head and Zennor and St Ives. And then, just across St Ives Bay one comes to the next lighthouse in line, Godrevy, whose winking light I used to see every night for nearly ten years during the time we lived at St Ives. Like so many outlying rock or island lighthouses Godrevy was put up after a particularly disastrous shipwreck on the villainous Stones, a reef stretching across part of St Ives Bay. As mentioned earlier, Virginia Woolf enhanced the fame of Godrevy in her novel *To the Lighthouse.* During a recent tour I took the opportunity to visit two more of the four lighthouses which are open to the public — Trevose Head, near Padstow, and the spectacularly situated St Anthony Head lighthouse at the entrance to one of England's great natural harbours at Falmouth. I shall always remember standing on that low headland beside St Anthony looking across to Pendennis Castle on the opposite side and in between seeing the white sails of yachts of all sizes and shapes, as well as the mountainous steel silhouettes of cargo ships bound for the docks at Falmouth. Nearer to home, there is the Longships, set on the Carn Brea rocks about a mile west of Land's End itself — a lighthouse so near to the land that the keepers and their wives can semaphore to each other! The wives live in a row of white coastguard houses on the cliffs at Sennen — yet because of the expanse of extremely dangerous waters they might as well be a hundred miles away as far as actual contact is concerned. I expect quite a few readers have leaned on a wall or rock at Land's End and stared out in wonder at the lonely lighthouse. If you have been lucky enough to have done so on a day of Atlantic gales you will surely have marvelled at the sight — a not infrequent one by any means — of huge waves whose spray reaches up to the window panes of the light lanterns, nearly 120 feet high. Altogether the Longships presents quite an eerie picture and not surprisingly there are many hair-raising stories about keepers going mad and drowning and so forth. Some of the most vivid accounts of the atmosphere are captured in a favourite old book of mine, which you can still find in second hand bookshops, *Watchers on the Longships* by James F. Cobb.

Another extremely functional Cornish lighthouse is the Wolf, but this is something very much out of the ordinary for, like the Eddystone off Plymouth, it is set far out to sea. I have often sailed close by and would estimate the Wolf rock to be about ten miles from the mainland. The lighthouse is an imposing and ingenious edifice, a 135 foot tower painstakingly built up with dove-tailed granite blocks on top of rock foundations at a total cost of £62,726. Being so far out to sea, the Wolf light is a great boon to sailors who can take cross-bearings with it as is the Longships and the Lizard and, for that matter, the two main lighthouses on the Isles of Scilly: the famous Bishop, and Round Island, on the north west side.

The Bishop's designer, James Walker, based its structure on the ideas of Smeaton's Eddystone, a series of two ton granite blocks set into pre-selected positions. Remembering that every piece of granite had to be shipped from the mainland and hauled into position, often in the face of the most inclement weather, it is little wonder that the whole project took seven years. The total costs of the Bishop are said to have exceeded £100,000 but all these expensive precautions are very necessary — records show that during one storm waves were so high that they tore a 5 cwt foghorn out of its fastenings! As readers of the national newspapers may remember, keepers on the Bishop have been marooned there by bad weather. Recently plans were in hand to build helicopter platforms on both Bishop and Round Island.

In all our consideration of the savage sea in Cornwall we have been mesmerised by the restless sea itself, as if it were a living thing, enveloping us endlessly in its constantly moving world. Of course this is true — yet there is another aspect of the sea-life of Cornwall which is worth mentioning, as it remains one of the most delightful of all pleasures which the proximity of great oceans has given to this strange land. I am thinking now of the boisterous, lively, crowded, bustling harbour-life to be found all along the coast of Cornwall, from busy fishing ports like Looe and its smaller companion, Polperro, in the south east corner, through Fowey and Mevagissey and small Lizard ports like Coverack and Cadgwith and Porthleven, down to the big Mount's Bay port of Newlyn on the South West. On the more inhospitable north coast of Cornwall the fishing ports are fewer and further between, but there are some marvellous miniature ones, like Port Isaac and Boscastle, as well as sizeable ports at St Ives and Padstow. Whether it be north or south, the Cornish fishing ports provide an endless source of interest, and I never tire of parking my car in some back street of Newlyn and then walking out along the famous North pier, where sometimes there may be berthed nearly two hundred fishing boats of all sizes and shapes (sometimes their masts can be seen from quite a distance, like a forest). Everywhere the air is filled with the smell of tar and paint and diesel, on every boat men in blue dungarees are bustling about either cleaning nets or repairing for a voyage, or maybe unloading a catch just bought in in rows of long plastic containers. Newlyn is surely one of the most interesting ports not only in Cornwall but in Britain, for its has remained very much a working harbour and is in fact the most important commercial fishery in the South West (more mackerel are brought into Newlyn than into any other port in the British Isles). As the harbour-master once said jocularly — thinking no doubt wryly of St Ives, which has, alas, given itself over to the holiday trade — 'Here we lay nets for fish, not tourists'. Nearly 200 boats operate from Newlyn, ranging from 90 foot trawlers equipped with Decca navigators, echo sounders, radio direction finders and telephones down to one-man dories and dinghies, and the total annual value of fish landings must be near the £1. million mark. The types of fishing carried out at Newlyn range from trawling and long-lining to shell fishing, though much of the latter is exported to France.

While Newlyn is a fascinating example of a large Cornish harbour (as is Mevagissey or Looe), some of the smaller ports are gems, and everyone should visit a traditional small port such as Porthleven or Coverack or Porthguance, where boats are drawn up on the steep beach, or even Polperro, half-submerged as it is by the tourists. In some of the small ports, like Polperro or Mousehole, great wooden bars are put across the harbour entrance in winter time, to keep out the huge seas. This is a form of obstruction not always used with peaceful intent — in the past at both Fowey and Newlyn, chains have been stretched across harbour entrances, in the first instance to keep out pirates, and in the second to keep *in* irreligious Scots fishing men who wanted to go to sea on a Sunday!

It is at these smaller ports that old fishermen will still be found sitting on the harbour wall, puffing their pipes, ready to reminisce about the good old days of seine netting and herring fishing and the like, now almost defunct. Seine netting in particular has a very romantic history. At Sennen Cove, where it was carried on until quite recently, huge crowds would gather to watch the annual occasion when the vast seine net would be taken out to enclose the entire bay (after a watcher had spotted a shoal of mullet or pilchards), the net gradually being drawn in by hundreds of willing hands until finally hundreds of thousands of fish were dragged up on to the beach. Similar seining took place in St Ives Bay where indeed in 1871, there was the largest shoal ever taken by any Cornish seine — masses of fish, four or five deep, which it was estimated, if placed in a single line, would reach from St Ives to John O'Groats and back again. The financial gains involved were enormous for those times — a profit of £8,000.

The sea and Cornwall, Cornwall and the sea — the permutations are endless for there is as much variety to be dredged out of one subject as the other. What about smuggling, that favourite pastime — once indeed practically a major industry — of Cornwall not so long ago? Cornwall is by no means the only English coastal county to have known the smuggling trade, but it was certainly one of the very busiest centres of what used to be known, euphemistically, as 'Free Trade'. It is important to remember that in olden days the smuggler was perhaps the most popular law breaker there has ever been — a kind of Robin Hood of the coast, who cheated the Government to bring luxuries within the reach of all classes of the community. He was everyone's friend, as Cyril Noall emphasises in his history, *Smuggling in Cornwall,* as welcome with his surreptitious parcels and packages at the squire's hall and the rectory as at the labourer's cottage — his only enemies being the Kings Men, officers of the Custom and Excise and their companions on the Revenue Cutters. Television viewers who watched Winston Graham's *'Poldark'* series will recall several episodes of daring coastal raids by smugglers, often running into ambushes laid by the wily

141

Customs men. Typically, like so much else in Cornwall, Cornish smuggling differed from that of most other parts of Britain. Elsewhere large vessels up to 300 tons were used and everything was highly organised by commercial groups — in Cornwall smuggling was very much an individual effort, using small cutters or fishing boats which would put into lonely coves along the Lizard Peninsula, or in Mount's Bay (where the name Prussia Cove commemorates the legendary exploits of John Carter, 'King of Prussia'.) Needless to say the Cornish fishermen of their day were very much involved in smuggling, for their intimate knowledge of every inch of the tricky coastline, coupled with an inborn skill in handling fast sailing luggers, gave them an enormous advantage.

The dealings of the Cornish smugglers reached their height in the eighteenth century when 'Free Trade' had in fact acquired the status of a major industry. Boats from Roscoff in Brittany were landing their goods with impunity on the beaches, often being met by a welcoming crowd of fishermen and tinners. The goods would then be loaded on to the backs of ponies and donkeys (sometimes men, too). Of course there were frequent encounters with the vigilant customs men, but they were only human and open to bribes, thus the saying that they wore 'fog spectacles with bank note shades'! One way and another few smuggling runs failed, and few smugglers were caught, and for two or three centuries it was almost a routine business along wide open beaches such as Lelant or Hayle and Gwithian, on the north coast, or further up, Newquay, Padstow and Bude. On the south coast, at several spots along the huge sweep of Mount's Bay, and in particular the coastline from Polperro to Plymouth sound, smuggling was carried out on a much bigger scale than anywhere else in Cornwall.

Cornish smugglers were not only daring, but ingenious — for a long time they even audaciously took their merchandise not merely into Falmouth Harbour, but right up the River Fal to St Mawes and Tresillian Creek, and even into Truro itself, thirteen miles from the sea! Some idea of the scale of this river trade can be gauged from the fact that when a smuggler's packet boat was seized by the preventative officers just below Truro she was found to have on board 120 kegs of brandy.

As with other sea occupations, smuggling has not altogether passed into myth and legends by any means — every year one reads of instances of smugglers being caught in Falmouth and Fowey and the larger ports (nobody knows what may still be going on in smaller ports!). What has perhaps now superseded smuggling, and is of course a more law-abiding profession, is treasure hunting. In recent years Cornwall has seen quite a boom in this, notably out in the Isles of Scilly, the most romantic venture there being the raising of the bullion from the wreck of Admiral Sir Cloudsly Shovell's *Association,* off the Gillstone Reef, an operation carried out by a team of divers led by Rowland Morris, author of the fascinating *Island Treasure.* Skin diving itself has opened up whole new worlds and insights in Cornwall, and for those who want to understand some of the mysteries of Cornwall and its sea then here, surely, may be the answer. Who knows? When diving off some craggy sea-swept rocks into the deep sea blue waters, you may swim down and down and encounter some strange whole hidden mysterious world, a lost land of Lyonesse indeed.

Chapter Nine

The Haunted Land

One day, friend and stranger,
The granite beast will rise
Rubbing the salt sea from his hundred eyes
Sleeping no longer.

CHARLES CAUSLEY

Cornwall is a haunted land. This is both a statement of fact and an expression of opinion, and one can be substantiated as easily as the other: there are books galore (see Bibliography) from which all sorts of relevant facts can be extracted — and as for the opinion, well first and foremost go there yourself and see and then form your own opinions. I have not the least doubt that whatever else you may feel, even if it is the same as the poet Walter de la Mare: fearful until he had crossed the Tamer back into civilisation again: the one thing you will not experience is indifference. A person would have to be blind and deaf, one might think, not to react to the atmosphere of Cornwall. Astonishingly enough, it is that very person, the now blind and deaf Cornish poet, Jack Clemo, from the clay-pits around St Austell who, looking back over many years to a time when he could see, can still visualise:

Clay land dawns and sunsets, the first golden rays of the sun striking the white peaks, setting the metal prongs and tip-wires glowing and shimmering while the gravel bulk remained in shadow, and then at evening the daylight fading mysteriously from the blurred grey masses and the weird spiked cluster of stacks... at night there was a fairyland touch with the dune lights, pit lights and tank lights twinkling, and the red glare of a furnace occasionally glimpsed through a kiln doorway.

That is a specialised view of a strange and man-created interior part of Cornwall, though one that in its way is just as weird and haunting as the effects of nature. However in the main Cornwall has been fashioned by nature, and here there are some wise words contained in Ithel Colquhon's *Living Stones:*

The life of a region depends ultimately on its geological substratum, for this sets up a chain reaction which passes, determining their character, in turn through its stream and wells, its vegetation and the animal life which feeds on this, and finally through the type of human being attracted to live there. In a profound sense also the structure of its rocks gives rise to the psychic life of the land: granite, serpentine, slate, sandstone, limestone, chalk and the rest have each their special personality dependant upon the age in which they were laid down, each being co-existent with a special phase of the earth spirit's manifestation.

West Penwith is made up of granite, one of the world's oldest rocks, a substance we associate instinctively with endurance and inflexibility — interestingly enough the basic elements of the Cornish character — and as Ithel Colquhon suggests, the fundamental fact about Cornwall is that if for some reason you do not like granite, then you will literally never be happy there. If, however, like most people, you experience an instinctive response to a granite boulder hung with grey and golden lichen, especially if set high on some lonely moor or above a raging sea far below, then you are likely to feel at home. And to feel at home in Cornwall, as I have tried to indicate in this book, is something of an experience which appears to have been shared in particular by artists and creative people of all kinds — something which in itself suggests that we are dealing with a very unusual environment indeed.

In considering the land mass of Cornwall, then, we have to remember first its tremendous age and second, the fortunate fact that despite all the ravages of wild weather and even now the intrusions of human activities of various sorts, Cornwall remains rich in pre-historic remains. Charles Woolb, 'Bard Don Delynyans of the Cornish Gorsedd' has suggested that for its size Land's End peninsula has the greater concentration of these than any other area in the county. In particular the area is scattered with high granite masses that, though obviously belonging to a dim past, nevertheless have a look about them of having been constructed. Many people feel that such constructions, whether quoits or old crosses, are really 'holy rocks', emanating quite powerful radiation forces (or as some would prefer to say, psychic forces). This all fits in with the now popular theory advanced by John Michel in his book on the old stones of Cornwall in which he suggests that Cornwall plays an all-important part in the scheme of things as envisaged by the ancient creators of ley stones (which can be identified quite easily from the air), a series of ancient stones linking one with another, as far as the eye can see, across much of Britain. These ley stones symbolically reflected a mystical philosophy of life and appear absolutely normal in a place like Cornwall. Of course it is important to recognise the right stones, the ancient ones, and not to be misled by more conventional erections: monuments and statues, such as the huge granite cross on top of Carn Brea to commemorate Sir Francis Bassett, of Knill's Steeple at St Ives which, in Ithel Colquhon's words, have no inner vitality and exhale a mausoleum's chill.

How different in quality ae the stones surrounding an ancient well! Either they have absorbed the virtue of the spring they guard or have themselves been 'hole rocks' before their incorporation within the shrine — often itself a perpetuation of the earliest lore though nominally converted. Old stone crosses, too, are full of psychic life: some are older than Christianity, examples of the masculine cross; others, like the Wendron God to whom hats were but lately still doffed, were sanctified menhirs before they were carved with the cross form. Some, indeed, are Christian, but had the Celtic Church not some praeternatural contact that later orthodoxies have lost or been denied?

Circles of stones play a large part in the mythology of West Cornwall. There ae at least half a dozen such circles, one of which, Boscawen near St Just, is made up of nineteen stones — the same number as is associated with the south-east of Stonehenge. (Once every nineteen years the Sun God was due to appear to his worshippers when the approximation of lunar and solar lie occurred, and nineteen years was the length of the Sacred King's reign.) Close to where my own home is at St Buryan there is the famous stone circle known as the 'Merry Maidens', on the road from Lamorna. Legend has it that the stones represent the forever-frozen forms of maidens who dance on a holy day. There are other strange stone edifices, like *Men an Tol*, with a ring like stone through which one is supposed to crawl in the nude as a cure for rheumatism. There is a similar stone, the *Tolven*, near the Helford River; also an adjoining large stone called the *Maen Pol*. Apart from such ancient statues, the Penwith moors abound with cromlechs and carns, not forgetting several interesting ancient villages, like Chyauster, just above New Mill, and Porthmeor, near Gurnard's Head. It is impossible to wander among such settlements, or to pass thoughtfully around huge stones like the Lanyon Quoit, or for that matter to explore the *Fogous*, that is man-made caves, of Pendeen, Boscastle, Lamorna, Hollangye and Carn Euny (the latter, in the care of the Ministry of Building and Works, being open to the public), without being constantly reminded of that saying of George

Meredith's about the past constantly being at the elbow of the Cornish.

This is the important thing to remember in considering the bleak bare granite, imponderable backbone of Cornwall, wheresoever you may wander: *it is always the land of the Celt.* Little wonder that for so many people Cornwall is still the home of the legendary King Arthur and that often around the coastline, as at Mousehole, you will come upon a 'Merlin's Rock' or at Sennen an immense stone called the 'Table Men' supposed to have served the King as a dining table (while of course Dozmary Pool on Bodmin Moor has long been recognised as the abode of the Lady of the Lake). The spirit of King Arthur in fact permeates most of Cornwall: Castle D'or, home of Iseult's husband, King Mark is set up the River Fowey; Lamorna Cove has associations with the name of Sir Modret by whom Arthur met his death; and having once seen an electrifying performance of *'Tristan and Iseult'* at the Minack Theatre on the cliffs at Porthcurno, I am quite ready to believe that it was from some such romantic cliff that Iseult's ladies stared anxiously out to sea, watching for the all-important glimpse of the sail of the ship bringing news of Tristan's life or death (the black sail, falsely hauled up, caused Iseult to kill herself). And, of course, this is without even beginning to consider the region of Tintagel and Boscastle, rich in legends of Arthur and Guinevere and company, with the impressive ruined castle set on its headland amid ruins of a Celtic monastery, and Merlin's Cove cut into the cliffs below.

Wherever the traveller wanders in Cornwall, whether it be along the sea-wracked shore or up among the inland moors, it requires very little imagination to summon back all kinds of haunting apparitions of the past, and of course there are numerous legends to fan the flame. One of the commonest is of the fearful spirit of John Tregeagle who haunts Cornwall from coast to coast, pursued eternally by friends or by the Devil with a pack of headless hounds. One of the numerous

148

herculean tasks he was set to earn penance for his sins was the perpetual emptying of Dozmary Pool. Fleeing from that he sought refuge in the weird crag known as Roche Rock, a landmark for miles around, with a fifteenth century chapel of St Michael's, including a hermit's cell, perched on the summit. Built of granite the building literally seems to grow out of the rock. Tregeagle is supposed to have thrust his head through the tiny chapel window for sanctuary, but disliked equally the hermit's exhortations inside and the shrieks of thwarted demons without, and so, the legend has it, 'howled louder than all the winter tempests', so that none of the local people ever dared go near the place. Not, that is, until by some further spell poor old Tregeagle had been wafted away to a lonely beach in North Cornwall where he was set yet another endless and hopeless task — making ropes of sand at the edge of the sea!

Headless horsemen, Zennor mermaids, sunken cities, lost lands, village wenches turned into stone — they are all part of what the contemporary Cornish poet D.M. Thomas aptly called 'the granite kingdom', a place whose scenery could indeed be said made to match its players. No wonder Cornwall has been described as sloping to hateful sunsets and the end of time. And yet — and yet, even then, even at Land's End, Cornwall has not ended. There is still that stretch of twenty-eight turbulent miles beyond which (and you can clearly see them on a clear day) lie those fascinating, fairy-like humps, the Isles of Scilly. Still more granite, still more legends, as in these lines extracted from a longer poem by Geoffrey Grigson:

> Here are the islands of dead hope;
> And where the bodies safely crouched,
> The megaliths, empty on the headlines lie,
> In the red, wind-shivering fern
> High on these islands of a grim goodbye...

And soon beyond the reddened fern, the rounded
Granite, gold on this green-black sea,
Day darkening with the night's destroying fear,
Must rise the flattened, huge and butter-
Yellow moon, which cannot care.

The Isles of Scilly are very much a part of Cornwall, having once been joined to the mainland. 'History fades into antiquity', in the words of scholar Molly Mortimer:

When one gazes upon the ancient face of Scilly to the antiquarian there lies in this small cluster of islands one of the richest treasure houses in England. History would indicate that the tiny jewelled archipelago was at one time venerated as a burial place of the ancients and regular archaeological excavations have uncovered many graves and tombs.

The aesthetic as well as the antiquarian eye can find complete satisfaction in Scilly. Once past the Wolf Lighthouse the shadowy shapes to westward turn into tiny peaks and ridges, blinding sand and granite ridges. Desolation develops into the Pool, Garrison and Quay of the metropolitan island, and the whole sweet circle sweeps into view. Here is long lean St Martin's; black and silver Tresco, looking like every child's dream of a desert island; fierce, windy little Bryher; hazy be-bluebelled Sampson, pink thrift shining over its fairy-like bay; and away in the west, haloed by its unholy rocks, St Agnes. This then is Scilly, of the hundred isles and thousand rocks; where the peacock shoals are always laced with foam and the water is coloured like the crystals that lie on the shore; jade, chalcedony, amethyst and topaz. Perhaps nowhere else could one find such conjunction of north and south. The seal and the porpoise watch the shark and the dolphin. The hardy northern guillemot rests on rustling palm. Outside the almost tropical gardens of Tresco, lie uplands of heather and bracken, trees stunted by gales. Yet you can light your fire with geranium and rosemary faggots, so high do these shrubs grow. All in all it is a temperate climate where no snake, toad or other poisonous thing lives...truly an unbelievably sweet world of wave-encompassed wonder.

Part of the fascination of exploring the land of Cornwall is literally walking down lonely overgrown byways, where often there is a sense of entering strange and secret worlds, quite possibly populated by some of the 'little people'. Even following the coastal paths — and it is worth remembering that thanks to the National Trust, very large areas of the Cornish coast can now be traversed by public footpath — it is possible to have this sense of other-worldliness, of remoteness from reality. In the *Cornish Review* I once published a fascinating account by M.A. Hollingham of a walk which began at St Ives and did a full semi-circle right out round the Lizard as well. After pointing out that anyone who had ever taken a leisurely sunny Sunday afternoon stroll along the Cornish clifftops and come back battered almost senseless by the sheer beauty of it all would understand why the only way to appreciate the coast is to see it on foot, he continued:

That last stretch from St Ives past Zennor Head and Porthmeor Cove towards Pendeen was the worst and made us fit — abruptly and cruelly — but it wasn't all sweat and curses. Alone in a desolation of mile upon mile of wild and windswept cliffs we were in another world; a world where man can only be an occasional unwanted intruder. It made us feel pioneers so that we were disappointed when we saw a distant figure fishing from a spit of rocks far below us. That loneliness gave us a sense of isolation that was to last throughout our walk... But at the same time, as scene after unsurpassed scene piled one on top of another, we wanted to cry out, 'Stop'. It's all too much, we can't take any more'. If you walk through the mining country south of Pendeen Watch, past the old and crumbling engine house at Geevor, you can feel the earth's sadness where it has been so pierced and wounded that its seeping blood stains red the sea around the rocks of the Averack... If you walk up to Land's End from Sennen Cove, you find yourself in a fantastic land where massive squared granite boulders rise from the sea, piled crazily against the cliffs like a set of giant child's bricks, half collapsed and forgotten in a corner.

The continuing of our walk had a cumulative effect: the coastline fading away from one climax of beauty, only to take on another, subtly altered mood before sweeping us up again. The low cliffs and sheltered greenness of Mount's Bay slowly giving way to the rising convoluted serpentine made a fitting prelude to the Lizard. It was late afternoon when we reached there, black angry clouds driven hard by the wind obscured the low sun and made the white-capped sea dark and seethingly wicked. A shaft of sunlight struggled through the clouds and illuminated a patch of water far out to sea so that it looked like a lake in the middle of some writhing mudland. And those cruel rocks; gaunt grinding teeth in that foam-flecked maniac hells-mouth, which has swallowed so many hopeless screams while devouring so many helpless ships and people. Punch-drunk with the ecstasy of that incredible scenery, greedy for more, we walked along to Cadgwith with the setting sun shadowing the menacing silhouette of the aptly named Black Head in front of us.

Cornwall has been described as oppressing all who come under its spell with that vague foreboding felt by a sleeper waking from sleep, haunted by the confused images of night — an untamed land, enduring sullenly the trappings of an age far from those remote twilights when with flint and stone man first sought to tame its wildness. Brooding over happenings with which his fate has small concern, the heights look down on square fields where with much labour a victory has been won over the castes of moor and boulder-strewn upland — and even in those small plots of green the granite shoulders its way through the soil and many among them are relics of victories won in vain, little broken dwellings whose builders have gone and whose walls have crumbled back upon the earth...

It really is extraordinary how Cornwall's qualities can make so strong an impact upon even the most inarticulate of people. Fortunately we also have the advantage of many articulate reactions as well. I can remember long conversations with one of the great Cornish landscape painters, the late Charles Simpson, at his gracious house in Penzance where he was fond of recalling that moment of the day, the hour of twilight, when the Cornish hills would seem to loom huge above the sea and the tokens of man dead or alive were alike swallowed up — as day departed the power in the granite seemed almost to rouse up to watch the approach of night:

The area of Cornwall which impresses the mind most strongly with this peculiar quality of brooding, of vengeful menace, of the unrest and terror added by man, of cataclysmic events beyond his sphere, lies between the cliffs at Land's End and the narrow watershed some few miles nearer sunrise. Here the waves along two opposing coastlines appear to strive which shall be first to wear down the resistance of the rocks and make an island of the westward hills. It is possible to gaze from sea to sea and listen almost at the same moment to waves breaking on either side, to hear the roar of surf swirling round the black cliffs to the north and long rolls sweeping up the southern shore, and thus in imagination to conceive the peninsular as an entity aloof from the mainland. Fantasies of the past surge round its people . The northern cliffs frown upon the sea, an unbroken barrier of rock, grey as the jackdar's mantle, sombre as the raven's wing. . . Dull tones of thunder-cloud and rain-storm find their match on the highlands, darkening the bracken to green of a leaden hue in summer, to swarthy, smouldering red in autumn; . . . the very sunlight is colder, bleaker, sadder than elsewehre. Those who wander on the moors enter the domain of fog. . . the shades of some dawn that never breaks, some paler counterpart of night. Sunsets there are, and golden skies, but they seem ruled by a capricious power who wills the sun to shine half in eclipse. The land has a countenance whose smiles only intensify its gloom and if there is laughter on the hills it is hollow as the cackle of an aged man.

The uplands, too, stretching southward from sea to sea have something of the aspect of a desert or plain, so sweeping are the curves of the moor as they meet the sky with monotonous regularity. This aspect of flatness conveys the sense of thwarted, sullen impotence so peculiar to the landscape.

In keeping with the panorama of moorland crag, and sea are the cries of birds. The curlew flutes its thin quavering notes across the wilderness of grass, and from a furze-bush the stonechat warbles its spring song — gayer sounds than the hoarse croak of the raven, but melancholy enough in such surroundings. There is sameness everywhere: furze, bracken and heather are blended in one tone. Upon this dun expanse some wizard hand plays a melody of sighing rhythm . . . the grass gives to the sky a mellow light and the sky conveys to the grass its greyness — the melody is transposed alternately from a major to a minor key . . . producing on the mind an effect of mysterious, dissolving harmonies.

Seen through the eyes of a landscape painter like Charles Simpson the mystery of the Cornish land becomes even more emphatic for, as he used to point out to me, even among the lesser pinnacles up on the moors there is still a sense that the granite might have been belched out from the earth as if in a last impatient shudder before an age of silence and waiting settled upon the shaping world. One looks out upon cairn after cairn of jagged rock piled above the plains of grass and feels that here there was once a striving. This is particularly so around Great and Little Galva, in Penwith, and the Hooting Carn at Kenidjack. There, for instance, on a western summit the castle's battlements are level with its curve and round the lower slopes ae chequered fields and square-built farms where from the castle's vantage point boulders used to be hurled; the rocks lie among the bracken as they fell, the walls of the fortress also lie and the long, rough escarpment of the hill remains the same.

Through this canopy of fog the wan light filters down upon the peninsular of Western Cornwall; often only at sunset there comes a momentary gleam of brightness on the higher moors. The fog lifts. A shaft of light strikes the summits of the hills, splashed with gold of furze and glinting stone. An isolated farm, a stack of masonry marking the site of an abandoned mine, the low straggling walls, quarries and tracks of bygone days scarring the land as though it had been torn by wide-stretched fingers in the frenzy of old despair — these glitter in the flame. Then the fog descends. It is the hour when the Spirit of Cornwall broods over the long ages of the past.

The haunting and brooding atmosphere of the Cornish landscape tends to be associated mostly with the wild and rugged coastline, where cascading seas and rearing cliffs meet in awesome conflict, though there are one or two inland areas like Bodmin Moor which can also create an immediate sense of

154

unease. An interesting aspect of the inland areas is the way man-made intervention has somehow accentuated the same general feeling of weirdness, of other worldliness. For instance, according to A.C. Todd and Peter Laws in their *Industrial Archaeology of Cornwall,* the face of about 45 square miles of the county around St Austell has over the past 200 years been transformed into a kind of lunar landscape, characterised by deep pits and quarries and huge grey and white pyramids of waste materials (just as the excavations go down to some 300 feet so do the mountains of waste rise up an equal distance). This part of Cornwall, stretching from Fraddon and Melder in the west nine miles eastwards to St Blazey, and from Roche in the north for five miles southwards to St Stephen, is china clay country. China clay, a stone containing special and peculiar properties of kaolin and feldspan was first discovered around 1745 by William Cookworthy at Tregonning Hill near Germoe, in West Cornwall. Later Cookworthy explored further east and finally found major sources of supply in the Austell area, where before long open-cast mining was begun by various small companies later forming the huge English China Clay Company (themselves now part of the International Rio Tinto Zinc Mining Group). In those early days the impact upon the county must have been quite an extraordinary one, as is indicated in this quotation from Mrs R.M. Barton's *History of the Cornish China Clay Industry:*

A scene then probably unique in the world. In all directions lay busy clay pits, round and oval ones; square pans filled with liquid clay; overhead launders (long wooden troughs for carrying liquid) attached to pumps forming a skeleton roof; the constant passage of bonnetted and aproned women carrying clay blocks to reeders, drying sheds or drying grounds. Children, who earned 7d a day, collected moss to fill the joints between the granite blocks of the pans which allowed moisture to pass through. The creaking of pumps, of horse whims and the rushing of countless water engines...

Today, under pressure from environmental groups, the china clay industry is endeavouring to encourage natural growth to cover the ancient waste tips with grass, though the dozens of huge water filled pits remain so dramatically overhung by 'white mountains' which motorists suddenly see rising high against the skyline as they travel either east or west. Because china clay is in such world demand the industry is likely to prosper and expand for a considerable time: production is running at 20 million tons a year and the clay is exported all over the world for use in making rubber, plastics, paint, pharmaceuticals, inks, dyes, cosmetics and (the largest proportion) paper. Possibly now the biggest single industry in Cornwall, next to tourism, china clay even has its own special ports, at Par and Fowey, where the whole area often bears the unmistakable snowy taint of the clay dust, blown hither and thither by perverse winds. At these ports, notably at the docks up the River Fowey, large cargo vessels can be seen flying flags of Sweden, Denmark, Germany, Cyprus, Spain, Algeria, even Japan, and this, too, adds to the colourfulness of the landscape.

Where china clay, still a thriving industry, continues to make a strong physical impact upon Cornwall, one or two older industries, which now operate only on a comparatively small scale, have nevertheless left even more emphatic marks upon the countryside. I am referring in particular to tin and copper mining. In the words of A.C. Todd and Peter Laws:

Those who may buy a cottage on a headland or in a valley winding down to the sea often hardly realise that from 1760 onwards Cornwall was as industrialised as the Midlands and the North of England. For almost 200 years it was one of the most important metal mining areas in the world, and became the setting for tremendous enterprises in the world of engineering, its blue skies shrouded by the smoke from a thousand chimney stacks, its wild life in fields, moors and lanes disturbed by the roar and clatter of machines. During the last century Cornwall yielded more than £200 million worth of tin and copper. Hundreds of shafts were sunk and thousands of miles of galleries

156

driven with forests of timber erected for their support. Mountains of ore and rivers of water were brought to the surface and fleets of ships were required to bring coal to feed the boilers and smelters. At the height of Cornwall's economic and industrial supremacy, from 1830 to 1860, it was estimated that more than 600 steam engines were at work, with scores of foundries manufacturing these giants of the art of pumping.

All this was soon to change: Cornwall, hub of the mining world, endured a tremendous slump and from a time when there were 300 water power mills, today, a hundred years later, there are now very few. The same startling collapse has taken place in the number of mines — where once there were hundreds, a few years ago the figure had dropped to two: at Geevor near St Just, and South Crofty, near Redruth — though with the revival of international demand for tin one or two new mines are now being opened.

Disastrous though this regression may have been upon the Cornish economy, geographically it has left a very pronounced mark, as anyone who wanders about any of the old dejected mining areas will quickly observe. Just as the china clay white mountains create a bizarre extra dimension to that eeriness with which Cornwall is already associated by nature itself, so, too, the relics of those busy tin-mining days remain, like ghosts, to haunt the landscape. Sometimes it is possible to stand on some hillock, as at St Day, and look around and see rearing up against the skyline a cluster of a dozen or more of the old granite minine chimneys, warning fingers of fate from the past (the wooden parts of course having long since been looted for firewood). Local authorities have been careful to fill in or block off actual mine entrances, but here and there, there are still some remarkable monuments to this past era — notably at Botallack on the north west coast near St Just, where parts of old engine houses can still be seen rearing up against the sky and sea. (And Botallack, incidentally, with its tiers of exposed corridors, makes a fantastic sight from the sea.) Then again there are the remains of the famous Levant Mine, scene of a great natural disaster in 1919 when parts of the mine shaft that extended under the sea collapsed with the loss of thirty nine lives. To stand amid the chaos of Levant Mine in all its stark abandonment, say Todd and Laws, is to realise the shattering challenge facing an industrial archaeologist:

Who, as he sits among the wreckage, somehow has to visualise again the complex of buildings growing as they did before the eyes of those old engineers and craftsmen — and then to try and visualise the natural landscape as it was *before* they occupied it and adapted it to their own needs.

Equally the industrial archaeologist has an important contribution to make to what might be defined as the aesthetics of industry: engine houses that take on the appearance of Cornish chapels; granite stairways in mines that are as beautifully designed as any in a church tower; factories that were made to look like the coach houses of the gentry; chimney stacks that, for their mathematical precision of construction, bear comparison with the columns of a Roman temple; and crushing mills that one could easily mistake for part of a mediaeval monastery. There is all this and more for both the professional and the amateur archaeologist in Cornwall, where a single capstan in a cove below the mining town of Pendeen let to the discovery that some Cornishmen spent their days winning tin from the darkness a thousand feet or so 'below grass' and their nights in searching for fish, choosing to name their cluster of cottages, St Peter's Row.

So perhaps it can be seen that the romance of these old and new industries, so much a part of the history of Cornwall, have contributed a very marked physical effect upon the Cornish landscape, and one that we must recognise to the full. Perhaps I may add a personal note of a walk I often make out of Penzance to see a friend who lives up near the top of Ding-Dong, where the crumbling ruins still stand of a once active mine of that name. Here, high among the hills of Penwith, looking round upon great natural cairns, gorse-covered moors, huge granite headlands, here and there strange edifices like the

Lanyon Quoit, it is impossible not to include in this visual impression the weird shape of that old mine chimney rising up to the very heavens, stemming from a Cornish past that was most certainly man-made and yet now, somehow, has become part of the eternal mystery.

While considering the effect of local industries upon the actual shape and appearance and atmosphere of the Cornish landscape one should mention one or two smaller examples — slate quarrying, for instance. Physically this has not had such a pronounced effect as it has in North Wales, nevertheless parts of Cornwall — most notably around Delabole in the North — quite large scale excavations have contributed decisively to the generally haunting atmosphere of the whole area around Tintagel and Boscastle. Here, briefly, is a portrait from an old handbook for travellers published in 1850 by the Royal Geological Society of Cornwall:

Two villages owe their origin to the Delabole quarries, Pengelly and Medrose. These quarries present one of the most astonishing and animated scenes imaginable. The traveller suddenly beholds three enormous pits excavated by the uninterrupted labour of centuries, slowly encroaching upon the domain of the farmer. Throngs of men are engaged in various noisy employments, steam engines are lifting with a harsh sound their ponderous arms and raising loaded trucks from pit depths. Masses of slates slowly ascend on guide chains stretched like shrouds of a ship from the platform to pit bottom. The largst quarry is 260 feet deep. The slates, after blasting, are placed on a truck which is drawn up to the head by a steam engine, water being pumped from the quarry by a water wheel, and is then taken by waggon drawn by two bullocks and a horse to the beach at Port Gavorne to be loaded into ships.

Today the Delabole quarry is still functioning, and is now 500 feet deep and over a mile in circumference. There are various smaller quarries around, which make a striking impression on the unsuspecting traveller with their unusual blend of blue and brown and grey, rising on either side of the route from Camelford into Tintagel like surrealist hillocks.

Granite is also quarried in Cornwall: at Penryn, Mabe, Stithians, Constantine, Wendron, St Breward, Linkinborne, St Just etc. Waterloo Bridge was built with Penryn granite, and even the tiny quarry at Lamorna Cove, near Penzance, supplied large quantities of stone for the construction of the Thames Embankment. Most famous of the granite quarries is the De Lank at St Breward, near Wadebridge, a name known to stonemasons all over the world — and this business still operates. It provided the stone for the Eddystone and Beacy Head Lighthouses, as well as for the construction of docks at Singapore and Gibraltar. Nor should one forget other quarried stones, such as Polyhant, near Launceston, and serpentine, found in large quantities on the Lizard Peninsula. To this day the Lizard industry continues through individual craftsmen, working in a material that has been described as a beautiful marble of a dark green colour variated with veins of purple, red, white and scarlet.

In the same way that quarries add to the atmosphere of a strange world, it may be said that Cornwall's other two major industries, farming and fishing, have also contributed colour and atmosphere. Because Cornwall, jutting out so boldly into the heart of the surrounding seas, is so severely exposed to winds, the farming pattern has been to cover the land with small fields protected everywhere by the ubiquitous Cornish hedge (made invariably of loam and lumps of granite.) This is particularly so near the coast, where the land often acquires a tidy appearance that contrasts strangely with the often awesome and majestic lines of the cliffs and scenery. On some of the inland areas, particularly on huge open moors like Bodmin Moor, farming is of a different style, with few hedges, just vast areas of undulating arable land, lonely as the proverbial cloud save for here and there groups of grazing cattle of various sorts, including the famous Bodmin black ponies and, of course, sheep. Here again, the contrast of the vast sweep of moorland and the ever changing skies, often suffused with racing billowing clouds, makes for an often unforgettable impression, what painter Lionel Misken envisaged as 'an almost brutally present structure suggesting petrified waves, crested at the tors, otherwise in deep wide undulations.'

The impact of the fishing industry has been touched on in an earlier chapter, but it also has a certain relevance to the landscape, too, for all round the Cornish coast there are picturesque little fishing ports with straggling cobbled streets leading up steep-sided hills lined with fishermen's cottages. I am thinking of such places as Mousehole and Newlyn in the South West, of Polruan and Polperro in the South West. From a distance one looks down upon a vista of toy-like fishing boats dotted about the waters of the harbour, of cottages which take on the appearance of doll's houses — a blended vision of Cornwall — as ever — as a place strangely apart and *different*. Sometimes, too, as at Feock and Rostranguet and Mylor, or at Fowey and Golant, on the south coast, or at Wadebridge on the River Camel on the North Coast, the fishermen element penetrates deeper into the countryside, flavouring some of the inland areas with the smell of the sea, the colourfulness of bright sails and painted boats, the tranquillity of fishermen in their blue dungarees sitting on cobbled walls watching the world go by.

Time and again, as I've already mentioned, writers have come to Cornwall, seen and been conquered. My old friend and fellow author, Frank Baker, often recalls his days as an impecunious writer when he stayed in a remote place near St Just:

In the Kenidjak Valley my love for Cornwall was born, and it has never left me, nor will it. As I descended into the valley after the long track from St Just's wind-riven square I did not at once see any sign of the cottage where I stayed; only the walls of the valley which rose up high on either side, great granite slabs jutting out, rich with scrubs of bright gorse which kept April alive the year round; and deep in the gorge the sun-coloured mine ruins with a crumbling chimney stack from where in another age fumes of arsenic had drifted into the air. Very ancient mines. And the lower went the twisted rocky track, the deeper into a world of the past the walker penetrated, as a silence holding only the roar of the distant sea and the remote cheep of a yellow-hammer, fell and claimed my being. I stumbled almost in a half run down this craggy path . . . and stopped suddenly in wonderment. Far down at the threshold of the valley, shouldering up against the sea which could not be seen, was the black spiny hump of Cape Cornwall, with all the air around it misted by azure spindrift glistening in the deepening dark gold of the sky itself.

Lest it may seem that all the mystery of Cornwall is contained in that far western tip (a view which the reader may well have sensed I incline towards) let me redress the balance by quoting briefly from some wise words of Michael Williams, who once wrote a book about riding on horseback across Bodmin Moor:

The most lasting impression of Rough Tor — for me anyway — are the faces. As you climb, faces look down at your perspiring efforts. Some belong to sheep and ponies. Others are grotesque masks in the rock itself, created by the wear, rain and wind of centuries. Memorable, too, are a cluster of rocks like coins stacked one upon the other, by some miserly giant perhaps. Here imagination stirs. The dividing line between fact and fiction blurs. Where does one begin and the other end? I have sat in the saddle on Brown Willy, grateful for a sturdy sure-footed cob, and watched the different worlds of Devon and Cornwall fade into a morning haze: a day when the wind slept and only birds and animals moved. I have wedged myself between rocks on Rough Tor and attempted to hide from the invisible knife of the wind — and both times I have been conscious of the same fact: Cornwall is a draughtsman's country. There is a sense of geometry in the landscape and even the sun, filtering through, intensifying the colours, cannot alter it.

It is indeed as a draughtsman's country that the land of Cornwall makes its impact upon us: as a gaunt skeletal figure

162

of stone, writhing and contorting into strange shapes, inhabiting a world of shadow and darkness where colour is neither particularly present nor really needed. In this bleakly defined form Cornwall may be said to achieve a curious kind of unity — the open and treeless surroundings of Tintagel in the east, for instance, being very similar to the bleakness of St Just, in Penwith in the West, and both surrounded by the same wide prospect of sea. Even on the south coast, though woodlands are to be found up one or two of the estuaries along the coast there is the same pattern of windswept treeless lands, the same awareness of a grim reality of life, whether by land or sea. Wherever you go in Cornwall — and indeed the *more* you travel and explore in Cornwall — I think more a perceptive visitor must come to recognise that here indeed is a granite kingdom that is very much its own domain. Perhaps more than that, he will be uneasily aware of a feeling put deftly into words by one of Cornwall's own poets, Charles Causley:

> One day, friend and stranger,
> The granite beast will rise
> Rubbing the salt sea from his hundred eyes
> Sleeping no longer.
>
> In the running river he will observe the tree
> Forging the slow signature of summer
> And like Caliban he will stumble and clamour
> Crying 'I am free! I am free!'
>
> Cast off your coloured stone ropes, signal the journey!
> And to the bells of many drowned chapels
> Sail away, monster, leaving only ripples
> Written in water to tell of your journey.

An appropriate acknowledgement of the perpetual mystery!

Chapter Ten

The Spirit of Cornwall

Those who desire to understand the Cornish and their country must use their imagination and travel back in time. Superstition flows in the blood. Rocks and stones, hills and valleys, bear the imprint of men who long ago buried their dead beneath great chambered tombs and worshipped the earth goddess. The stones, like the natural granite cast up from the earth by nature, defy the centuries. The present vanishes, centuries dissolve, the mocking course of history with all its triumphs and defeats is blotted out. Here in the lichened stone is the essence of memory itself...

DAPHNE DU MAURIER

The spirit of Cornwall is what this book is all about. Nothing could be more fascinating to consider — nothing more difficult to explain. How does one explain Land's End in the grip of the wild Atlantic, a world 'full of the energy of storm, fiery in haste, and yet flinging back out of its motion the fitful swirls of bounding drift, of tortured vapour tossed up like man's hands as in defiance of the tempest . . . the whole surface of the sea one dizzy whirl of rushing, writhing, tortured undirected rage, bounding and crashing and coiling in an anarchy of power'? Such scenes defy rational explanation and we can only come to agree with that perceptive observer, Ruth Manning-Sanders, when she remembered drowned sailors of the past hailing their names above the moaning of the waters:

It is then that the sense of the primordial, the strange and the savage, the unknown, the very long ago, fills the dusk with something akin to dread. It is then that the place becomes haunted: a giant heaves grey limbs from his granite bed, a witch sits in that stone chair on the cliff...

This is the sort of thing, intangible and mysterious as it may often seem, which I firmly believe constitutes the true and inner spirit of Cornwall: hopefully some of the chapters of this book, especially those quoting reactions of writers and artists, will have born out this viewpoint. As mentioned in the introduction, Cornwall simply cannot be treated as just another English county. It has always been and will surely remain a place apart, a strange kind of timeless land in which past and present and future are all weirdly combined in a welter of images and experiences. Here I think we touch on an important word. The spirit of Cornwall is something each person has to *experience:* it is simply not something that can be picked up from some guide book or survey, admirable though many of these are for purely reference purposes. Probably nowhere in the British Isles has been the subject of more guide books than Cornwall — yet with a handful of exceptions they do not attempt to interpret the inner meaning of Cornwall. In a very real sense a reader would be just as likely to achieve this aim by throwing aside all these piles of pamphlets and booklets and simply wandering off across 'the granite kingdom', that place in which he would at once be made to feel aware not merely of an immediate past but of a huge and endless past stretching to the infinite. For instance try seeking out some of the 400 old Celtic crosses or standing stones which are studded around the countryside. Carved out of very old grey granite, crude and simple, often surprisingly large, with shafts up to 20 feet, these crosses really do seem to speak across the centuries.

Nevertheless, even if the spirit of Cornwall cannot be totally captured or explained, at least we can summarise some of the aspects of which it is made up. First and foremost there is the sheer and overwhelming *atmosphere,* that condition which so many writers and artists have reacted to often violently — as in the case I quoted of Walter de la Mare being so afraid that he could not feel at peace until he was safely back in Devon the atmosphere of what painter Charles Simpson called 'an untamed land, enduring sullenly the trappings of an age far from those remote twilights when with flint and stone man first sought to tame its wildness; a time of legend and mystery.' Sir John Betjeman put it more simply when he described how the sky widened as you approached Cornwall and it seemed as if a sense of sea hung in the lichenous branches as over the west glowed a mackerel sky. Thinking of old friends he once knew in Cornwall he wondered if they were one with the Celtic saints and he concluded, with a sense of uplift, that as he reached his Cornish destination he, too, became part 'of a sea unseen.' The fact is that lingering behind all these exterior impressions there is a sense of something deeper and terribly potent — we are acutely aware, as Charles Causley said, that, 'one day, friend and stranger, the granite beast will rise rubbing the salt sea from his hundred eyes sleeping no longer."

What a marvellous and haunting image that evokes, of a land — rather like the illustration of Margo Maeckleberghe's swirling Atlanta paintings — in which immense energies are crouching, waiting to be unleashed. Yes, if nothing else, we can say that atmosphere is a basic part of the spirit of Cornwall: an atmosphere that arises directly out of land and sea, cliffs and moorlands — indeed, as I have pointed out earlier, even from man-made creations like the white mountains of the clay pits, the regular lines of ley stones, the brown and blue piles of Delabole slates, even the picturesque forests of mastheads of hundreds of fishing boats lining the protective quays of fishing ports. To take just this last example of the human side of life in Cornwall it should always be remembered that it is neither an easy life nor a safe one — and risk, too, plays an important part in the make up of the spirit of Cornwall. This was brought out by the novelist Wilkie Collins writing about a walking tour in Cornwall with Charles Dickens in 1842. Quite unexpectedly he came upon the lovely old church of Mawgan on the North Coast:

Within the churchyard the bright colour of the turf and the grey hues of the moulding tombstones are picturesquely intermingled all over the uneven surface of the ground, save in one remote corner, where the graves are few and the grass grows rank and high. Here the eye is abruptly attracted to the stern of a boat, painted white, and fixed upright in the earth. The strange memorial, little suited though it be to the old monuments around, has a significance of its own which gives it a peculiar claim to consideration. Inscribed on it appeared the names of ten fishermen of the parish who went out to sea to pursue their calling on one wintry night in 1846. It was unusually cold on land — on the sea, the frosty bitter wind cut through the bones. the men were badly provided against the weather; and hardy as they were, the weather killed them that night. In the morning the boat drifted on shore, manned like a spectre bark by the ghastly figures of the dead — freighted horribly with the corpses of ten men all frozen to death. They are now buried in Mawgan Churchyard and the stern of the boat they died in tells their fatal story and points to the last home which they share together.

Another man-made activity especially a part of life in Cornwall which has contributed to this elusive 'spirit' has been tin mining. Wherever there is a hole in the ground you can be sure to find a Cornishman at the bottom of it, searching for metal, goes the old saying — and indeed the face of Cornwall is pock-marked with such holes by men who searched and scoured beneath its skin for tin and copper, though the only thing to be found at the bottom of most of them now is rubbish and water, as Frank Ruhrmund pointed out describing a visit to Geevor Mine, one of the few working mines that have survived.

The door of the cage clanged shut behind me; it was too late to change

167

my mind; I was trapped, my moment of truth had arrived. There was the ringing of bells and then suddenly without warning we were off — plunging straight down into the bowels of the earth. I though of the cold Atlantic outside and hoped it would remain calm. We reached the 100-foot level. This was where I got out. I staggered from the cage: my legs were soft and spongy my head buzzed and I felt as I did the first time I flew in an aircraft — terrible. The entrance to the level was sealed by a door of steel. Open it revealed a huge black hole, hewn from solid rock. It smelled of hard work and I wondered who it was who began such a tunnel, who drilled the first tiny tentative hole that started it all? The mine was still, as if asleep, the only sounds the faint tip-tap of dripping water and the distant hum of a generator. I thought about past disasers; the major ones like the flooding of Wheal Owles and the collapse of the man-engine at the Levant and of many minor ones that brought injury and death to more than a few; the horror of the moment and the subsequent grief and hardship inflicted upon countless families. Thoughts of the vast weight and power of the sea above me crept into my mind; I felt very tiny, insignificant and a little afraid...

Cornwall is made up of so many many things peculiar to Cornwall itself — like the old serpentine stone workers, of the Lizard working on stone dug from ploughed fields some way back from the cliff face. This craft goes back a long way and depends entirely on the fact that the Ice Age never reached so low as the Lizard, and so the stone beneath the fields, as also that on the beaches and cliffs, did not weather in the same way as in other parts of the island with the result that at the Lizard they have what is called serpentine stone. Its beauty and variety is due to the veining and mottling of the stone by talc, magnesite and irox oxide... and it is in fact not unlike marble.

And then, still close to the land consider the words of Prudence Jones of the Ministry of Public Building and Works, which controls Carn Euny at Sancreed, near Penzance:

The mystery of the Sphinx, the lost continent of Atlantis, the location of El Dorado — these are some of the world's mysteries that may never be sold. Why travel to the ends of the earth when, here in

168

Cornwall, is a puzzle awaiting solution? What is the mystery of the *fogous? Fogou* is a word corrupted from the old Cornish word for a cave. *Fogous* are, in fact, man-made caves. They are underground or partly underground structures of great antiquity consisting of a passage chamber with sometimes connecting passages or rooms. They appear to serve no useful purpose, being damp, dark and cold, and yet the effort and time put into their construction with nothing more than human strength and ingenuity is evidence of their importance to those who laboured over their building. They are thought to be of the Iron Age period and built around 100 B.C. The Carn Euny *fogou* is connected with a prehistoric village of the Iron Age situated on a hill over looking the sea in three directions and from where on a clear day the outline of the Isles of Scilly can be seen. One can stand on a grassy bank and not know that there is a tunnel or passage beneath one's feet though both ends of this tunnel are open. The original entrance slopes gradually downwards from ground level and today the first few yards are unroofed. Then the passage is found to divide, leftwards to the main part of the *fogou* and right to a shorter, low passage leading unto a circular chamber. This round chamber has a stone covered floor with a drain that leads off into the main chamber and thence downhill. The walls of the circular chamber are corbelled with granite rocks and now stand to a height of over 9 feet, that is, the floow of the chamber is about 10 feet below ground level. The diameter at the floor is roughly 15 feet but the walls gradually narrow upwards. The stones are of uncut granite, held together without any mortar and are small at the bottom gradually increasing in size towards the top. This beehive chamber is said to have had a stone roof but there is no evidence of this now and it is open to the sky. Except under the midday sun it is always dark down this 'hole in the ground,' how much more so when it was completely roofed? What was a *fogou* built for? Who went to all this trouble two thousand years ago? It was obviously a communal effort and was not built in a day. Was it built for storage? Some say it was but what can one store in a damp, dark hole in the ground? It is not unknown in winter for the main passage to be half-filled with water. Burial? There doesn't seem to be any trace. Could it have been a place of refuge, being partly concealed underground? It has been called a subterranean retreat but would more likely to have been a death trap — retreating from one's enemies the occupants could easily have been starved to death or smoked out. Was there any religious significance about a *fogou?* Great care and very much hard work was involved in the construction which suggests something important was the motive.

Whatever may be the secret of the *fogous,* or many other weird parts of the landscapes, we can never forget, as well, all those mysteries associated with the sea. I have written at some length about this aspect which encloses Cornwall in its vice-like grip. Perhaps one should remember, also, the quieter side of the sea life. M A Hollingham, writing about his childhood at Trevone Bay on the North Coast for the *Cornish Review,* remembered delightfully,

Long lazy hot summer days that I would pass browning on the beach, swimming and surfing in the sea, then walking barefoot the mile or so back to the village for lunch, through the heat of the mid day, which took my friend's talk and laughter, the buzzing of the bees, and the song of the skylark, and the distant calls of the gulls, to hang them on the clear summer sky of my memory. Then down again to the beach in the afternoon for long picnic teas on the sand. Or days when I would go, often alone, across the rocks and pools of Rocky Bay, shrimping, fishing and just turning over stones in pools to see what was underneath. And days when I would walk up from the beach on to the cliff with the large round hole in the middle, at the bottom of which was a cave that led out to sea. At high tide, and in rough weather, the sea would smash against the rocks at the bottom of the hole, and it was for all the world like peering over the edge of some vast boiling, bubbling cauldron. At low tide one could climb down to the bottom of the hole and walk through the cave to the cliff base, then climb round into the next cove and up and up back to the top of the cliff... Although all the people that I knew have gone, the village, and especially the beach and surrounding cliffs, have seen very little change in the twenty-five years that I have known them. Many times in the last few years, although living hundres of miles away, I've been drawn back to Trevone Bay and its cliffs. Each time that I've come, I've not been disappointed. The innocent, happy childhood that I knew there cannot be recaptured, but leaves a glowing memory, and I find a peace, a serenity, on those cliffs. For something very fundamental in me responds and is refreshed, and draws inspiration

170

from there. On a winter's evening, when all the people have gone and I walk up on to those cliffs, it is a timeless thing. I could be in any age of man's history. Although many people must know and love that place as well or better than I, for me, alone on those cliffs, it is as if no one had ever set foot there before me, or that there was no one else in the world. I feel that if I have any gods, then I am very close to them there.

One thinks, too, of such peripheral yet important matters such as the bird life of Cornwall, again somewhat unique. Surrounded by the sea on all but its eastern boundary, the rugged coastine and its offshore waters provide a unique harbourage for sea birds of many species and for impressive land birds, which find safety and seclusion for their nests on battered cliffs. The backbone of the country, comprising wild moorland, attracts birds of a different breed and manner — owls, whinchat, curlew, snipe, and others. Sheltered and wooded valleys are the homes of our song birds, visiting warblers from the sunny South and water-loving birds. Last, but far from least, there are numerous estuaries up which great Atlantic tides, twice in every twenty-four hours, bring up from the sea an exhaustless supply of marine food for the sustenance of not only many water fowl but also of travelling (and wintering) waders from and to their breeding grounds in the far North. During the last two or three decades, according to the late B. H. Ryves, the Cornish ornithologist, more than 240 species of birds have been recorded in Cornwall, 112 of which have been proved to breed. Pride of place of resident birds is taken by the chough, Cornwall's traditional emblem, a rare and elegant bird with red legs and long curved red bill. Then there are Montagu's sharriers, one of the rare hawks in the British Isles, as well as peregrines, buzzards, owls and crows. Among sea birds there are no less than 36 species, the largest being the gannet whose almost dazzling whiteness enhanced by black tipped wings rivet the attention. The commonest resident gull is the herring gull, sacrosanct among fishermen, and among

171

diving birds are the shag and the cormorant; auks and puffins, fulmars and shear-waters are among others — while among water fowls there are spoonbills, whooper swans, wild geese, shelduck, mallard, teal, divers sawbills and grebes of five varieties.

Surfing, too, is a part of the spirit of Cornwall. Hardly anywhere else in England can you experience that marvellous sensation of freedom, of literally throwing yourself, your whole being, upon the crest of some gigantic wave and being born along through the air and washed up like some magic mermaid upon long white sands. Sands — white, bleached sands, like those of Sennen or Fistral or Watergate or Widemouth — they, too, are part of this same quality. Surfing and sand, rock and cliffs, moors and carns — everything, it seems, is very physical in Cornwall, and certainly one's reactions are very physical, earthy, *felt*. But there are many other things to be considered. The old language for instance still being earnestly revived by a new generation of scholars, mindful of the late Grand Bard's promise: 'One generation has set Cornish on its feet; it is now for another to make it walk' — and certainly the growing popularity of the Cornish *Gorseths*, now linked with similar ceremonies in Britain and Wales, has been a great encouragement. We may never live to hear the Cornish language spoken in everyday use again, but many of its earlier expressions, like the *Ordinalia* plays held in the open air theatres like Pirran Round, are likely to be performed more widely. Along with the language, Cornwall will certainly cling firmly to all those long established traditional events I have described earlier, like the Helston Furry Day, the Padstow Hobby Horse, St Columb Hurling: like special occasions such as 'Tom Bocock's Night' at Mousehole, just before Christmas, when hundreds of people gather from far afield for a fish pasty supper at the Ship Inn — and of course like those memorable midsummer Night Eve bonfires lit on a string of hills around Cornwall, from Land's End to Launceston.

Perhaps in the end we come closest to understanding the meaning of the spirit of Cornwall if approaching the matter through the eyes of those very 'furriners' whom locals are so firmly keep at a wary distance — at least for the first 100 years! It is interesting to note how all-persuasive is the influence of the place upon the stranger. Writing in the book *My Cornwall*, Colin Wilson makes the point that whereas many writers living in Cornwall seem to fit the environment — Daphne du Maurier, Jack Clemo, Ronald Duncan — he cannot see any connection between his own work and the small Cornish village Gorran, near Mevagissey, where he has lived for two decades. 'And yet because Cornwall has been such an enormous part of my life I suppose it has entered into my bloodstream.' Colin Wilson goes on to specify the classlessness of life in Cornwall, the fact that locally a writer or a painter is accepted quite naturally for what he is as a human being. As a result, and this I feel is all part of the spirit of Cornwall, there is a marvellous sense of cosmopolitanism about life in places such as St Ives and Newlyn, Mevagissey and Fowey. Artists and fishermen and tin miners and dockers and craftsmen and shopkeepers; retired people and working people, rich people and poor people — they all seem to merge into a pleasant whole community. Idealistic? Perhaps, to some extent, about the people. But about the place, never.

The only entrance to our cliff was through this gate to the top. It was no place for strangers. There was a deep cleft biting into the land, a sheer fall to the sea below, guarding one boundary of the meadows; and the other boundary disappeared into boulders, brambles, gorse and, in summer, a forest of bracken. Below were the rocks, granite and blue elvan pitted with fissures, huge ungainly shapes each part of the whole which sloped without plan inevitably to the sea. Here the seaweed, draped like an apron, thickened the water at low tide; and gulls, oyster catchers, and turnstones poked among it, uttering wild cries. There was the sense of loneliness and yet of greatness, this was unmanageable nature, the freedom man chases.

Those words from Derek Tangye, one of several autobiographical writers whose enthusiasm has helped to draw many people to Cornwall, reach tentatively to the heart of the matter. In Cornwall, as in few other places, one can truly embark on the eternal search for that freedom which man chases, forever and ever without quite attaining it. And perhaps one of the wonderful things is that, like a disease, once experienced Cornwall never leaves you. It is always there, in all its mystery. As the late James Turner once remembered in *Sometimes Into England*:

We had come across England during the night over Bodmin Moor in the dawnlight, passed through Wadebridge and along the road to rock and Pityme. The narrow lanes, the gaunt and sometimes forbidding chapels, the harts tongue fern and violets, even the old iron bedsteads in the hedges, must be exactly as they were when we sped through them without looking on our way to the headland and childhood holidays. The little stone bridge at Tredinnick, the hamlets of Penrose and Trenance, anyone could name a hundred such places, seem just the same as they must have been decades ago. Only perhaps the great moonscape of china clay pits around St Austell may have grown outwards and increased. And how fitting those white hills are in a a country where trees are scarce and whose main characteristic is toughness. And yet they were all there waiting for me, just as the rocks, when I came back thirty years later, were waiting for me and had been for years!

> What in me do they await, and why this welcome;
> Granite arms reaching out to engrain me,
> Eternity of rock turning a centimetre to regard me
> Coming, a simple fragility of flesh and straining tendon
> Down the deep gully down
> To its caverns?

The spirit of Cornwall, in the end, has eluded me, lost somewhere in those granite arms reaching out to engrain us: let us, wisely, leave this as the best of endings, one that remains forever a challenge.

Bibliography

Many thousands of books have been written about Cornwall, ranging from essays on antiquities to thriller novels, from official histories to unofficial racy autobiographies, from historical romances to dry-as-dust official reports. Obviously it would be impossible to list them all, so here I have assembled what I hope is a fairly catholic selection of some of the more interesting volumes published in recent years. The books are listed here alphabetically by author's surnames.

We Bought An Island Evelyn Edith Atkins (Harrap, 1976)
In The Roar Of The Sea S. Baring-Gould (Methuen, 1915)
Folk Songs Of The West Country S. Baring-Gould (David & Charles, 1974)
The Call Of Cornwall Frank Baker (Robert Hale, 1976)
Hawker Of Morwenstow Piers Brendon (Jonathan Cape, 1975)
Cornish Water Mills D. E. Benney (Bradford Barton, 1972)
Portrait Of Cornwall Claude Berry (Robert Hale, 1971)
Victorian & Edwardian Cornwall John Betjeman & A. L. Rowse (Batsford, 1974)
Essays In Cornish Mining History D. Bradford Barton (Barton, 1961)
Billy Bray: The King's Son F. W. Bourne (Epworth Press, 1937)
Collected Poems, 1955-73 Ronald Bottrall (Routledge, 1974)
Life In Cornwall In The 19th Century R. M. Barton (Barton, 1970)
Cornish Phrase Book Christopher Bice (Lodenek Press, 1971)

The Natural History Of Cornwall William Borlase
(Robert Hale, 1970)

A Week At Land's End J. T. Blight (Dalwood, 1973)

Climbing In Cornwall Toni Carver (James Pike, 1973)

Peter Lanyon Paintings Andrew Causey (Aidan Ellis, 1971)

Collected Poems Charles Causley (Macmillan, 1951-1975)

The Echoing Tip Jack Clemo (Methuen 1971)

The Watchers On The Longships J. F. Cobb (Darton, 1948)

Bodmin Moor Ernest Coleman (David and Charles, 1975)

A Cornish Quintette: 5 One-Act Cornish Plays (Lodenek Press,
1973)

Cornwall Information Handbook (Cornish Tourist Board, 1980)

History of Polperro Jonathan Couch (W. Lake, 1871)

Cornish Feasts and Folk Lore M. A. Courtney (Folk Lore
Society, 1973)

The Folklore Of Cornwall Tony Deane (Batsford, 1975)

Tristan And Iseult In Cornwall E. M. R. Ditmas (Forrester
Roberts, 1970)

Cornish Names Piers Dixon (Piers Dixon, 1973)

Follow A Wild Dolphin Horace Dobbs (Souvenir Press, 1977)

The Saints Of Cornwall Gilbert Doble (Dean & Chapter
of Truro, 1970)

The House On The Strand Daphne Du Maurier (Gollancz,
1969)

The Monumental Brasses Of Cornwall E. H. W. Dunkin
(Kingsmead, 1970)

The Cornish Song Book Ralph Dunstan (Reid, 1929)

The Hurlers: Cornish Stone Circles C. W. Dymond (Institute of
Geomantic Research, 1977)

The Story Of China Clay English China Clays, Ltd, 1970)

Shipwreck John Fowles (Jonathan Cape, 1974)

The Owl's House (& Other Novels) Crosbie Garstin (Werner
Laurie, 1956)

The Cornish Language Around Us Richard Gendall (Lodenek
Press, 1975)

Island Camera: Isles Of Scilly In The Photography Of The Gibson Family (David and Charles, 1972)

Gorseth: History Of The Gorsedd (Gersedd of Bards of Cornwall, 1947)

Poldark Novels Winston Graham (Bodley Head, 1960)

Britain Observed: Landscape Through Artists' Eyes G. Grigson (Phaidon, 1975)

A History Of Cornwall Frank Halliday (Duckworth, 1975)

Footprints Of Former Men In Far Cornwall R. S. Hawker (Lane, 1903)

Complete Sculpture Of Barbar Hepworth, 1960-69 (Lund Humphries, 1971)

Days In Cornwall C. Lewis Hind (Methuen, 1945)

Historic Houses, Castles And Gardens In Cornwall (Tor Mark Press, 1970)

Walking In Cornwall J. R. Hockin (Methuen, 1942)

The Novels Of Silas And Joseph Hocking (Ward Lock & Frederick Warne)

Richard Trevithick James Hodge (Shire Publications, 1973)

Cornish Customs And Superstitions Robert Hunt (Tor Mark Press, 1970)

Sea Fishing Around Cornwall J. M. Hussey (Tor Mark Press, 1970)

Idle Rocks Zofia Ilinska (Mitre Press, 1972)

Inns Of Cornwall (Matlance, 1974)

Killer Mine Hammond Innes (Collings, 1973)

The Fogue Kenneth Ireland (Dobson, 1977)

A Grain Of Sand Erma Harvey James (William Kimber, 1976)

Cornwall And Its People A. K. Hamilton Jenkin (David and Charles, 1970)

Orphans Of The Sea Ken Jones (Harvill Press, 1970)

The Path Of The Sun: Biography Of Bryan Pearce Ruth Jones (Sheviock Gallery, 1976)

The Art Of Cornish Wrestling Bryan H. Kendall (Cornish Wrestling Association, 1974)

Humphrey Davy: Pilot Of Penzance James Kendall (Faber, 1954)

Cornish Shipwrecks Richard Larn (David and Charles, 1969)

A Potter's Book Bernard Leach (Faber, 1976)

Cornish Tales Charles Lee (Dent, 1941)

The Widow Woman Charles Lee (Dent, 1912)

The River Fowey Wilson Macarthur (Cassell, 1948)

The Old Stones Of Land's End John Michel (Garnstone Press, 1974)

Journals Of Caroline Fox Wendy Monk (Paul Elek, 1972)

Portrait Of The Isles Of Scilly Clive Mumford (Robert Hale, 1970)

An English Cornish Dictionary R. Morton Nance (Cornish Language Board, 1973)

Artists Of The Newlyn School, 1880-1900 (Newlyn Gallery, 1979)

My Cornwall Du Maurier & Nine Others (Bossiney Books, 1973)

Levant: The Mine Beneath The Sea Cyril Noall (Barton, 1970)

Smuggling In Cornwall Cyril Noall (Barton, 1971)

The Fighting Blacksmith: Biography Of Bob Fitzsimmons Gilbert Odd (Pelham, 1976)

Boats and Boat Building In West Cornwall A. S. Oliver (Barton, 1971)

Flowers Of The Cornish Coast Jean Paton (Tor Mark Press, 1970)

The Ports & Harbours Of Cornwall Richard Pearse (H. E. Warne, 1963)

Birds Of Cornwall Roger Penhallurick (Tor Mark Press, 1970)

Thomas Hardy In Cornwall Kenneth Phelps (Lodenek Press, 1975)

Cornish For Beginners Peter Pool (Cornish Language Board, 1970)

Novels Of "Q" (Sir Arthur Quiller Couch) (J M Dent & Sons)

Padstow's 'Obby 'Oss And May Day Festivities Donald Rawe (Lodenek, 1971)

Petroc Of Cornwall: A Play Donald Rawe (Lodenek, 1970)

Selected Poems Peter Redgrove (Routledge, 1975)

Rocks And Minerals Cedric Rogers (Ward Lock, 1973)

The Hard Rock Men: Cornish Immigrants John Rowe (Liverpool University Press, 1974)

A Cornish Childhood A. L. Rowse (Cape, 1974)

The Tamarask Dora Russell (Paul Elek, 1975)

Roger Hilton: Paintings And Drawings Serpentine Gallery (Arts Council Great Britain, 1974)

Evening Star: Story Of A Cornish Fishing Lugger Ken Shearwood (Barton, 1972)

The Story Of The Cornish Language A. S. D. Smith (An Lef Kenewek, 1969)

Autobiography Of Howard Spring (Collins, 1972)

St Michael's Mount John St Aubyn (Jarrold, 1974)

The Way To The Minack Derek Tangye (Michael Joseph, 1972)

Facing The Sea Nigel Tangye (William Kimber, 1974)

The Granite Kingdom D. M. Thomas (ed.) (Barton, 1970)

Industrial Archaeology Of Cornwall A. C. Todd and Peter Laws (David & Charles, 1972)

The Importance Of Being Cornish In Cornwall Charles Thomas (Institute of Cornish Studies, 1973)

The Principle Antiquities Of The Land's End District Charles Thomas and Peter Pool (Cornwall Archaeological Society, 1969)

Harbour Village: Yesterday In Cornwall Leo Tregenza (William Kember, 1977)

School House In The Wind Anne Treneer (Cape, 1950)

Sir Humphrey Davy Anne Treneer (Methuen, 1963)

Introduction To Sea Shore Life In Cornwall Stella Turk (Barton, 1971)

The Stone Peninsula: Scenes From The Cornish Landscape
James Turner (William Kimber, 1975)

Cornish Harvest: Anthology Short Stories Denys Val Baker (ed.)
(William Kimber, 1974)

Haunted Cornwall: Supernatural Stories Denys Val Baker (ed.)
(William Kimber, 1973)

An Old Mill By The Stream Denys Val Baker (William
Kimber, 1973)

A Summer To Remember Denys Val Baker (William Kimber,
1975)

Letters From A Cornish Garden C. C. Vyyyan (M. Joseph,
1972)

Paradise Creek Leo Walmsley (White Lion, 1974)

Early Photographs: Penzance And Newlyn Reg Watkiss
(Dalwood, 1975)

From A Cornish Landscape David Watmough (Lodenek, 1975)

Essays In Cornish Nationalism James Whetter (MK
Publications, 1973)

The Dark Land Mary Williams (William Kimber, 1975)

Supernatural In Cornwall Michael Williams (Bossiney Books,
1974)

An Introduction To The Archaeology Of Cornwall Charles
Woolf (Barton, 1970)

Letters Of Virginia Woolf, Vols 1 and 2 (Hogarth Press, 1975
and 1976)

Bryan Wynter: Paintings 1915-1975 (Arts Council of Great
Britain, 1976)

The Cry Of A Bird Dorothy Ygelesias (William Kimber, 1973)

GENERAL FICTION

		Cyril Abraham	
Δ	042697114X	THE ONEDIN LINE: THE SHIPMASTER	80p
Δ	0426132661	THE ONEDIN LINE: THE IRON SHIPS	80p
Δ	042616184X	THE ONEDIN LINE: THE HIGH SEAS	80p
Δ	0426172671	THE ONEDIN LINE: THE TRADE WINDS	80p
Δ	0352304006	THE ONEDIN LINE: THE WHITE SHIPS	95p
		Spiro T. Agnew	
	0352302550	THE CANFIELD DECISION	£1.25*
		Lynne Reid Banks	
	0352302690	MY DARLING VILLAIN	85p
		T. G. Barclay	
	0352304251	A SOWER WENT FORTH	£1.95
		Michael J. Bird	
Δ	0352302747	THE APHRODITE INHERITANCE	85p
		Judy Blume	
	0352302712	FOREVER	75p*
		John Brason	
Δ	0352305355	SECRET ARMY: THE END OF THE LINE	75p
		Barbara Brett	
	0352303441	BETWEEN TWO ETERNITIES	75p*
		André Brink	
	0352305916	RUMOURS OF RAIN	£1.95
		Jeffrey Caine	
	0352302003	HEATHCLIFF	75p
	0352395168	THE COLD ROOM	85p
		Ramsey Campbell	
	0352304987	THE DOLL WHO ATE HIS MOTHER	95p*
	0352305398	THE FACE THAT MUST DIE	95p
	0352300647	DEMONS BY DAYLIGHT	95p*

BARBARA CARTLAND'S ANCIENT WISDOM SERIES

	Barbara Cartland	
0427004209	THE FORGOTTEN CITY	70p*
	L. Adams Beck	
0427004217	THE HOUSE OF FULFILMENT	70p*
	Marie Corelli	
0427004225	A ROMANCE OF TWO WORLDS	70p*
	Talbot Mundy	
0427004233	BLACK LIGHT	70p*
	L. Adams Beck	
0427004241	THE GARDEN OF VISION	70p*

† For sale in Britain and Ireland only.
* Not for sale in Canada. • Reissues.
Δ Film & T.V. tie-ins.

GENERAL FICTION

Δ	0426187539	R. Chetwynd-Hayes **DOMINIQUE**	**75p**
	0352303514	Magda Chevak **SPLENDOUR IN THE DUST**	**£1.50***
Δ	0352395621	Jackie Collins **THE STUD**	**85p**
	0352300701	**LOVEHEAD**	**95p**
	0352398663	**THE WORLD IS FULL OF DIVORCED WOMEN**	**75p**
Δ	0352398752	**THE WORLD IS FULL OF MARRIED MEN**	**75p**
	0426163796	Catherine Cookson **THE GARMENT**	**95p**
	0426163524	**HANNAH MASSEY**	**95p**
	0426163605	**SLINKY JANE**	**95p**
	0352302194	Tony Curtis **KID ANDREW CODY AND JULIE SPARROW**	**95p***
	0352396113	Robertson Davies **FIFTH BUSINESS**	**£1.25***
	0352395281	**THE MANTICORE**	**£1.25***
	0352397748	**WORLD OF WONDERS**	**£1.50***
	0352301880	D. G. Finlay **ONCE AROUND THE SUN**	**95p**
	0352304073	**THE EDGE OF TOMORROW**	**£1.25**
	0352304995	Norman Garbo **THE ARTIST**	**£1.50***
	0352395273	Ken Grimwood **BREAKTHROUGH**	**95p***
Δ	0352304979	Robert Grossbach **CALIFORNIA SUITE**	**75p***
Δ	035230166X	**THE GOODBYE GIRL**	**60p***
	0352304359	Elizabeth Forsythe Hailey **A WOMAN OF INDEPENDENT MEANS**	**£1.25***
Δ	0352305142	Peter J. Hammond **SAPPHIRE AND STEEL**	**75p**
	0352301406	W. Harris **SALIVA**	**60p**
Δ	0352304030	William Johnston **KING**	**£1.25***

† For sale in Britain and Ireland only.
* Not for sale in Canada. • Reissues.
Δ Film & T.V. tie-ins.

GENERAL FICTION

		Heinz Konsalik	
	0352303956	**THE WAR BRIDE**	95p
	0427003210	**THE DAMNED OF THE TAIGA**	75p
	0352303883	**NATASHA**	95p
	0352304022	**THE CHANGED FACE**	95p
		Jeffrey Konvitz	
Δ	0352398981	**THE SENTINEL**	70p*
		Dean R. Koontz	
	0352301643	**NIGHT CHILLS**	85p*
		Andrew Laurance	
	035230412X	**PREMONITIONS OF AN INHERITED MIND**	95p
		Ellie Ling	
	0352304154	**THE FIRST SPLASH**	75p
		Pat McGrath	
	0352303328	**DAYBREAK**	95p
		Lee Mackenzie	
Δ	0352396903	**EMMERDALE FARM (No. 1)** **THE LEGACY**	70p
Δ	0352396296	**EMMERDALE FARM (No. 2)** **PRODIGAL'S PROGRESS**	70p
Δ	0352395974	**EMMERDALE FARM (No. 3)** **ALL THAT A MAN HAS . . .**	75p
Δ	0352301414	**EMMERDALE FARM (No. 4)** **LOVERS MEETING**	70p
Δ	0352301422	**EMMERDALE FARM (No. 5)** **A SAD AND HAPPY SUMMER**	70p
Δ	0352302437	**EMMERDALE FARM (No. 6)** **A SENSE OF RESPONSIBILITY**	70p
Δ	0352303034	**EMMERDALE FARM (No. 7)** **NOTHING STAYS THE SAME**	75p
Δ	0352303344	**EMMERDALE FARM (No. 8)** **THE COUPLE AT DEMDYKE ROW**	75p
Δ	0352304103	**EMMERDALE FARM (No. 9)** **WHISPERS OF SCANDAL**	75p
Δ	0352304510	**EMMERDALE FARM (No. 10)** **SHADOWS FROM THE PAST**	75p
Δ	0352302569	**ANNIE SUGDEN'S COUNTRY DIARY (illus)**	£1.25
Δ	0352304340	**EARLY DAYS AT EMMERDALE FARM**	75p
		David Martin	
Δ	0352304288	**MURDER AT THE WEDDING**	95p
		Graham Masterton	
Δ	0352396164	**THE MANITOU**	70p*
	0352395265	**THE DJINN**	75p*
	0352302178	**THE SPHINX**	75p*
	0352395982	**PLAGUE**	95p*
	0352396911	**A MILE BEFORE MORNING**	75p*

† For sale in Britain and Ireland only.
* Not for sale in Canada. ● Reissues.
Δ Film & T.V. tie-ins.

Wyndham Books are obtainable from many booksellers and newsagents. If you have any difficulty please send purchase price plus postage on the scale below to:

Wyndham Cash Sales
P.O. Box 11
Falmouth
Cornwall
OR
Star Book Service,
G.P.O. Box 29,
Douglas,
Isle of Man,
British Isles.

While every effort is made to keep prices low, it is sometimes necessary to increase prices at short notice. Wyndham Books reserve the right to show new retail prices on covers which may differ from those advertised in the text or elsewhere.

Postage and Packing Rate

UK: 30p for the first book, plus 15p per copy for each additional book ordered to a maximum charge of £1.29.
BFPO and Eire: 30p for the first book, plus 15p per copy for the next 6 books and thereafter 6p per book. **Overseas:** 50p for the first book and 15p per copy for each additional book.

These charges are subject to Post Office charge fluctuations.

GOOD DOG, BAD DOG

MORDECAI SIEGAL

&

MATTHEW MARGOLIS

A SIGNET BOOK

NEW AMERICAN LIBRARY

TIMES MIRROR

SIGNET TRADEMARK REG. U.S. PAT. OFF. AND FOREIGN COUNTRIES
REGISTERED TRADEMARK——MARCA REGISTRADA
HECHO EN CHICAGO, U.S.A.

SIGNET, SIGNET CLASSICS, MENTOR, PLUME, MERIDIAN AND NAL
BOOKS are published by The New American Library, Inc.,
1633 Broadway, New York, New York 10019

First Printing, October, 1974

8   9   10   11   12   13   14   15

PRINTED IN THE UNITED STATES OF AMERICA

For
Pete, Princess, and Silver . . .

Three Lucky Dogs

Contents

The authors wish to express their gratitude and appreciation to Mark Handler for his skill and sensitivity as photographer for *Good Dog, Bad Dog*.

To Beverly Margolis and Vicki Siegal a special note of admiration for their patience and assistance.

A special thank you to Don Gold and Hy Shore for the application of their very special gifts to this book.

Introduction

> If you pick up a starving dog and make him prosperous, he will not bite you. This is the principal difference between a dog and a man.
>
> —MARK TWAIN

Now that the commitment has been made to own a dog, it is reasonable to want to know how to take care of him. After all, these bundles of fur are totally dependent creatures and innocently look to their owners for food, shelter, medical attention, and love. Everything connected with their survival depends on the big guys, the humans. And in the human world a dog's survival often hinges on his ability to respond to a direct command. "Pete, stay!" "Silver, come!" "No!" "Down!" "Sit!" These are not arbitrary orders shouted from the Gestapo Handbook. They are scientific commands given to a trained animal whose correct response may save his life in city traffic or rural hazards. These commands will also allow for a satisfying relationship between dog and master. If a dog is not housebroken, not able to be silent, not able to keep from destroying furniture or property, not able to obey when required, then his survival is in jeopardy. Many people give up their dogs after a few months of abject frustration, and the future of those animals is then in grave danger. This is why obedience training is not only valuable but necessary.

With the many books available concerning dog training, one might ask what's special about this one. To begin with, the premise of this book is that the owner is being trained how to train his or her dog. Equal emphasis is given to teaching the owner as well as the animal.

As owner-operator of the National Institute of Dog Training, Inc., coauthor Matthew Margolis has trained approximately five thousand dogs *and their owners* in their homes. He is one of the pioneers in the techniques of owner-animal training in the home. The benefits of his experience are herewith offered.

This is the first dog-training book that attempts to dig beneath the surface of its own method and explain how the technique works. Within these pages are offered a basic obedience training course that has proven itself over and over with thousands of dogs of all breeds. No training book has ever gone beneath the surface to understand the behavioral characteristics of specific breeds and how to use that understanding in training. This one does. It is the first practical guide to training your dog *at home*. It emphasizes affection, kindness, and authority. It is based on the idea that dogs are nice.

PART 1

The Basic Obedience Course

1/Success

GOOD DOG, GOOD OWNER

Being a dog is a boring job. Most of his life is spent either sleeping or waiting to be fed. Chances are the dog is bored beyond belief. This is especially true if his owner does not know how to communicate with him, to convey what is wanted, or to spend the necessary time relating so that a rapport exists. Dogs are in a foreign country and do not understand the language. Which may explain why they seek the company of other dogs. Most dog owners are kind and generous people. They need only to develop consistent goals and principles to enjoy the many years of companionship and protection that a dog gives.

The difference between a good dog and a bad dog is whether or not he makes his owner feel like a benevolent master who is always in control. As lord of the manor, it is the owner's noble obligation to offer shelter, hearty nutrition, proper medical attention, exercise, affection, and training. In return the dog should respond with love, joy, undying devotion, and *absolute* obedience. Although it seems a bit medieval, this is approximately the ideal dog-master relationship. Successful training helps achieve this goal. This course deals exclusively with obedience because it has been proven through experience that the entire dog-master relationship improves greatly after an effective training course.

THE PROPER FRAME OF MIND

To successfully train a dog, the owner must maintain the cool objectivity of a "pro." This means not allowing frustrations to interfere with relating to the dog. Many mistakes are going to be made by the dog as he proceeds from lesson to lesson throughout the course, and the owner's patience will be put to the test over and over again. The dog must not be yelled at or punished in any way. If the owner has had a trying day he must either postpone the lesson or stay alert not to abuse the dog because he didn't get that promotion, or his wife dented a fender, or his teen-age daughter moved into a co-educational dorm. One must exercise patience, kindness, and an understanding of emotional limitations and personal in-adequacies. Many a kicked dog has been a stand-in for the boss, the wife, the husband, the mother-in-law. Before ex-pressing anger at the dog, ask if he really deserves it. There is no place in this obedience course for abuses. Forget the word *punishment*. Replace it with the word *correction*.

WHY TRAIN A DOG?

The answer to this question has to do with why one buys a dog at all. There are many reasons why people keep dogs. Pleasure, companionship, protection, child education are a few, but mainly it's to enjoy the animal. No living being will love you as completely as a dog. Training will at once remove the obstacles standing between the owner and the beneficial objectives of dog ownership, thus allowing many trouble-free years with the animal.

Without training, cute puppy behavior soon develops into annoying adult habits. These annoying habits sometimes become severe problems and permanently damage the dog's temperament. But with a trained dog you will never have to cope with dog fighting, being dragged down the street, being jumped on, or having furniture destroyed. Obedience training also eliminates stealing food from the table, defecat-ing indoors, throwing up in the car, or the hundreds of other problems that make it unpleasant to own an animal. If a dog does any combination of these things he is not a bad dog. He is merely untrained. This is a correctable situation; it is well within the owner's grasp to change it.

Dogs are like babies, and as there is no such thing as a bad baby, there is no such thing as a bad puppy. Dogs are shaped by environmental influences as well as the genetic characteristics of the dog's bloodline. If a dog is trained properly he will behave like a gentleman and cause very few problems throughout his life. A good definition of training is *teaching a dog to respond to his master and doing what is expected of him the minute a command is given.* Any dog can be trained and any owner can train him.

DISPELLING MYTHS FROM THE DARK AGES

It is important to forget the hearsay methods of dog training that have been handed down through the ages like snake oil in a medicine show. Chances are it was Attila the Hun who first rubbed his dog's nose in his own mess and yelled and screamed at him. Forget that "method." Forget all methods that brutalize and are abusive, such as swatting with a rolled-up newspaper. It teaches the dog nothing except to fear long cylindrical objects (including your hands) and to run when he sees them. It is merely another form of punishment, and that accomplishes nothing positive beyond giving you emotional release.

Do you hit your dog? Of course not. But some confused, frustrated owners do. A flinching, cowering, neurotic animal is a giveaway. The owner says in protest ". . . but I really love Tinkle. I only kicked her because she was a bad dog." This obedience course shows a better way to make a dog behave and replaces antiquated techniques. Forever resolve not to hit, kick, pinch, punch, gouge, slap, knuckle, tweak, bang, strike, nip, or bite your dog. Please refrain from ever using your hand for anything other than hand signals (used in giving commands) or affectionate praise or love. Never use your hand for threats, violent gestures, or even disciplinary pointing. Pointing your finger at the dog and saying "Naughty, naughty" produces the same negative effect. Pain, fear, and terror retard or prohibit communication. It is also inhumane.

Imagine entering a taxi in a foreign country. The driver asks "Where to?" in his native tongue. You stare at him and shrug, not knowing the language. He then goes berserk and smacks you hard on the snout. It would seem painfully unreasonable, to say the least. Some dogs face this horror every day of their lives. If hitting a dog was the least bit useful, why would it have to be done so often? Your dog can be trained with absolute results without being punished. This is an opportunity to stop feeling guilty by giving your dog a punishment-free life. This will enable you to enjoy your friend, the dog.

WHEN TO BEGIN TRAINING

Training can begin at age three months for puppies of all breeds. By this we mean housebreaking (or paper training), the command "Heel" (to the extent of getting the puppy used to the leash), and the command "Sit." At age four and a half months the entire course may be taught.

WHO SHOULD PARTICIPATE
IN THE TRAINING

Ideally, every member of the family should learn the new techniques in order to avoid confusing the dog. For obvious reasons, only one person should introduce the training to the animal. After the dog has learned each new command, the instructor then teaches the rest of the family what to do and how to do it. If everyone participated in the training at the same time, it would become more of a chaotic party than a lesson for the dog and the session would go out the window. What with cross-conversations, inconsistent commands, and the general tumult, the dog's attentiveness would disappear.

It is best to teach the dog a command with no one else around. It may take from one to three sessions for him to respond immediately to the new command. Once he does, do not turn him over to the rest of the family until he has had time to rest and absorb what he has learned. Give him at least five hours before showing the other members of the family. Then take them one at a time and teach them how to execute the new command. This will give you the responsibility of correcting them with patience.

THE BASIC OBEDIENCE COURSE

No training session should last longer than fifteen minutes. Dogs tire and bore very easily. If you work a dog more than fifteen minutes he is going to respond to every distraction imaginable. Try to be extra patient and understanding during the first few sessions. He is going to be denied every impulse that is natural for him. It will be a whole new world of discipline and obedience. You are going to create conditioned responses in his brain that will make it impossible for him to disregard a command. This represents a major mental chore for the dog and will make him moody and irritable when the first sessions are over Allow for this by letting him sleep after the sessions. Sleep is probably what he'll want.

These minor considerations for the animal come out of your understanding his immediate problems. Every chapter will contain a section entitled "Beneath the Surface of the Training." With every new command, this section will explain the natural instinct of the dog and how you are going to change or manipulate that instinct. The result should be a greater understanding of the dog in relation to the command. It is important, however, to attempt to analyze your own dog. He is a *student* and like all students has his positive and negative qualities. Every dog has a different personality. How does *your* dog react in certain situations?

The best way to train your dog is to utilize his good attributes. If he is very affectionate then that should be the key to getting a good response from him. He will respond to the giving or withholding of affection. With other dogs too much affection will not bring good results. He may assume that every time you praise him he can then revert back to doing as he pleases. In other circumstances a withdrawn dog will possibly respond better to praise and affection. Determine if your dog is affectionate, stubborn, spiteful, outgoing, withdrawn, afraid of noises, etc. Of course it is safe to assume that a three-month-old puppy is going to be playful, outgoing, energetic, and generally responsive to affection. They often make the best students.

Pick a suitable area where the training is to be given. Inside the home is fine, providing there is ample walking space and a minimum of distractions. Outdoors, a quiet, secluded area is best. It is futile to teach a command such as "Sit" when there are eight dogs in heat hanging around, plus an airplane crash, and ten young boys playing baseball.

Communication is the prime factor in training a dog. He does not speak or understand English. His intelligence level is that of a small child. Therefore you must seek his level of understanding. He will respond mostly to a tone of voice. Like an actor, you must pretend firmness, softness, or playfulness through vocal tone and attitude. If you have ever communicated with an infant you will understand what is meant here. It's almost the same thing. "Goo-goo" makes a baby smile. A firmly said "No" makes him let go of your glasses. Once you have established lines of communication you are halfway finished with the training.

2 / Equipment

There are enough manufactured dog items to completely fill a supermarket—more than one could use in a lifetime. If you bought them all you could create a do-it-yourself Spanish Inquisition. Cattle prods, throw-chains, and various electrical gadgets would be more suitable for counter-intelligence interrogations. Very few, however, are useful for training purposes.

A great hindrance to acquiring practical training equipment is the "rhinestone and paisley" syndrome. Several years ago a Park Avenue client contracted for an obedience course for her dog. Her silver-gray poodle was about as clipped and manicured as they came. When the rather grand lady was asked for the dog's training equipment, she opened a closet door and revealed over fifty collars and leashes of every color, style, and description. She became self-conscious after the trainer gasped. She explained that she always bought Pipa a new collar and leash whenever she purchased a new clothing ensemble for herself. She and her Pipa were at all times fashion coordinated. However, she did not have the very few items necessary to properly control the dog. Unless one is interested in making "Best-Dressed Dog of the Year," there are few items needed to train a dog.

THINGS THAT *WON'T* BE NEEDED

A spiked collar. A spiked or pronged collar is a choke collar with bent prongs on the underside, the ends of which dig into the animal's neck when pulled on its slip device. These prongs, though blunted, make dozens of tiny impressions around the throat and effectively restrict the dog's movement when jerked into operation. It is true that they can be useful when used properly by a professional trainer, but the chance of misusing it and seriously injuring your dog is great. One jerk with a pronged collar is worth fifteen jerks with a regular choke collar. However, inexperienced dog owners tend to overdo it and make the animal suffer or become permanently damaged.

A leash made of chain. No matter how long or short, it is almost impossible to tell ahead of time when it is going to snap. If it should break while in city traffic the dog might bolt, run out in the street, and the rest is too unpleasant to think about. One can see where a leather leash is wearing thin or losing its stitching.

Thick, short leashes. They are useless for training purposes. They may look very masculine with a Doberman or Shepherd on the end of them, but they are very ineffective for employing the various training techniques that will be discussed in the coming chapters.

Leather collars. For reasons that will become clear, they work against the training technique. The exceptions to this are the long-haired breeds such as Afghans, Sheepdogs, etc. In that situation a leather collar is preferable because a metal one tends to rub the fur away and create permanent ring marks or bald spots.

THINGS THAT *WILL* BE NEEDED

A six-foot leather leash. This is used in every command except where otherwise indicated. It will allow the proper distance for control when teaching the dog to "Sit." Six feet of leash will also allow you to walk behind him while still exercising control. A leather leash, by the way, will not hurt your hand or the dog's chest when employing various training techniques.

Leashes come in various widths. The size of your dog should guide you in choosing the proper width, although five-eighths of an inch is recommended as the most comfortable width without sacrificing strength. Toy breeds require a narrower width such as the half-inch or smaller. The key to buying this equipment is strength and comfort. A fancy, multicolored nylon leash may look beautiful but might break and then you won't have a dog.

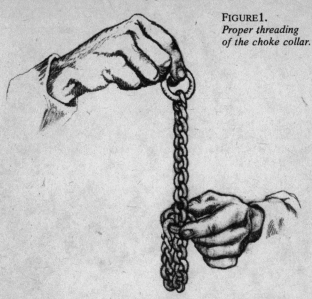

FIGURE 1.
*Proper threading
of the choke collar.*

A twenty-five-foot clothesline. Used as a long leash, this rope is implemented when teaching "Sit-Stay" *off-leash.*

A fifty-foot clothesline. This length of rope is employed as a leash when teaching the dog to "Come When Called" *off-leash.*

A jeweled choke collar. A jeweled choke collar is one that has small metal links which are welded very close together. This type is the strongest and releases its grip from the dog's neck quickly and smoothly. The wide-linked choke collars sometimes jam as one link entangles in another. For correct threading of the jeweled choke collar, see Figure 1. The term "choke" collar is a misnomer. It does not choke the dog. It "corrects" the dog by tightening around his neck when the leash is pulled. If the collar is placed around the dog's neck properly it will release quickly, thus avoiding any pain. (See Fig. 2). *Do not use a metal choke collar for Toy breeds and small puppies.* These dogs are too fragile for this equipment. Either use a leather collar or slip the end of a nylon leash through the hand loop, thus effecting a slip knot around the animal's neck.

FIGURE 2.
*Left: correct way for dog to
wear the choke collar.
Right: incorrect way.*

A *"throw can."* This is another misnomer. It is not really used for throwing. Similar to a New Year's Eve noisemaker, it is used to startle a dog and get his immediate attention. Take an empty soda can and slip fifteen pennies into it, taping the opening closed. By rattling it up and down you get a demanding sound. This is used primarily for puppy problems such as housebreaking, chewing, jumping, going into the garbage, chasing the baby, etc. Shake the can and say "No" in a firm voice. The noise becomes associated with the word "No" and stops the puppy from continuing his indiscretion.

This is all the equipment one needs to successfully complete the obedience course. The outlay of money is nominal.

These items are standard and available in any pet supply outlet. Please resist the temptation to substitute these items with homemade, inadequate versions or storebought, overly complex versions of the same things. Purchase exactly what is suggested. This equipment is uncomplicated, inexpensive, and highly functional. Once the equipment is procured you are ready to begin the course. Good luck.

3/Housebreaking

One of the great agonies for dog owners is housebreaking. Here is a method to solve that problem. There are many reasons why a dog is not housebroken, but the prime cause is the inability to communicate what is wanted from him. Most new dog owners are extremely inhibited and embarrassed by the whole subject of housebreaking. If dealing with the functions of the animal body is too embarrassing, how then can one teach the animal to control those functions? Many dog owners behave like six-year-old children making "toidy" jokes in a Gilbert and Sullivan operetta. "Muff-Muff make do-do." "Princess made ta-ta." Nothing is worse than hearing a grown person say of his 185-pound Mastiff, "Horace makes tinkle on the bed." The worst ever recorded was, "Poofie makes chocolates in the house!" It is desirable to avoid such euphemisms as *surprises, plops, wee-wee, ca-ca, eh-eh, gifts*(!), *presents, numbers one and two, feces, movements, etc.* A dog defecates. A dog urinates. Let's be brave about it.

DEFINITION OF HOUSEBREAKING

It is simply, teaching your dog to relieve himself, outside, on a schedule most convenient for you.

BENEATH THE SURFACE OF THE TRAINING

There is no such thing as a partly housebroken dog. Many an owner has said something like, "Fang is completely housebroken . . . except he dumps on the bed after we change the linen." Either he is housebroken or he isn't. Some people say their dog is housebroken when they mean he's paper-trained. There is a considerable difference between the two. When a dog is housebroken he never, but *never,* uses the house for his toilet, on or off the newspaper.

Many people do not understand why their dog does not know what to do when taken outside. Merely taking him outside does not mean that he knows what he's being taken out for. The biggest problem between dog and owner is that the dog would love to please but doesn't know how; and the owner would love to teach the dog what he wants but doesn't know how to communicate to the dog. This method solves that problem. There is nothing worse than a dog who is not housebroken. It is the first and most important phase of domesticating an animal. Many a dog and owner have parted company at this phase of their relationship. Many a good and loving dog has been saved from being given away or destroyed after the owner was introduced to this housebreaking method.

PROCEDURE AND TECHNIQUE FOR HOUSEBREAKING

This technique is the most humane ever devised. With it there is no confusion for the animal. Each phase has its importance and each phase should be followed the way it is outlined. There are four major steps:

1. Proper diet and scheduling
2. Using an odor neutralizer
3. Confining the dog
4. Proper correction (not punishment)

This method is ideal for dogs between three months and three years old. However, good results have been gotten with dogs as old as six years. Of course you will not get the same results with a six-year-old as with a puppy, but the method does work. The ideal age to start housebreaking your dog is when he is approximately twelve weeks old. By that time one assumes he has visited a veterinarian and has had his permanent shots and there is no chance of his catching distemper, leptospirosis, or canine hepatitis. The method should take no more than two to four weeks. You should find a great improvement in the first week. If the dog does not respond, it is possible that he has a medical problem and should be examined by a veterinarian. If you have been paper training your dog, pick up the papers and forget that technique. Otherwise the animal will become totally confused.

PROPER DIET AND SCHEDULING

Feed, water, and walk your dog properly. He needs a stable, well-balanced diet consisting of correct amounts of fat, proteins, carbohydrates, vitamins, and minerals. The ideal dog food is pure meat added to some form of cereal. Canned meat products mixed with commercial cereal are adequate. Commercial dog food has all the vitamins and minerals essential for your dog's well-being and it is recommended. Table scraps are a hit-or-miss affair. When changing the dog's diet, do not do it all at once. Gradually mix the two diets over a three-day period so that the change is not sudden. Otherwise it will cause diarrhea. A dog's stomach is very sensitive to changes of food.

Feed, water, and walk the dog at the same times each day to achieve favorable results. Consistency is the key to this method. The following rules must be followed without variance:

1. Do not vary your dog's diet.
2. Snacks or between-meal treats are forbidden.

Putting your dog on a proper schedule. Here is the ideal schedule for a three- to five-month-old puppy (follow the established diet pattern for older dogs): seven-thirty in the morning—feed, water, and walk him; eleven-thirty in the morning—feed, water, and walk him; four-thirty in the afternoon—feed, water, and walk him; eight-thirty in the evening —water only and a walk; eleven-thirty in the evening—just a walk.

At feed time allow fifteen minutes for the dog to complete his meal and then take it away, no matter how much he has left in the bowl. Allow him a few minutes to drink water. *He is not to be given food except at the scheduled times.* (This dietary schedule is for the duration of the housebreaking period only.) Water should be made available at all times.

Please consult a veterinarian on all matters pertaining to your dog's diet.

The more one restricts the time for food and water, the closer one comes to scheduling the dog's bodily functions. A dish with four or five ice cubes may substitute for a bowl of water, thus satisfying the dog's thirst while reducing his water intake. Once again we advise you to consult a veterinarian about the specific needs of your dog.

The minute the dog is fed and watered, take him out for his walk. Once he has relieved himself, praise him and take him inside immediately. He will soon begin to understand why he is being taken out.

The length of time a dog should be walked must not exceed fifteen or twenty minutes. If taken on a long walk before or after he has performed his bodily functions the impact of *why* he is being taken out will have been diminished and the method will not work. This is exactly why most dogs do not know what is expected of them when they are taken outside.

Schedule for nine-to-five working people. Take the dog out immediately after waking up. Bring him back inside, feed and water him, and then walk him once again so that the routine is established. When you come home from work repeat the process. Take him out, back in for feeding and watering, and then out for another immediate walking. It would be good for the dog if you could arrange for someone to repeat this cycle at lunchtime. Before going to bed walk him one last time without a feeding. Because a small puppy cannot hold his water for eight or nine hours, it is advisable to confine him to an area that he can urinate in without causing any household damage.

If the dog has a favorite outdoor area let him go there to sniff around. Many dogs develop a favorite spot and it should not be discouraged.

When this program is first begun, do not be frustrated if the dog does not relieve himself for the first two or three rounds of feeding, watering, and walking. He may hold out for as long as twenty hours. Bear in mind that he is being forced to break his old habits and do something new for the first time. If he holds out for too long, then insert a glycerin baby suppository in his anus after his feeding and watering. Take him outside. You will get results. After he relieves himself, praise him so that he knows that going outside pleases you. All this is temporary until the dog is housebroken.

USING AN ODOR NEUTRALIZER

The second phase of housebreaking, and probably the most important, is getting rid of the dog's past urinary and excretory odors from the house. This is accomplished with an odor neutralizer, which is available in pet stores and pharmacies. When used properly it will completely eliminate these odors, sometimes discerned only by the dog, by neutralizing them rather than perfuming or covering them with a stronger scent. Place twenty drops of the liquid neutralizer into three quarts of hot water. With this mixture mop all areas where the dog has messed. If all such areas are neutralized, dogs will relieve themselves indoors less frequently. When your dog has to relieve himself he seeks an area where he or another dog has gone. This can be borne out by observing him outdoors. He sniffs around for a very specific spot before he performs.

It is important to note that no ordinary cleaning product neutralizes these odors. Ammonia, bleach, and detergents of every kind fail for one reason. They are not designed for this purpose. Consequently, the dog's odor remains long after the mess has been cleaned away. A liquid odor neutralizer does its job every time. If your dog urinates in the house, your first step toward success is to odor-neutralize the spot frequently. This process should be repeated each and every time the dog has an accident in order to prevent him from returning to the scene of the crime.

CONFINING THE DOG

The third phase of housebreaking is *watching* and *confining* the dog. For whatever the reason, there are many times when the dog must be left alone in the house. This, very often, is precisely when he chooses to relieve himself. It is rare that he will attempt it before your eyes after the first experience with your scorn. Therefore, confine the dog when he is left alone. Confinement, however, does not mean tying him up. He is simply contained in a small area where he cannot stray. Psychologically, a dog will never defecate in an area where he must remain. His habit is to go as far away as possible, relieve himself, and then go back to his own area. The area of confinement must be large enough for him to walk around without feeling punished. Otherwise, he'll bark and try to get out.

When you are home the dog should be allowed to run around loose, *providing you watch him.* If he is going to relieve himself, be in a position to correct him immediately. The key to watching and confining is that the dog will not mess in his own area if he can help it. However, if he is never let loose to run around the house it becomes too much like punishment, and that will work against this method.

PROPER CORRECTION

The final phase of housebreaking is the technique for correction. Under no circumstances should a dog be punished for relieving himself in the house. He cannot be justifiably punished for his ignorance; he can only be corrected.

Never correct a dog unless you catch him in the act. A few minutes after the deed has been done, the dog has no mental capacity to connect your wrath with whatever he did wrong. It is confusing to him and you will only get a puzzled whimper. That's why punishments have little or no effect and only lead to frustration for dog and owner. Catch him in the act or it's no good.

When the dog messes in the house in front of you, there is only one way to correct him. Do not rub his face in it. Do not say "shame." Do not play negative games with the newspaper or other threatening objects. *Startle* and *impress* him with the word "No." This is where you use the "throw can." (See Chapter 2.) When the dog is in the act of urinating, shake the can vigorously like a party noisemaker. This should be accompanied with a harsh "No." Whatever he is doing, he will probably stop. When he does, immediately take him outside to finish what he started. *This is the only way that you can show the dog what you want him to do.* You are catching him in the act, stopping him, taking him outside to finish, and then giving him tremendous praise when he finishes.

The difference between shaking the can and slapping a newspaper in your hand is the difference between getting his attention or threatening him with a slap or blow. Do not instill fear in the animal. Stop him in the middle of his action so that he can be taken to the proper place for it. The correction really comes from the harsh "No." With a large dog it may be necessary to throw the can on the floor (behind your back, preferably) to stop him. During this period, if necessary, leave the leash and collar on so that he can be taken outside quickly with no delay. The idea is to correct, not punish.

Many people are mistakenly convinced that dogs mess in the house for spite or revenge, usually for having been left alone. This is incorrect. It is for reasons of anxiety, nervousness, or fear that he behaves this way . . . or simply because he is not properly housebroken. Very often an owner comes home and finds the dog behaving in a fearful, shameful, or generally guilt-ridden manner. The owner knows the dog has messed somewhere. It is because of this behavior that an owner is convinced the dog messes in the house for spite. It simply isn't true. The dog cringes when you come home because he associates your arrival with punishment. He does not understand what he has done wrong in the specific sense. If the dog is left alone in a new place or in a situation that makes him nervous or frightened, he will uncontrollably defecate. It has nothing to do with his ability to perform as a well-behaved, housebroken pet.

Many methods of housebreaking are negative in approach. Consequently, the dog half understands. He knows he's done something wrong. But he gets little or no instruction for what he should be doing. The first emphasis of this method is prevention and the second is instruction. This was once illustrated to a client who called the trainer at home at three in the morning after he had been asleep for several hours. A frantic voice asked, "Mr. Margolis?"

"Yes," he mumbled.

"This is Mrs. Baxter. You're training my little Filbert."

"Yes," he answered, "but it's three in the morning. What do you want?"

"You told me to call you if Filbert had an accident. Well he made do-do on the rug. What should I do?"

"Clean it up," he said as he hung up the phone. That's instruction.

4 / Paper Training

In the world of dogs, pouring over the Sunday papers has an entirely different connotation. Next to reporting the news, the greatest service rendered to the public by newspapers is to provide an inexhaustible supply of paper-training equipment. Paper training is an ideal alternative to housebreaking for many reasons. The convenience of not having to use the streets at all hours of the day and night speaks for itself. Inclement weather and rigorous work schedules are also good reasons for wanting to stay off the streets. But possibly the best reason of all is one that most city dwellers are familiar with. That is, the aesthetic problem involved in soiling the city streets and sidewalks with dog litter.

In large urban areas such as New York City, where over six hundred thousand dogs reside, many nondog owners have created a major public issue of this subject and have lobbied for restrictive legislation against dogs and dog owners. The authors do not believe that legislation is an effective answer to this problem. However, paper training offers an excellent alternative to this irksome situation. If paper training were adopted by enough considerate dog owners it would mean the end of one more aspect of the pollution problem in American cities. For those who love their dogs but are also concerned with ecology, the end of the conflict lies in paper training.

DEFINITION OF PAPER TRAINING

This means that a dog will urinate and defecate on paper in your house or apartment, in a designated area of your choice.

BENEATH THE SURFACE
OF THE TRAINING

The main reason a dog prefers to urinate on paper is because the urine disappears by absorption. That you remove the papers after he uses them is soon understood. No animal wants to be around his own body waste. Another reason why paper training works so well is that dogs prefer to toilet on the same spot they did previously. It has to do with the territorial instinct for claiming specific areas as their own. Because of a dog's highly developed sense of smell, he is capable of detecting scents of which we are completely unaware. Consequently, after he has soiled one spot he is drawn back to the same place simply because he can smell it. Only a powerful odor neutralizer can prevent his smelling it.

Paper training is most successful when introduced to the animal as a puppy. If the choice is made to paper train, you must not change over to housebreaking. Too often a pup is taken away from his litter before ten weeks and cannot be taken outside for housebreaking. The owner uses newspapers, indoors, as a temporary measure. It is a mistake to then take the puppy away from his paper procedure. This offers nothing but confusion to the little dog. As a result the dog starts having one accident after another in his attempt to interpret your wishes. These accidents often occur on an expensive carpet or in a corner of your bedroom during the night. The dog is then punished or shamed or burdened with unjust guilt while the owner suffers from frustration and rage. This is also the beginning of neurotic behavior in most animals.

The rule should be that you do not take a puppy into your house before he is ten weeks old unless you are firm in your resolution to paper train him. In the case of dogs that have already been housebroken, it is only fair to say that the changeover will be difficult and will demand a great deal of patience.

PROCEDURE AND TECHNIQUE
FOR PAPER TRAINING

There are four steps to paper training:

　　1. Proper diet and scheduling

  2. Confining the dog
  3. Using an odor neutralizer
  4. Proper correction

These steps are primarily geared for puppies, although they can be used for older dogs if you take a little more time and exercise greater patience. What should be done first is to pick an area in the house that is convenient for this purpose. Designate it as the permanent paper place for the dog. Here is where he will always relieve himself and feel confident that you will not be angry when he uses it. This will be where you *paper* the dog. Some of the more convenient places to use are the bathroom, the kitchen, the pantry, the basement, or any place where you're least likely to be offended when the dog uses it. Do not, however, pick a place that is inaccessible for him. The easier it is for him to get there the more success you will have.

PROPER DIET AND SCHEDULING

Feed, water, and paper the dog properly. He needs a stable, well-balanced diet consisting of correct amounts of fat, protein, carbohydrates, vitamins, and minerals. As discussed in the housebreaking chapter, the ideal dog food is pure meat mixed with some form of cereal. It is not advisable to make sudden dietary changes. Because of intestinal sensitivity, this will cause diarrhea. First, consult a veterinarian for the nutritional needs of your dog. Then, combine the new food mixture with the old one. Phase the old one out over a three-day period.

Feed, water, and walk the dog at the same times each day to achieve favorable results. Consistency is the key to this method. By timing an animal's intake of food you can determine when he will relieve himself. It usually takes food from six to eight hours to pass through his system.

Putting your dog on a proper schedule. The dog must be given the opportunity to use the paper a minimum of four times a day. He is to be fed, watered, and papered—*in that order.*
  Here is the ideal schedule for a three- to five-month-old puppy (follow the established diet pattern for older dogs):

seven-thirty in the morning—feed, water, and paper; eleven-thirty in the morning—feed, water, and paper; four-thirty in the afternoon—feed, water, and paper; eight-thirty in the evening—water only and paper; eleven-thirty in the evening—just the paper.

At feeding time allow fifteen minutes for the dog to complete his meal and then take it away, no matter how much he has left in the bowl. He is not to be given food except at the scheduled times. Keep an ample supply of water available at all times. A dish of ice cubes will limit the dog's water intake yet quench his thirst. The more you restrict the time for food and water the closer you come to scheduling his bodily functions.

The minute the dog is fed and watered he is to be allowed to use the paper. Praise him each time he urinates or defecates on the paper and then remove him to another room. He will quickly understand what the paper is for.

Schedule for nine-to-five working people. Take the dog to the paper immediately after waking up. Allow him to use it. Once he does, you may immediately feed, water, and then paper him once again so that the routine is established. He is then to be confined in one area (outlined in greater detail later in this chapter) with the newspaper laid out for him. You are now able to leave the house for work. On coming home, repeat the process: feed, water, and paper. Before bedtime place him on the paper one last time without a feeding or watering. Because a small puppy cannot hold his water for eight or nine hours, it is advisable not to give him the run of the house. Confine him to one small area.

The length of time a dog is allowed to use the paper should not exceed ten minutes. If he hasn't performed in that time chances are he's not going to and he should be removed. Sometimes sprinkling a little water on the paper encourages him to use it. An effective technique is to save one sheet of previously soiled paper to place underneath the new sheets. The smell will give him the idea of what is wanted. When first beginning this program do not be frustrated if the dog does not relieve himself for the first two or three rounds of feeding, watering, and papering. He may hold out for as long as twenty hours, especially in the case of older dogs. If your patience wears thin you may use a glycerin baby suppository. Insert it in the dog's anus after his feeding and watering. Although a bit indelicate, it produces the desired result. After he relieves himself give him a great deal of praise so that he knows that using the paper pleases you. That is essentially what he wants to do.

CONFINING THE DOG

From the first moment you start this program, after selecting the proper place, lay newspaper over the entire room in a three- to five-sheet thickness. Do not miss a spot. This must be done for the first five days. If the dog is placed on an area that is completely covered with paper he has no choice but to do the right thing. Immediately after he uses the paper pick it up, but save one sheet that is soiled and place it underneath the fresh sheets the next time around. If the dog is a very young puppy he may use the paper nine or ten times a day. He will sniff, circle around, or let you know in some way that he wants to use the paper. Learn his signals. As he gets older he will go at less frequent intervals.

After the fifth day, start narrowing down the amount of space you cover with the newspaper. Pick up the soiled paper but replace it with less and less paper, until after several days you are laying down only as much paper as he needs. By this time he will probably have confined himself to one favored spot in the room. Of course, if in the first five days you notice that he has already started using one small area then that is the time to start using less paper. In any event, this process should not take more than two days after the first five days of totally covering the room with paper.

Every pet owner is sooner or later faced with the problem of leaving the untrained dog alone. It is a nagging dilemma for any pet owner, but more so for the novice. One usually comes home to a house littered with urine and fecal matter. If the dog has ever been yelled at for his indiscretions he will wait until left alone to do his worst. This is why confining the dog is important. Do not misinterpret this to mean that you should tie the dog down. Select a small, convenient area where the dog cannot stray and confine him in it. *This area must be where he uses his papers.* It is extremely unpleasant for a dog to relieve himself in the same area where he must remain. It is for this reason that confinement acts as an aid in this training. The area of confinement must not be so restrictive that the animal has no room to walk around. That would be like punishment and cause him to bark and try to escape the confinement. If his papers are available he'll use them and walk to the other portion of his area. This too helps the training process.

To avoid making the puppy's life oppressive, allow him to run around loose when you are home. This is desirable *providing you watch him.* Always be prepared to correct him if he begins to relieve himself off the papers. If he is never let loose to run around the house it becomes too much like punishment, and that will work against this training method.

USING AN ODOR NEUTRALIZER

When the dog makes a mistake and relieves himself in the house in a place that is not covered with newspaper, there are two things that must be done. First, there is the correction which will be dealt with in "Proper Correction," which follows. The second thing is to get rid of the odor quickly. This is important. Even when the spot is washed the smell is discernible to the animal. That is why ordinary cleaning products are useless for this purpose. Ammonia, bleach, detergents, and various household sprays do not work. Only a strong liquid odor neutralizer actually eliminates the scent. Place twenty drops of neutralizer into three quarts of hot water. Mop all soiled areas with this mixture.

A dog cannot help himself once he gets the scent of his own urine or defecation. Even though we cannot smell it ourselves, he does, and is inevitably drawn to it. Dogs mark their territory by urinating on key parts of it. Other dogs come along and mark the same spot. When walking your dog you can observe that he is smelling for his or another dog's odor. That is why you should neutralize the odor of all indoor areas where the dog has relieved himself. By removing the scent of his own waste matter you will prevent him from repeating his indiscretion on the same spot.

PROPER CORRECTION

Under no circumstances should a dog be punished for relieving himself off the paper. He can only be corrected. *Unless you are actually there to stop the dog as he begins to relieve himself, it is useless to correct him.* Punishments, indeed, not even mild corrections, have any effect in the dog's mind if a few minutes have elapsed between his act and your correction. His mental processes are quite limited in this respect.

This brings us to the meaning of "correction" as the word is used throughout this training program. To *correct* the animal is to communicate to him that he has displeased you. In paper training, as in housebreaking, the technique of correction involves use of the word "No," which must be said in a firm tone of voice. The objective is to startle the dog and thereby impress upon him your displeasure. However, this can only be communicated to him if he is in the middle of his wrongdoing. If one's voice is too mild or if the dog does not respond to the firm "No," it can be accompanied with the noise of the "throw can." (See Chapter 2.)

As the dog relieves himself off the papers rattle the pennies inside the can vigorously and simultaneously say, "No," firmly. That much noise will have to stop the dog. It is precisely at that moment that he should be taken to his papers. Praise him for having stopped what he was doing at your command. Allow him to finish his act, on the papers. Then once again give him a great deal of praise. *This is the only way that you can show the dog what to do.* It is, quite literally, a teaching process.

Paper training, like housebreaking, should not be approached from a negative perspective. If it is, the dog will only understand half the training. He will understand that he has displeased you, but he must be made to understand what to do so that you will be pleased with him. Communicating to him what you expect is the objective of all dog training. Keeping the dog off the carpets and the city streets is the objective of paper training.

5 / Proper Use of "No" and "Okay"

Spoken words are vocalized symbols that are used to communicate information, emotion, or combinations of the two. But for the purposes of dog training, words are used as tools for manipulating behavior. In this context we weigh our words carefully when training a dog to submit to our will. Two very valuable words are "No" and "Okay." These tools should not be used in a wasteful and unproductive manner. To wit, "Sidney, *no,* get your head out of the garbage." Or, "*Okay,* Sidney, what did you do? Now you're gonna get it." In dog training the words "No" and "Okay" are used for very specific purposes and do their job well. The trick is to use these words *only* to accomplish their designated tasks.

DEFINITION OF "NO"

The word "No" is applied to stop the dog from doing anything that is considered undesirable. It is never accompanied by other words or phrases.

BENEATH THE SURFACE OF THE TRAINING

The most common cause of a dog's confusion is inconsistency in the commands given by his owner. When you want the dog to refrain from jumping on the furniture, stealing food from the table, messing on the floor, or any other bad habit, use only one corrective word: "No." Too often an owner will use ten different corrective words in the course of one day. Words such as "Stop! Don't! Please! Bad dog! Shame!" only communicate anger.

"No" is the most authoritative and negative sound in the language. It is almost impossible to say this word in a positive way. The most timid personality can get the idea across to the animal with "No." If used consistently, the dog will always associate "No" with a bad thing and stop what he's doing instantly. The objective is to create an instant response in the animal to the word "No."

It is important that the word "No" never be associated with the dog's name. If it is he will associate his name with a bad thing. The consequences are great. For instance, in all action commands the dog's name is used before giving the actual command, i.e., "*Silver,* heel"; "Pete, come." But if the dog associates his name with a bad thing, he will never come to you on command or do anything associated with his name except slink away in fear. With a little practice you will discover that "No" used as a correction without any other word will do the job perfectly.

One other point is necessary with this correction. Do not use the word "No" more than once with each correction. Correct the dog with precision rather than a display of emotion. Most dogs respond badly to hyperemotionalism and pick it up as part of their own behavior. If you shout "No, no, no" in a shrill voice you might create a nervous, high-strung, and very neurotic animal. The way to make the correction is with a firm, authoritative vocal sound that comes from the diaphragm. This is accomplished by taking in a deep breath and allowing the stomach to expand with air. Say the word "No" as you release the air. With practice, your tone will resonate and become deeper. One deep-sounding "No" will get the job done, free from emotional damage to the dog. Your voice should indicate a no-nonsense attitude rather than an angry shout, or worse. The point of the command is to get his attention and mildly startle him. Don't make him collapse with fear and urinate uncontrollably in the wake of thundering wrath. "No" simply gets his attention and indicates to him that he is doing something wrong.

The reverse of this problem is using the correction in too mild a manner. Do not take on the tone and style of a doting grandmother with whining, nagging phrases like, "Ohhh, what did you do now, Wolfgang?" Well, sly little Wolfgang knows he has a sucker and can get away with just about anything. It is quite common for an owner to avoid authority in his corrections for fear of losing the animal's love and attention. The truth of the matter is that the animal is grateful to know, once and for all, what he can and cannot do. His respect and love grow in leaps and bounds when he knows *exactly* how to please his master. The dog wants to get along and be accepted with love and affection. If given praise for what he does properly and authoritative corrections when he is behaving badly, he will consistently work for the praise. Dogs, like children, have a keen appreciation for consistency and justice.

PROCEDURE AND TECHNIQUE FOR "NO"

With a firm, authoritative voice give the command "No" for any situation where you want the dog to stop what he is doing. Never use his name. Give him time to respond to the command. Some dogs obey immediately, while others take a second or two before complying. Depending on the breed and temperament of the individual dog, it will take between one and five seconds. One "No" is all you should say. Once the dog has obeyed, praise him for it. This is the beginning of making him work for praise. It is not the word itself that gets the results. It's the *way* you say it. The sound must come from deep within the stomach and indicate a cool authority rather than an emotional anger. You should not have to repeat the correction, otherwise something is wrong. Try using more firmness in your voice. Under no circumstances hit the dog. The word "No" is a key factor in correcting the dog during all training sessions.

The correction "No" is also used with a "throw can" in conjunction with housebreaking and paper training. The "throw can" is explained in detail in Chapter 2. When the dog misbehaves and doesn't respond to "No" as well as he should, shake the can behind your back and then deliver the vocal correction. Dog training is the rare exception where "No" accentuates the positive.

DEFINITION OF "OKAY"

This word is used in several ways. It is used when calling your dog as an affirmative prefix to his name. "Okay" is also a release from training sessions and a release from walking by your side when he has to use the street to relieve himself.

BENEATH THE SURFACE
OF THE TRAINING

"Okay" is a positive command. It should represent a pleasant experience for the dog. The word is essentially a release from discipline. But it is more than that. It is an important word when calling the dog to you. When the dog is far away you must raise your voice to be heard. It could sound like a reprimand and would tend to make the dog hesitate. It implies, "You'd better get here or else." But when you prefix the command with a cheerful "*Okay,* Pete, come," it automatically assures the dog of a happy reception. It is almost impossible to say "Okay" negatively. It seems to make its own cheerful sound because it forces the tone of voice to go higher. Since all the dog wants is love and affection, the use of "Okay" will indicate that everything is fine.

PROCEDURE AND TECHNIQUE
FOR "OKAY"

If one uses the word "Okay," then everything *should* be okay. Do not use the word in any negative context or you will render it useless as a training tool. The word is still considered a command even though it is a light, breezy one. It should make the dog aware that something pleasant is going to happen.

As a release. Assuming he is housebroken, a good dog walks by his owner's left side when on his way to the area in which he relieves himself. He is only allowed three feet of the leash while the rest is gathered up in the owner's hand. This prevents him from leaving the owner's side. When they arrive at the designated place, the owner says "Okay" in a pleasant tone of voice and allows the extra length of the leash to slip through his hand. The dog should then be led off the sidewalk and into the street. He will soon begin to understand what is expected of him if he is *consistently* made to walk by his owner's side until he arrives at the designated area. "Okay" will become a very important word for him. If the dog's need is urgent, stand clear. It has happened that an owner was forced to change his trousers after releasing the dog.

"Okay" is also used when a training session is finished. "*Okay,* Pete; that's all" should bring a joyful response, unless the dog is exhausted from his lesson, which is often the case. Even so, "Okay" will be a welcome sound. This should always be true throughout the dog's life.

6 / The Corrective Jerk

The "corrective jerk" has nothing to do with the latest dance step or the neighborhood chiropractor. A dog does not speak any language known to man, but there are two basic things he does respond to: your pleasure and your displeasure. The very first thing he must learn is that there is only one way to perform—your way. Therefore, it is important to learn how to communicate your displeasure when he does not perform correctly. Hollering at him or hitting him may get across the idea that he was bad, but then his mind is in no condition to go to the next step, which is—what he should have been doing. The most effective communication technique is the "corrective jerk." It is *the* primary corrective action in this obedience course and will be used over and over again. Its importance cannot be stressed enough. Once this technique is learned, you will have a valuable teaching and corrective tool for as long as you have a dog.

DEFINITION OF THE "CORRECTIVE JERK"

The six-foot training leash is attached to a choke collar which hangs loosely around the dog's neck. The leash is held in the right hand as the dog sits or stands on the left side of the owner. Both are facing the same direction. Three feet of the leash dangle from the collar, across the owner's knees, while the remaining three feet are gathered in the owner's right hand. The leash is jerked to the right, sideways, away from the owner's right thigh. The word "No" is said in a firm tone of voice when the jerk is executed. The jerk is quickly executed so that the right hand returns to its original position in a fraction of a second. During the execution of the jerk the choke collar tightens around the dog's neck giving him a mild sensation. As the owner's right hand returns to its original position,

the choke collar is automatically released and once again
hangs loosely from the dog's neck.

BENEATH THE SURFACE
OF THE TRAINING

This technique will be disturbing and a bit of a shock to the
dog when done for the first time. Although it does not hurt, it
does startle him. The firm "No" reinforces the jerk and leaves
no doubt that the dog has displeased you. This is how he will
learn right from wrong. Whenever the dog refuses to execute
a command or indulges a bad habit, deliver a corrective jerk.
*However, immediately following each corrective jerk, give
him great praise and tell him how good he is.*

It is better to deliver one firm jerk, executed correctly,
than many jerks that are not quite so hard. In the end, ten or
fifteen niggling tugs will not only irritate and exhaust the
animal, but will also produce very poor obedience. Excessive
use of this technique will make any dog "jerk shy." If the
firm "No" is applied with every corrective jerk, eventually
the word, without the jerk, will suffice. This will be the beginning of a conditioned reflex to which the dog will respond
for the rest of his life.

PROCEDURE AND TECHNIQUE
FOR THE "CORRECTIVE JERK"

The first step is learning to hold the leash properly. The six-
foot training leash is held in the right hand as it connects to
the choke collar. The dog is by your left side. Both owner and
dog should be facing the same direction.

Place the thumb of the right hand into the very top of the
loop and hold the rest of the leash with the entire hand. (See
Fig. 3.) Depending upon your height, only two or three feet of
the leash should be hanging across the front of your knees
from the dog's collar. The remainder of the leash hangs from
the right hand, barely touching the outer right thigh. This
means that you are holding both the loop and approximately
half of the leash with the right hand. This allows for a firm

FIGURE 3.
How to hold the six-foot training leash.

hold and absolute control. If the dog should bolt, your thumb will hold the leash firmly in your hand.

To properly execute the corrective jerk. Start by facing the same direction as the dog. He is by your left side with the leash attached to his choke collar. Hold the leash in your right hand. Both hands are hanging down from your sides. The leash is quickly jerked to the right, sideways, away from the outer portion of the right thigh. This is always accompanied by a sharp "No." The arm moves like a spring, your wrist and forearm only being used, as the right hand returns to its original position immediately after the jerk. (See Fig. 4.) The choke collar will have tightened around the dog's neck for a split second and then returned to its loose position. The action is to jerk and then release. The entire movement should take no longer than one second. (See Fig. 5.) Any longer than that may hurt or injure the animal.

When jerking the dog. It should not be so hard as to force his legs to leave the ground. That would be more like a punishment than a correction. The dog may whine or cry out after the first few corrective jerks. Do not be disturbed by this. The worst you may have done is pinch his neck. More than likely the animal is trying to manipulate you into letting him maintain control over the situation as he might have been doing up till now. Some dogs are criers and will emit a shrill squeal to force you to stop making them do what they don't want to do. This is a ploy and does not indicate that the dog is

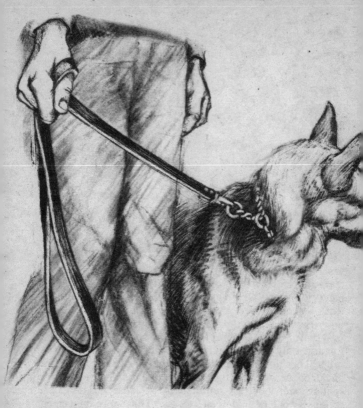

FIGURE 4.
The "corrective jerk."

FIGURE 5.
The "corrective jerk." The right hand holds the leash with several inches of slack. In one quick motion the leash is snapped to the right side and immediately returned to its original position.
All photographs
by Mark Handler.

experiencing the slightest bit of pain. Maintain a firm attitude and never let the dog control the situation.

Praise. Immediately following the corrective jerk, give the dog a great deal of enthusiastic praise. Compliments such as "Good boy," "Good dog," "Atta boy," etc., are very effective. Make the praise verbal and do not pet him. A pat on the head very often indicates to a dog that the lesson is over and he can relax. Verbal congratulations are his reward and he needs them in order to know that he has pleased you. This is an aspect of training where many people go wrong. It seems embarrassing to walk down the street talking to your dog. But it is the best thing for a successful training program. Do not be inhibited in expressing affection and enthusiasm for a job well done. Talking to an animal is not as eccentric as it may seem. One talks to an infant even knowing he doesn't understand one word. What one is communicating is approval through emotion. Most humans and domestic animals respond to it. Communicative vocal praise produces greater results than most head pats and body rubs. In this way you are expressing approval without sacrificing disciplinary demands.

When teaching yourself how to execute the corrective jerk, do not practice on the dog. It will exhaust him and create confusion. The correction is merely a tool to be used when

teaching the other commands. It is not an end in itself. It would make a lot more sense to practice on a broom handle or stairway banister until you have learned to execute it correctly. *Do not correct the dog for something he didn't do.* It is counterproductive and unfair. The corrective jerk is a technique—not a person.

7/ "Sit"

Have you ever seen a dog ignore his master when given a command? It is painful to watch the man's face redden and his voice progress from one octave to another as he yells, "Sit. . . . Sit. . . . SIT. . . . *SIT!!!*" Perhaps you've been that man. He has no idea how to communicate with his dog and he doesn't know what to communicate. Commands should be precise and consistent. For that reason each command is defined at the beginning of every chapter. The same command should not be given with a different expectation each time. The command "Sit" is incorrect if used to stop a dog from barking, from running, or from urinating on your friend's leg. None of these have a single thing to do with "Sit."

DEFINITION OF "SIT"

On command, the dog sits erect with all his weight on his haunches. His body is upright and his front legs are straight and slant inward at the top to a slight degree. His mien is proud, his head straight, and his eyes are looking forward.

BENEATH THE SURFACE
OF THE TRAINING

Sitting is a natural position for a dog. But having him sit on command requires patient training and a good understanding of why and when you want him to sit. His inclination to sit occurs when he is curious and wants to observe. The command is one of the best techniques to gain quick control of his behavior when something is overexciting him or distracting him from your purposes. If the doorbell rings, for example, he may start barking or running frantically to the door. In order to control this burst of energy and avoid scaring your caller half to death, undercut the dog's reaction by controlling his behavior. Putting him in the "Sit" would accomplish this if the dog could respond to that command in the middle of his mischief. But he cannot because of his limited mental capacity. He must be made to stop what he's doing first, and then he can be commanded to do something else. Therefore, give him the command "No" first, and "Sit" immediately afterward. If the dog were to get loose while on the street, it would be a life-saving factor to be able to trigger the mechanism in his brain that makes him sit at your command. If trained properly he cannot refuse your command unless he is running at top speed or is involved in an intense dog fight. But even then you will have some control.

From this chapter to the end of the obedience course it is important that you do not feed the dog before beginning training sessions. Otherwise he will be too sluggish to respond properly. Starting with "Sit," every command taught thereafter will require every ounce of concentration the dog possesses. If his stomach is full he will not want to learn. It is also important to allow the dog to relieve himself if the session is conducted outdoors.

PROCEDURE AND TECHNIQUE
FOR "SIT"

Whenever teaching this or any other command you must have absolute control and attention. The main tools for exercising this control are the six-foot leash and the choke collar. Nothing can be accomplished without them.

Since this will be the first command the dog will be taught, try to make it as easy as possible for him by giving him the benefit of little or no distraction at all. Take him to a quiet, out-of-the-way place in your neighborhood or to a secluded room indoors. There should be no audience! It will be less inhibiting for both you and the dog. If the lesson is being conducted outdoors, allow the dog to relieve himself before beginning. Otherwise he will not be able to concentrate.

Like most commands, "Sit" requires that you *do not* use the dog's name before giving the command. Only prefix his name to those commands that involve forward motion. The two forward or action commands in this course are "Heel" and "Come."

The leash. Because the leash and the choke collar are of primary importance, their use will once again be described as in Chapter 6. The six-foot training leash is held with the right hand and the dog stays by your left side. Both dog and owner face the same direction. Place the thumb of the right hand into the very top of the loop and hold the rest of the leash with the entire hand. Only two or three feet of the leash should be hanging across the front of your knees from the dog's collar to your right hand. It is easier to maintain control with a shorter length of leash.

Giving the command. Once positioned correctly with the leash properly placed in your hand, give the command "Sit." With your *left hand* push on his haunches until he is in a sitting position. If this is done too hard or too fast it will startle him and he will jump up and move around. Give the command with gentle authority and push on his haunches slowly. When he reaches the proper position praise him. (See Fig. 6.) "Good boy. That's a good dog. Attaboy." Try not to use your hands when giving praise. If he's a puppy he may nip. An older dog may take an affectionate stroke or pat on the head as a sign that the lesson is over. Develop a tone of voice that suggests praise and satisfaction with the dog's performance.

From this point on it is simply a matter of repetition. Repeat the process until he begins to sit without the use of your left hand. It will not take very long. This is the teaching process. It is very important that no correction be given during the teaching process. It is pointless to correct him in something he has not yet learned.

Once he has learned to respond to "Sit" and he fails to do so, the corrective jerk is then used. In this first session repeat the teaching process ten or fifteen times and give him a rest. Do not give him a reason to believe it is now playtime. Just stop and walk around a little, but do not release him from the session. After the break, go back to the command and repeat it again another ten or fifteen times. Both halves of the session should not last more tnan fifteen or twenty minutes. It is quite possible that he will have learned the command in the first session. If not, give him another session, but wait at least one hour. You may give two sessions a day.

FIGURE 6.
*The teaching technique for the command
"Sit." The left hand pushes the
dog into proper position as the
command "Sit" is given.*

Using the corrective jerk. If the dog is still having problems learning the command after several sessions, employ the corrective jerk. With the dog close to your side, take up all but two or three feet of the leash. Give the command "Sit," and gently pull or jerk up on the leash with your right hand and push his haunches down with your left. Once he is in the sitting position give him his praise. This is vital. Repeat the command; pull him with the right hand; lower him with the left. As he sits, give him his praise. Repeat this process until he sits immediately after your command. Do not give him time to consider the command once it is given and never say the command more than once without forcing him to respond properly.

This leads us to the basic training formula of this course: command, correction, and praise. It applies to the teaching of every command. Assuming the dog has been taught the command and he knows it, apply the corrective jerk whenever he does not respond properly. If he ignores you or simply doesn't obey when you say "Sit," snap the leash to the right and sharply say "No!" He will sit because he has been reminded to do so. Remember the formula: command, correction, and praise. If he responds to your command then go right to the praise. If not, execute a corrective jerk and *then* give him his praise. The secret of successful dog training is immediate praise after every correction or command. The dog knows he has pleased you and begins to work for your approval. Verbal praise will spare you the discomfort of fifteen years of bribery.

8 / The "Heel" and "Automatic Sit"

If a human being is referred to as a "heel" it is accepted that he is a bounder, a rotter, one who will take advantage of attractive females and doublecross his friends. If he is "well heeled" he is equipped with much money. But a well-heeled dog is quite another matter. This refers to a dog who *walks in heel,* which is to say, a dog that does not pull his master down the street like an Alaskan sled. The bounding energy of a dog out for his first walk offers little pleasure unless he is trained to "Heel," especially if he is the size of a small horse.

DEFINITION OF "HEEL"

Heeling is having the dog walk on your left side with his head next to your thigh. He walks when you walk and stops when you do. When executed properly, the dog never leaves your side. (See Fig. 7.)

BENEATH THE SURFACE
OF THE TRAINING

Don't throw this book across the room and say, "I'll never get Killheart to do that for me." Although it sounds like a great deal to accomplish, it's not as hard as it seems. The alternatives are unpleasant. If the dog does not "Heel" properly you will either be yanked down the street like a Brahman bull rider at the Rodeo or you will be dragging him along the sidewalk with fifteen meddling "animal lovers" giving you enough guilt to wear away the lining of your stomach. Heeling is not a trick and is not too difficult to teach. Because it does not conform with the natural instincts of the dog, he must be taught to do this with patience, diligence, and repetition.

Everything out of doors is new and exciting, especially to a young puppy, and the street holds a thousand adventures in sight and smell. His natural inclinations are toward curiosity and the indulgence of animal impulses. As in every lesson, do not feed your dog before beginning a training session. Otherwise he will be too sluggish to respond properly.

If the session is conducted outdoors, allow the dog to relieve himself. Otherwise he's in no condition to learn something new. Find a quiet outdoor area with a minimum of distraction. The dog's first response to the outside will be to run ahead, straining at the leash as he pulls you down the street. In his excitement he becomes an absolute ingrate and forgets all you've done for him. Thus it becomes important to teach him that you are the most important factor when out for a walk or a training session.

The dog's spirit is going to be high as he is walked to the training place. Not wanting him to dread each session, try not to discourage his pleasant, happy feeling.

In order to succeed in training your dog you must learn to communicate. This implies that there is a kind of language to be developed. Dogs are like babies that never grow up. An infant responds to the tone, volume, and pitch of the voice speaking to it. Dogs respond in much the same way. The word "No" delivered in a firm tone will stop most dogs in their tracks.

Gaining the dog's attention without a correction is accomplished by pitching the voice high and speaking as you would to a baby. "That's a *good* boy!" Affection and praise are given softly and sincerely. If the dog is trained to sit on command, he will do it properly if you say "liver." It is all in the voice.

PROCEDURE AND TECHNIQUE FOR THE "HEEL"

Limit each session to fifteen minutes and conduct no more than two sessions a day, spaced at least one hour apart.

Proper position. The first step in teaching the "Heel" is putting your dog in the proper position. Place him in the "Sit" position on your left side. Choosing the left side is merely

FIGURE 7.
"Heel" and "Automatic Sit." After the
command "Heel" is given, start out with your
left foot. Allow several inches of slack in the
leash. The dog's head is even with your left
thigh. When you stop, the dog does as well
and goes into the "Sit" position.

traditional. It began as a safety factor for hunters who carried their weapons with their right arm while the dog walked astride on the left.

Using the six-foot leash, hold it in your right hand as if you were going to execute the corrective jerk. Both arms should hang loose and unbent. Always allow two or three feet of slackened leash to drape across the knees. Do not hold the leash with two hands. That would merely be holding on to the animal. Do not let the right hand rise to your chest. You cannot jerk properly unless the right hand is by your side.

Using his name. Once you and the dog are in the correct position and ready to go, give the command, "Pete, heel!" Use his name this time because "Heel" is an action command and it alerts him to move into a forward position. Saying his name first gets his attention. Once his name is said, the dog's focus should be on you. He should be ready to move. At the command, "Pete, heel," start walking by starting with your left foot. The reason one starts with the left foot is because it is closer to the dog's eyes and he will move when you do. In this way you will move together. Remember, the objective is to have the dog walk at your side.

If the dog runs ahead. The first problem you will probably encounter is the dog's desire to run ahead. The best way to solve this is to allow him to run to the end of the six-foot training leash. As he reaches the end of it make a quick right turn. At the moment of impact give a loud, authoritative "Heel." Immediately walk in the opposite direction. The dog will have been jolted and forcibly turned in the direction you are walking. (See Fig. 8.) Once again his primitive instincts will have been totally thwarted by your will.

Certain breeds will cry out in shock louder than others. Do not express the slightest concern or sympathy. Keep walking at a brisk clip and the dog will catch up. When he does, adjust the leash to the length with which you started. If the dog shoots ahead of you again, repeat the procedure. Make a quick right turn, say "Heel," and walk in the opposite direction. This business of turning in the opposite direction is hard on the dog. Therefore he must be praised as he catches up. The praise will help teach him what walking in "Heel" means. It tells him he is good if he walks by your side. It also keeps his attention on you, which prepares him for any stops or turns. *The technique for praising the dog varies from breed to*

FIGURE 8.
*If the dog runs ahead after
being commanded to "Heel,"
make a sharp turn in the
opposite direction and continue walking.*

breed. Either give immediate praise after the sudden turn or withhold it for a few seconds, depending upon the breed of the dog. Some breeds need immediate approval, while others take it to mean they are released from the lesson. Check Part III and find the page pertaining to your breed for this specific information.

Lagging behind. The dog's tendency to run ahead will diminish with each fifteen-minute lesson. Once he is no longer running ahead, be prepared to cope with the problem of lagging behind. This problem is easily solved by extending verbal encouragement if the dog fails to keep up with you. Tell him what a good dog he is, and literally entice him to catch up. A lavish invitation to walk by your side will keep his attention fixed on you and will probably solve the problem. What is desirable is to help the dog develop the habit of keeping his attention on you whenever he is taken for a walk.

Walking by your side. After three or four lessons it will be time to teach the dog his exact position when walking with you. Up to this point he will have been keeping one or two lengths ahead, which is all right. But now he must learn to always walk with his head lined up to your left thigh, no far ther ahead or behind.

As before, start with the dog in the "Sit" position. Give him the command, "Pete, heel." Start walking with your left foot. Every single time the dog's head moves beyond your thigh execute a corrective jerk, sharply say "No," make an immediate right turn, say, "Pete, heel," and continue to walk in the opposite direction. Praise him. This procedure should be repeated again and again until the dog is walking in the prescribed position. It is possible for the dog to learn this in a single fifteen-minute session. However, keep repeating the technique for as long as it takes him to learn it. Do not work the dog for more than fifteen minutes at a time and give him an hour's rest between lessons. Only two lessons a day are permissible.

Too shy to walk. Occasionally a dog is either too shy or too frightened to walk at all on his first encounter with the outside. This is usually associated with puppies. He will cower with fear and probably duck under your legs or look for the protection of the nearest wall. The objective is to rid the dog of his fear. Too much authority will only tend to reinforce his terror and uncertainty. First, try to start him out on the "Heel" command. If he will not walk, step in front of him and go down on your knees. Gently call him with affectionate entreaties and playful calls. Get him to come. Do this about three or four times until he comes every time that you bend down. Once he is doing that start backing away as he comes. Keep lengthening the distance he has to go. Once he is on his feet and walking, stand up, turn, and walk together. If he is a particularly stubborn dog and freezes at this point, keep walking, pulling him along until he gives in. Be careful not to scrape his paw pads too hard along the sidewalk or other hard surfaces. The pads are sensitive and will bleed easily. This could create a trauma which will make the problem acute. If the struggle continues, take him to a park. If the dog again freezes, keep walking as you pull him along the grass. This will prevent a traumatic injury and force the dog to walk with you.

Jumping. If your dog is overexuberant and continually jumps on people on the street during his training session, employ the corrective jerk at the moment of his infraction and sharply say "No." It is important to note that if the dog is corrected for jumping on people, then it must be consistently enforced both indoors and outdoors.

Walking out of "Heel." If the dog is overly affectionate he is probably wrapping himself around your legs. Obviously, this creates an absurd situation. It could be insecurity or acute sensitivity. This is the only instance where one uses the left hand while walking in "Heel." Place the dog in the proper position as you walk, all the while giving him encouragement. His head must always be lined up with your left thigh. If he continues to wrap around your legs, walk and hold him in place with the left hand, utilizing the corrective jerk less frequently than usual and manipulating him more with a soothing tone of voice.

In the beginning it is more important to stress the proper position than the other aspects of heeling. Never use excessive authority to a nervous or frightened dog. Affection and gentleness are the only techniques that will rid him of his fear.

Walking inward. Another problem is when the dog begins to turn inward while heeling, causing both owner and dog to step into each other's paths. This is usually poor navigation on the dog's part and nothing more serious than that. The corrective jerk is the only way to solve this problem. As soon as the dog walks into your path, execute a corrective jerk. At the same time sharply say "No." Then make a left or right turn, depending on how far inward he has gotten. As you turn, your knee will gently force him to turn with you. Praise him. Then say, "Pete, heel." Continue walking. Praise him. Do this every time he gets underfoot.

Whenever the dog becomes distracted, tries to wander off, or turns the session into play, do this: give the corrective jerk. Sharply say "No." Then say, "Pete, heel." Continue to walk. Praise him.

DEFINITION OF THE "AUTOMATIC SIT"

When the dog is walking in "Heel," he must stop when you do and sit without being given a command. He then waits until he is given the next command, which is usually "Heel."

PROCEDURE AND TECHNIQUE FOR THE "AUTOMATIC SIT"

This is accomplished by letting the dog know that you are going to stop. By simply slowing down, he will be alerted to a change of some kind. Because he watches you most of the time, he will slow down, too. As you come to a full stop, give the command "Sit." Do not use the dog's name on this command. *The verbal command is used during the teaching process only.* If the dog fails to sit, use the corrective jerk as a reminder. Do not forget to praise him after he successfully obeys each command, even if he did so after a correction.

If he does not sit. Do not give the command more than once. This should be a firm rule throughout the training. You cannot stand in the street saying "Sit, sit, sit, sit, sit" *ad nauseam* until he finally obeys. Use the corrective jerk and in a sharp voice say "No!" The dog will understand this and sit for you. Praise him for obeying.

To reiterate: slow your pace and gradually come to a full

stop. If the dog does not sit, give the command "Sit." If he does not respond, give him a corrective jerk and a sharp "No!" If he responds properly, praise him with enthusiasm, even though he was corrected. This is his motivation.

In that rare instance when the dog does not respond to the corrective jerk accompanied by the "No," give him a corrective jerk and the command "Sit!" Then slowly pull the leash upward as you force the dog to sit by pushing his haunches down with your left hand. One usually never gives a command with the corrective jerk. It causes the dog to associate a negative emotion with that particular command. However, in this extreme instance it becomes necessary.

How you give the corrective jerk is the key to this problem. One or two hard jerks will save much time and frustration for both you and the dog. He must know that you mean what you say. It will be useful to remember that the word "Sit" is a command and the word "No" is a correction. The commands are given with firmness. The corrections are given with an authoritative tone of voice.

Because every training session should end on a high note, the lesson ought to be terminated when the dog has completed his task successfully for the first time. Obviously, he is not going to be perfect in his execution of your commands for several weeks. Therefore the instant he performs his new command correctly, end the lesson and extend lavish praise. This will help him to remember what he has just learned and to look forward to performing properly the next time. Try to instill in him the idea that training is fun.

9/ "Sit-Stay"

Now that you have taught your dog to "Sit" and to automatically "Sit" after walking in "Heel," the next command is perfectly logical. You want him to "Stay" in his sitting position. It's not as simple as it sounds. Dogs take you at your word, quite literally. If given the command "Sit," a trained dog will sit—for an instant and then move on to whatever interests him. His obligation has been fulfilled, from his point of view. If expected to remain in a sitting position for any length of time, he must be commanded to do so.

DEFINITION OF "SIT-STAY"

Once again, on command, the dog sits erect with all his weight on his haunches. He remains in this position until released from the command . . . no matter what!

BENEATH THE SURFACE OF THE TRAINING

This command is used when you do not want the dog to move. When leaving your home, if the dog follows you to the door, you know he'll dash out the minute it is open. Give the command "Sit" and he'll obey. But as soon as you start to leave he'll be out of the house too. Therefore, give the next command, "Stay."

This command goes against every instinctual impulse the animal has. Most dogs, especially puppies, will follow you to the edge of the world and jump off if you do. The dog wants to go where you go, do what you do, as the song says, then he'll be happy. The pattern is set in the first months of ownership. The dog grows up following you wherever you go, underfoot, in the kitchen, on the couch, and in the bed. By now he is so used to being with you he looks up at you as if you were a lunatic when first given the command "Stay." He will completely disregard the command and race you to wherever you're going.

After the dog has been taught the command "Stay," there will still be times when it will be almost impossible for him to obey. For instance, if there is a party going on in your house he will have a nervous breakdown trying to comply with your command and ignore his impulse to join the fun. Either remove him from the scene or invite him in to be admired and ogled. The same applies if you're cooking a steak in front of his nose. Also, don't expect him to remain in a "Stay" position for eternity. If he will remain in position between fifteen and thirty minutes then he is extraordinary and has been well trained.

The command "Sit-Stay" is not designed for off-leash discipline in the city. If such a foolish thing is attempted, one might well be considered an executioner. The dog in the city may obey perfectly outside for six months, off-leash. But it only takes one infraction of the command for him to chase another dog or pigeon and lose his life to an oncoming automobile.

"Sit-Stay" should be taught indoors with the six-foot leash. Learning the command on the six-foot leash is so vital that there must be no distraction at all. Do not go outdoors for this command until you reach that section of this chapter that calls for working with the twenty-five-foot line.

PROCEDURE AND TECHNIQUE FOR "SIT-STAY"

Teaching this command involves three elements: a voice command, a hand signal, and a pivoting technique on the ball of your left foot.

The voice command and hand signal. Place the dog in the "Sit" position on your left side. Allow him thirty seconds to settle down and get comfortable. Both dog and owner should be facing the same direction. Give the command "Stay" in a firm voice. Because this is not an action command, do not

FIGURE 9.
"Sit-Stay." Start out facing in the same direction as the dog. Give the verbal command accompanied by the correct hand signal. The dog should remain in position when you move directly in front of him and when you move back.

prefix the command with the dog's name. The leash is held in the right hand. Upon giving the command flatten your left hand with all fingers closed together (as for a salute) and place it in front of the dog's eyes four inches away. Do not touch his eyes. Simply block his vision. (See Fig. 9.) The hand signal is given simultaneously with the voice command. As the right hand holds the leash, the left hand extends in front of you four inches and then moves leftward to block the dog's vision. The hand signal is a deliberate but quick gesture. Therefore, you return your left hand to your side two or three seconds after having blocked the dog's vision. Eventually, the dog will respond to this hand signal without the vocal command.

A pivoting technique for the ball of your left foot. You and the dog are facing in the same direction. The objective now is to make one deliberate turn without moving the dog so that you will be facing him. Do not step off with your left foot as you normally would in the "Heel." Step off with your right foot and turn toward the dog. The left foot is used as a pivot and revolves in place. It is all right if the left foot must move a very short distance. Once your body is turned and facing the dog, bring the left foot back to where the right foot has landed so that both feet are together. (See Fig. 10.) If you move your left foot before facing the dog, he is going to assume it's time to "Heel" and start walking.

The secret of teaching him to "Stay." As you pivot in front of him, hold eighteen inches of the leash straight up so that the leash and collar are high on his neck. The remainder of the leash dangles in a slackened loop from the bottom of your right hand. In this position the dog cannot move as you turn to face him. What you are doing is holding him in a fixed position with the extended leash. If the leash is held properly there will be eighteen inches of taut leash extended upward. Do not hold the leash too tightly or he may choke or become frightened and struggle to run.

It is this strict leash control during the pivotal turn that communicates the idea "Stay." The entire movement should be accomplished with dispatch so that he does not have time to think about turning or walking. Keep him in position and get in front of him without wasting a motion. It is going to take ten or fifteen tries before he gets the idea. Do not forget to give the dog praise once you have made the turn and he has remained in position, even though he had to be held there with the leash. (Do not use his name when giving the praise. He will try to move if you do.) Once you are in front of the dog, remain still for ten or fifteen seconds, leash still held high, so that he begins to absorb what's expected of him. This technique of stepping in front of the dog is only used in training. If you are training a puppy do not be too strict.

Backing away as the dog remains in "Stay." Once the dog accepts the leash control as you stand in front of him, it is then time to back away as he remains in "Stay." While still holding the leash above the dog's head, transfer it to the left hand, placing the thumb inside the loop at the very top. With the right hand, grasp the leash eighteen inches above the collar and hold it loosely. The leash must be able to slide through the right hand once you start to move away from the dog. (See Fig. 11.) The technique will eliminate any slack from developing as you move away. This is important. If the leash slackens you will be unable to force the dog to remain in "Sit-Stay."

Using the right hand as a guide for the leash to slide through, begin to back away slowly. If the dog starts to move forward,

FIGURE 10.
Simultaneously giving command and hand signal, pivot on the ball of the left foot.

and he will, give the command "Stay." As you do, step in toward the dog, pull the leash through the right hand and hold it eighteen inches over the dog's head. Keep the leash tight so that it forces the dog to "Sit." (When stepping in, try to pull the leash slightly to the side as you extend it upward. This will avoid hitting the dog on the chin with the metal clip.) The correction will stop the dog from moving. As he repositions himself give him praise for stopping. Wait a few seconds and then continue to back away. Slowly continue to slide the leash through your right hand as you move. You will probably be able to go a little farther back this time before he begins to move again. The instant the dog moves forward repeat the procedure: Give the command "Stay." Step in toward the dog and hold the leash tightly over his head. Praise him for stopping after he repositions himself. Continue to back away until you reach the end of the six feet of leash. Reinforce this instruction by repeating the entire process ten times.

Walking around either side of the dog as he remains in "Stay." It is now time to condition the dog so that you can walk around him or to either side without his violating the "Stay" command. Usually when you walk to the dog's side or behind him while he is in "Stay," he will turn his head to watch and then turn his entire body to face you. This is a violation of the command. If he is allowed to move that much then it will soon become permissible to move away completely. He must remain in the same position in which he was originally placed. A certain amount of head turning is inevitable, but that is all.

Once again, standing in front of the dog, hold the leash tightly eighteen inches above his head with your right hand. Take one or two steps to the right without loosening up on the leash and then return. Do the same thing again but move to the left. This will condition the dog to your side movements while he is still held in place. Repeat this ten times. Return to the original "Sit" position with the dog at your left side and repeat the entire lesson to this point five times.

Walking behind the dog as he remains in "Stay." Once again hold the leash with your left hand. Standing in front of the dog, slide your right hand in on the leash and extend it over the dog's head about eighteen inches. As you hold the dog in place, begin a brisk but deliberate circular walk around the dog. If he starts to move tighten up on the leash and repeat the command "Stay." When walking around the dog take large steps. The command should be given in a low, soothing voice that reassures. However, it is the subtle use of the leash that is your line of communication.

The leash is comparable to the reins of a horse. Although it is extended upward, it does not tighten unless the dog tries to move. The moment he stops moving you loosen up a bit. A horse respects a rider the minute he mounts him if the rider knows how to handle the reins. The same applies to a dog. If an owner is in control, with the use of the leash and collar, the dog will respect him and submit to his authority.

The minute he observes a lack of consistent control he is going to disobey. In turn the owner will get frustrated and angry and the lesson will be shot.

Because "Stay" is difficult for your dog to learn, do not attempt to teach everything in one training session. Give him a chance to learn it slowly. Sometimes it takes several sessions for the dog to get accustomed to your pivot. When teaching more than one phase of this command in one day rest one hour between each phase. Do not teach more than two sessions a day. Dogs tire and bore easily and after a point lose their ability to pay attention. It is more important that

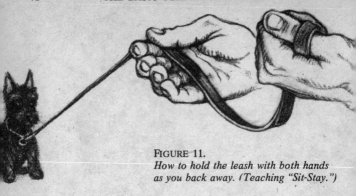

FIGURE 11.
*How to hold the leash with both hands
as you back away. (Teaching "Sit-Stay.")*

the dog learn well and obey when given a command than learn quickly and forget the command two days later.

"SIT-STAY," OFF-LEASH, OUTDOORS

Now that you and the dog have learned the basic "Stay" command we come to the very difficult aspect of that command, and that is "Stay" while off the leash. Taking the dog off the leash is a very dangerous practice and there are few occasions when it is justified. But assuming you are in a safe, no-traffic locale or a fenced-in area, it can be taught with patience and diligence. Off-leash training is optional.

A twenty-five-foot clothesline. In order to teach the "Stay" off-leash, you will need a twenty-five-foot training leash or clothesline. However, before going into this lesson make certain that the dog is thoroughly trained to sit in the "Stay" position with the six-foot leash attached to his collar. If he cannot accomplish that then teaching him the "Stay" off-leash will be a waste of time. The point of the long leash or clothesline is to keep extending the distance between you and the dog while he is placed in "Stay." He may "Stay" at six feet, but will he "Stay" at twelve feet? It is desirable for him to respond off the leash, but he will never accomplish that if he is not *perfect* while on the leash. There is no shortcut or substitute for accomplishing this command.

The same technique. In teaching "Stay" off the leash, you use the same technique outlined in teaching the "Stay" while on-leash with one difference. You keep extending the length of the leash two feet each time the dog holds the position properly. Starting with eight feet of leash proceed by walking around the dog after placing him in "Stay." Each time he holds still extend the leash another two feet. At the dog's back, during your circular walk around him, take up some of the leash by sliding it through your right hand so that you will be much closer to him. In that manner a correction can be given if he moves. When coming around the other side let out the leash to the length you started with. If the dog moves during any part of this procedure execute a corrective jerk and a sharp "No." It is good form to correct the animal now that he has learned the basics of the command.

Extend the clothesline two feet at a time. Do not go from eight feet to twenty feet in one or two lessons. It is important to go methodically in two-feet increments. He must learn to "Stay" at six feet, eight feet, ten feet, twelve feet, and soon to the end of the line or it will be a waste of time. At eighteen or twenty feet it will be difficult to deliver an effective corrective jerk. However, by accompanying the corrective jerk with the sharp "No" at the shorter distances, the "No" itself will almost suffice at the longer distances. That is, providing your "No" has always been very firm. By this time he is associating your "No" with the corrective jerk and will understand on a vocal level alone. Once he starts responding to your "No" while on the leash, it will have the same effect with the leash removed. This conditions the dog psychologically to associate the firm "No" with the hard corrective jerk. Eventually he will stop whatever he's doing when corrected vocally.

At the end of his rope. Once twenty or twenty-five feet of line have been reached it is not unusual for the dog to break and run the other way, even though he has been placed in "Stay." He may see another dog or go butterfly chasing. In this event let him reach the end of the line and then jerk him in the opposite direction with full force and yell "No" as loudly and as harshly as you can. This is the ultimate correction and will be long remembered by your dog.

You are now ready to try him off the leash. Do not attempt this unless absolutely certain he will remain in "Stay" for the full length of the twenty-five-foot leash. When ready for the big moment be certain you remove the leash in a closed-in area. If he breaks or moves once having been placed in "Stay," deliver a very firm "No." If he does not respond properly *do not punish him.* Simply go back to the twenty-five-foot line and work him some more. Eventually he will respond properly.

Another aspect of "Stay" has to do with placing him in that position and leaving the room. It can be useful and convenient from time to time. Place the dog in the "Sit" position. Hook the six-foot leash to his collar and let it drop to the floor. Start out by placing him in "Stay" and leaving the room. Do not forget to use the hand signal. Return in five seconds. If he did not move, praise him. Do this ten times. The next step is to leave the room for ten seconds, return, and praise him for his good performance. It is assuring him that you are not really leaving. Gradually increase the length of time out of the room until he will "Stay" by himself for at least five minutes. Once again, do not do this off the leash until it is certain that he will "Stay" without moving. The leash, even though it is not being held, represents the line of authority between you and the dog. He knows and respects it. A good way to practice this command is to put it in operation right away during everyday household situations. If he approaches the garbage can when the lid is off, put him in "Sit-Stay" until it is covered. The same applies when the doorbell rings or a visitor enters the house. This kind of practice plus his regular lessons will help round off his schooling perfectly.

Once the dog has completely learned the meaning of the command "Stay," you can, with confidence, leave him in a room alone, or talk with friends or tradesmen as he sits still. This command will also keep him out of intimate situations that do not concern him. Every dog is a born voyeur and the command "Stay" could save your marriage. Work hard on this one!

10/"Down" and "Down-Stay"

Professional dog trainers often are confronted with seemingly difficult problems that are easily solved. One recent client is a musician who owns a magnificent Basset Hound. He named his dog "Cat." In the parlance of contemporary musicians this designation is a compliment. (The name gathers no blue ribbons in Dogdom, however.) It seems that Cat had a problem. He couldn't sit like a dog. Owing to his long, heavy body and his short legs it was impossible for him to "Sit-Stay" for more than a few seconds. His "Sit" was sloped at a ten-degree angle. He looked like a jacked-up car with a flat tire. Too much weight rested on those short front legs and Cat had to get off his "dogs" quickly. It was then that the "Down" and "Down-Stay" was taught.

Even though you may not own a Basset Hound, your dog may have Cat's problem to some degree. The "Sit-Stay" position is a temporary one and is used for short periods of time. But if the dog is to stay in his corner while guests are being entertained, employ the "Down" and "Down-Stay." It's more comfortable for the dog and dictates a longer staying time to him. It was a great relief for Cat and will be for your dog, too. Does all this seem confusing? Well, think of poor Cat, the dog!

DEFINITION OF "DOWN"

The dog is on the ground, head erect, eyes looking forward. The front legs are extended and the hind legs relaxed with the rear weight resting on both haunches. The hind legs should be equally tucked under in a straight parallel.

BENEATH THE SURFACE
OF THE TRAINING

The "Down" position is probably the most comfortable one for the dog. But it may take the longest period of time to teach. Sitting and walking are natural movements for a dog and are assimilated as commands quite easily. But going down on command is unnatural for him, even though he sleeps and rests in that position. Quite often the command "Down" is given as a remedy for undesirable behavior. "Down" should be used only as a command. As outlined in the "Sit-Stay" chapter, you cannot go directly into a command when the dog is misbehaving until a correction has been made first.

In the "Procedure and Technique for Down,' " which follows, you will see that a hand signal is used to help the dog perform properly. The hand signal entails using your unbent, extended arm in a slow downward sweep with the flattened palm of the hand facing the ground. This hand signal may be problematic if the dog has been hit. When he sees that hand come down, his first reaction will be fear. Naturally, he will think he is about to be hit again. The dog probably will have the same reaction when someone reaches out to pet him. He will either run away, flinch, or literally bite the hand that feeds him. This condition is called "hand shy."

If your dog is hand shy you must cease hitting him. It is now time to convince him that hands reaching out to him or commanding him mean something good rather than the smack on the snout they too often represented in the past. If the dog has been hit over a long period of time, or has been hit severely, then it is too late. He will never be able to be taught this command with a hand signal. You will have to rely on the voice command only. You may try extending your hand while lavishing him with praise and affection. If applied long enough this may possibly recondition the dog's reaction. However, if it's not too late, refrain from ever using your hand for anything other than hand signals or affectionate praise or love. This rule also precludes the use of the hand for threats, violent gestures, or even disciplinary pointing. Pointing your finger at the dog and saying "Naughty, naughty" produces the same negative effect.

There are many occasions when the "Down" and "Down-Stay" are useful and make life more comfortable. When you're having company for dinner it is extremely difficult for Gusman to keep his nose out of things. In the "Down" and "Down-Stay" position he is able to participate in the festivities without getting into trouble. These commands are extremely useful outdoors, if, for example, you want to sit on a park bench without being disturbed by a dog pulling on his leash. The main reason this position works so well is because it is comfortable and relaxing for the dog.

Because of the difficulty involved in teaching this command, it is important to be alone with the animal. Do not expect him to learn it in one lesson. Take as long as is necessary. Maintain only two sessions a day, spaced at least one hour apart. Each session must be confined to fifteen minutes. Before starting each session work the dog in his other commands in order to get him in the proper frame of mind. Only teach as much in one day as the dog can absorb. It is interesting to note that the dog will learn "Down" and "Down-Stay" better than any other command he has been taught. The reason is that more time and diligence are required in the teaching than any other aspect of this course. You will also be using these commands more often than any other during the course of a single day. These sessions will prove to be the most rewarding. There is nothing more gratifying than raising your hand in the air when the dog is five or ten feet away and watching him go down as you lower your hand.

PROCEDURE AND TECHNIQUE FOR "DOWN"

Putting the dog down as you stand by his side. Always place the dog in a "Sit-Stay" position to begin each session. Stand by his right side as in the "Heel," holding the leash in whichever hand is most comfortable. Both you and the dog face the same direction. Kneel down on your left knee. In a firm voice give the command "Down," and with your free hand pull his two front paws forward so that he has no choice but to ease himself to the ground. Place your index finger between his two paws so that you can grip both of them with one hand. (See Fig. 12.) The reason for separating his paws with your finger is so they do not get crushed together.

To recap: you and the dog are facing the same direction as in the "Heel." The dog is in the "Sit-Stay" position. The

FIGURE 12.
"Down" and "Down-Stay."
When pulling the dog's paws
forward to teach him "Down"
be sure to separate them
with your index finger. This
avoids pain for the dog.

leash is held in the right hand. Give the command "Down," and as you kneel reach in front of the dog, take his two front paws in your hand (separating them with your index finger), and pull them forward, forcing him down.

For the command "Down" the vocal intonation is different from all others. The very word must be said in an exaggerated manner so that the sound suggests to the dog a downward motion. The tone of your voice should descend in pitch as .he dog obeys the command and goes down. Stretch out the middle part of the word so that you do not finish saying it until the dog has reached the ground. This is done by elongating the "ow" part of "D-o-w-n." Somewhere in the middle of the elongated "ow" the voice should descend so that it accompanies the downward action of the dog. It looks like this on paper: "DOWWWWWwwn." Dogs do not understand words as well as they understand intonations. "DOWWWWW-wwwn" is a sound they remember all their lives.

Maintain control with the use of the leash. If the dog gets up in the middle of the session use the leash to place him in the "Sit-Stay" position again. Do not give him a corrective jerk or any other kind of correction. That is never done when teaching a new command. Actually, the leash is used primarily to keep the dog in a sitting position as you slowly give the command and pull his paws forward.

Each time the dog goes down give him praise and congratulations. At this stage, however, he may roll on his side. Give him praise, anyway. It is for going down on command (even though he was pulled). The important thing at this stage is that he learn the most fundamental meaning of the command "Down." He may play or get frisky once he is on the ground. Let him. That can always be corrected later. This procedure should be repeated ten or fifteen times until he offers no resistance when his paws are pulled forward. If you're very lucky he may begin to go down without your hands pulling him.

Putting the dog down as you stand in front of him. The object here is to get the dog to go down while you stand in front of him, face to face. This is important if he is to obey the command when he stands a good distance away from you.

Again, put the dog in the "Sit-Stay" position. Move in front of him and proceed as before. Kneeling on one foot, give the command "DOWWWWWwwwn," and pull his front paws forward with your right hand. The position of the leash is a little more awkward this time because it will be held above and to the left of the dog's head with your left hand. The leash becomes very important here. Some dogs will have a tendency to walk toward you if you are facing them. The dog must be held in place with the leash without a formal correction. You will probably not have to repeat this step as often as the first one since it is mostly the same movement but in a different position.

Repeat this procedure ten or fifteen times and quit for the day.

The hand signal for "Down" as you stand by his side. You now start introducing the hand signal with the voice command. To do so go back to the side position. Always start out in this position because it makes it easier to control the dog. It offers fewer distractions and allows the hand to manipulate the leash with greater authority. If the dog has ever been hit, or for some inexplicable dog reason doesn't like this command, he may attempt to bite when you use the hand signal. Begin the lesson in the side position because it offers greater safety.

You are now in the "Heel" position, but with one knee on the ground. Hold the leash with your right hand and leave your left hand free. The leash is extended to the right of the dog in front of your body. There should be absolutely no slack in the leash. Allow about twelve inches from his collar to your right hand. If the dog tries to jump up on you in a playful manner simply raise the leash so that he has no room to do anything but sit. Command him to "Sit," give him a "Good boy," and return your right hand to its original position.

Stay in a cheerful mood and do not say anything harsh. This is the crucial part of the lesson. Bring your left hand up above the dog's eye level and slightly to the right of his head. Keep it flattened, fingers closed, palm down. With your right hand make sure that the leash is taut. This is very important. If your left hand is positioned properly it should be in sight of the dog's peripheral vision.

Give the dog the vocal command "DOWWWWWwwwwn" as you begin to lower your left hand to the ground. As your hand goes down it will press on the leash where the metal clasp connects with the collar ring. (See Fig. 13.) The dog is pushed to the ground by the force of the hand against the leash. Because the dog sees your flattened hand push him

FIGURE 13.
*"Down" and "Down-Stay."
Teaching the dog to go down
by pushing the leash downward with the left hand
while kneeling by the side of
the dog.*

down, he will always associate that hand gesture with his cue to go down. It should not take too many repetitions for him to offer little or no resistance. The point is that he has already been taught the meaning of the vocal command "DOWWWWWwwwn" and will know what to do. Of course, it took the first two steps to get to this point. If the dog resists or offers opposition, just keep pushing down and don't worry if the collar tightens up. Once he's down, lavish him with praise. If he really fights hard on this lesson stop immediately, tell him he's a good boy, and go into the "Heel" and the "Sit" and then start over.

Exercise patience and the strictest control over your temper. The dog cannot be intimidated into learning this lesson. He must be brought around to it with persistence and the reassurance that it pleases you. Reposition yourself and place the dog in "Sit-Stay." Hold the leash tautly in your right hand and kneel. Place your flattened left hand on top of the leash near the clip, give the command "DOWWWWWwwwn," and push the tightened leash to the ground. When the dog touches the ground congratulate him with a "Good boy" in a cheerful voice. Let him know that you are very pleased with him. This is very hard work for the dog and it will tire him quickly. Every ounce of concentration he possesses is being utilized. Give him at least an hour's rest after this session.

The hand signal while standing in front of him. You are now going to be standing in front of the dog. He saw the hand from the side force him down. Now he is going to see it from the front. It was important that your hand was first seen from the side. It represented no threat of hitting him. It will now be easier for him to accept the hand signal from the front because he is familiar with it.

From "Heel" place the dog in "Sit-Stay," then step in front of him. Hold the leash, with the left hand, to your left side. This gives you greater control as you push down. Kneel on one knee, raise your right hand, palm down, on top of the leash and push it to the ground. At the same time give the vocal command "DOWWWWWwwwn." Once the dog is on the ground he may try to nip playfully at your fingers. As long as it doesn't hurt it is permissible and can be corrected at a time when he knows the command perfectly. If, however, the dog tends to hide or play between your knees, exercise control with the leash by placing him in "Sit-Stay" and starting all over. Repeat this entire step until the dog is performing with no resistance. This is as far as you should go in one day. End the session on a happy note and continue the next day. Resist the temptation to show the new command to your friends and relatives until it is absolutely certain the dog has thoroughly printed it in his mind.

Without kneeling. Review the training of the preceding sessions. The object of this step is to get the dog to respond to "Down" with a vocal command and a hand signal as you stand in front of him *without kneeling.* Stand in front of the dog and stay about eighteen inches away. Place the dog in the "Sit-Stay" position. Hold the leash with your left hand. If he tries to get up, tighten the leash by raising it above his head. This will hold him in place. Even if the dog doesn't obey the command properly he will be forced to sit and wait for you to correct him or reinstruct him.

For this step leave half the leash slack (three feet of the six-foot training leash). Raise your right arm and flatten your hand, palm down, as if for a salute. Give the vocal command "DOWWWWWwwwn." As you say the command start lowering your arm. Bring the flat of your hand to the top of the slackened leash, which should be held at an angle to your left. (See Fig. 14.) The dog should go down without having to be forced by the leash. Give him an enthusiastic "Good boy" and repeat the step ten times.

From a farther distance. After a short rest repeat the procedure but from a farther distance. You were eighteen inches away before, now extend the distance to three feet. You are still at a distance where the dog can be corrected if he gets too playful or does not respond to the command properly. If he starts to move away or come forward, give him a corrective jerk and a firm "No." It is acceptable to use the corrective jerk now because the dog is quite familiar with the command. You are no longer teaching the basics of the "Down" but rather the refinements.

Once again, raise your arm with a flattened hand as if for a salute. While saying "DOWWWWWwwwn," bring your arm down with the palm facing the ground. Only this time, the hand goes past the leash without touching it. (See Fig. 15.) This is the hand signal as it will always look. Visually it is the lowering of the arm as it returns to its natural position by the side of the body. At this point the dog thinks you are

FIGURE 14.
"Down" and "Down-Stay."
Pushing the leash downward
while standing in front of
the dog.

FIGURE 15.
"Down" and "Down-Stay."
Proper hand signal for
"Down."

FIGURE 16.
Proper hand signal for "Down."

going to touch the top of the leash and force him down. His response will be to go into the "Down" position in anticipation of being pushed down. The movement will soon become natural for him and will never require anything more than a lowering of your raised arm. (See Fig. 16.) Once the dog knows this position, you will be able to execute the command with the hand signal or with the voice command only. Practice giving the command "DOWWWWWwwwn" without the hand signal. Repeat the vocal procedure alone several times and then switch to giving the signal alone. End the session by using both hand signal and voice command. Remember, a great quantity of praise is necessary in this lesson. Lavish the dog with praise every time he performs properly. But never use his name during his praise or he's going to get up and walk toward you.

If the dog acts confused when you give the hand signal without the voice command, repeat the signal several times. If he still does not respond then go back to giving the hand signal accompanied by the voice command. Immediately afterward, try the hand signal alone. This process should reinforce his understanding of what is expected of him. What's important is the consistency between your hand descending and the tone of your voice descending in the elongated command "DOWWWWWwwwn." Once he executes the command to your satisfaction, stop work. End the lesson on a high note.

An alternate method for oversized dogs. The technique outlined in this chapter will always work if applied properly. However, there is one exception. If the dog is oversized it will be awkward or difficult to use the leash in the same manner. Therefore, instead of pushing the leash with your flattened hand, use your foot. By this it is meant that the leash is in the right hand and held in place with the left foot. (See Fig. 17.) The trick is to run the leash under your shoe in the space between the heel and the sole. Sliding the leash through the arch gives leverage to your hand and will force the dog to the ground while you lower your left arm as described before. Give the voice command "DOWWWWWwwwn" and slowly pull up on the leash as you lower your left arm past his eyes. Do not pull up on the leash too quickly or you'll have a fight on your hands. Be careful not to hurt the animal, otherwise this will always be an unhappy command for him. Do it slowly, gently, and firmly. Extend the voice command

FIGURE 17.
*"Down." Method for teaching
"Down" to an oversized dog.
Run the leash under your
shoe in the space between the
heel and the sole.*

to match the time it takes to pull him to the "Down" position. When he is in position give him an expansive, "Good boy!" Once he's down and tries to get up, simply hold the leash with the sole of your shoe so he won't be able to move. Use this technique only if the dog is too large to push down with your hand on the leash. Substitute this "pull-up" method wherever it is indicated that you "push down" on the leash. It may be necessary to switch from left to right hand when using this "pull-up" method. Everything else remains the same as described before.

A word of caution. If your dog is overly aggressive, temperamental, or a "fear biter" excessive force will make him bite or react in a hostile manner, such as with deep throat growls. If this is the situation then the "pull-up" method is definitely out, no matter how big the animal. The "push-down" method may be too dangerous as well. Use the front-paw method exclusively. Even at that it will have to be done gently and with great patience. Instead of pulling his paws out in front of him, gently and slowly push his front paws from behind until he slumps to the ground, grudgingly, but without aggressive resistance. Give the voice command "DOWWWWW-wwwn" as you push his paws and coax him soothingly. It's like the old conundrum, "Where does a five-hundred-pound pussycat sleep? Anywhere he wants!" If it still does not work, then avoid this command or engage the services of a professional trainer. This problem will not arise with a young dog or puppy. It only happens with older dogs who have had enough time to develop bad habits or nervous, neurotic behavior caused by too little training given too late.

DEFINITION OF "DOWN-STAY"

The dog is on the ground, head erect, eyes looking forward. The front legs are extended and the hind quarters relaxed with the rear weight resting on one haunch or the other. He remains in that position until he is released by the person who placed him there. (See Fig. 18.)

FIGURE 18.
"Down" and "Down-Stay." These are the various ways a dog may position himself while in "Down-Stay." The Weimaraner and the Maltese are in perfect position. The Husky has found his own variation of the position.

PROCEDURE AND TECHNIQUE FOR THE "DOWN-STAY"

If the dog has learned the "Sit-Stay," then it is simply a matter of using the same technique for the "Down-Stay."

After placing him in the "Down" give the command "Stay" in a firm voice. Because it is not an action command do not use his name before or afterward. Upon giving the command, flatten your left hand with fingers close together as for a salute and place it in front of his eyes. Your hand should be four inches in front of them. The hand signal is given simultaneously with the voice command. It is a deliberate but quick gesture which temporarily blocks the dog's vision. Assuming the animal has been taught the "Sit-Stay," that's all there is to be done. If he does not respond properly, then review the chapter dealing with "Sit-Stay" and give the dog a few brush-up lessons.

One last note. The commands "Down" and "Stay" are not corrections. If the dog jumps up on a stranger, the couch, the bed, the dinner table, or into the cat's litter box do not yell "Down" and expect him to respond properly. He will become confused. A firm "No" is the only way to make a correction. From there you can employ any command you wish. "Down" will do very well.

11 / "Come When Called"

The dog's name prefixed to the word "Come" is all that's necessary in getting the animal to "Come When Called." As pointed out earlier, language is not your dog's *forte*. Adding "Okay" to "Silver, come" gives a note of good cheer and reassurance that you're not angry with him. Anything more than that will louse up the command and draw a blank in the dog's mind. "Okay, Silver, come," is all it really takes, once the dog has been taught the command. More than that adds confusion, uncertainty, and a lack of response.

There are two cautions concerning this command. The first has to do with older dogs. "Come When Called" must be considered for puppies and young dogs only. The second has to do with the indoor-outdoor use of the command. If your dog lives in the city it is extremely hazardous to allow the dog off the leash. Therefore, consider it very carefully before teaching "Come When Called" out of the house. it could result in the death of the animal. On the other hand, using the command indoors is very practical and offers a convenient way to get the dog to where you want him to be.

DEFINITION OF "COME WHEN CALLED"

The dog comes to you when you call him and goes into a "Sit" position in front of you, regardless of any distractions. (See Fig. 19.)

FIGURE 19.
"Come When Called." Give the verbal command and hand signal and pull the leash toward you. Use both hands, one after the other. The dog sits when he reaches you.

BENEATH THE SURFACE
OF THE TRAINING

This is probably the command that people want most and have the least idea how to execute. It makes the greatest demand of the dog. Most of his life is spent playing and pursuing all distractions that cross his path. Now he is being asked to respond immediately by shifting his focus and using all his concentration to please you. When a dog is indoors there is nothing for him to do but come when you call him. But when he is outside there are smells, sights, other dogs, children, people, moving objects, and noises that command his attention. To get him to resist all that and obey your command is quite a chore.

In order to teach him to come to you when he's *off-leash* it is necessary to start by teaching him *on-leash*. There is no way to teach this command without starting on-leash. Before getting him trained off-leash you must go through a training process of gradually extending the length of the leash. *Never try this command off-leash until he is obeying perfectly on-leash.* It is too dangerous.

The most important rule to remember is *never* to call the dog to you in order to reprimand him. If you use his name or the command "Come" and then correct or punish him he will never come to you again. Avoid statements like "Princess, come. What did you do? Shame, shame! Don't you ever do that again!" Some people even go further by hitting the dog after he has obeyed the command. Each command must be dealt with individually. If the dog obeys a command, praise him. If he "Comes When Called" it is a betrayal of the rules if you scold him. Besides, using his name for correction will only make him associate the sound of his name with "Uh oh. Here it comes." No one in his right mind will run enthusiastically to get hollered at or punished. If the dog needs correction for an infraction of the rules *you must go to him to do it.* In that way his ability to "Come When Called" will not be impaired. A dog should feel that coming to you is a good thing. He should always feel confident that it is a pleasant experience. This attitude is achieved by lavishing him with praise every time he obeys. If you are consistent, he will always come to you.

It is important in teaching this command that the dog never get into the habit of hesitating when called. He should respond immediately. His reward for coming is the praise, but it should be established from the beginning that he must come on the first command. His immediate response could be important to his safety in the city. More dogs are killed in the city by automobiles than by natural causes. This consideration alone makes the command a very valuable one.

PROCEDURE AND TECHNIQUE FOR "COME WHEN CALLED" —ON-LEASH

Begin indoors or out. An area that offers a few distractions is not objectionable as a training place. Use the six-foot leash. First put the dog through his basic commands, i.e., "Heel," "Sit," "Sit-Stay," "Down," "Down-Stay," etc. Then put him in "Sit-Stay." Begin the lesson facing the dog.

Place yourself in front of the dog slightly less than the full extent of the six-foot leash. Holding the leash with the left hand (thumb in loop as described in previous chapters), allow a very slight amount of slack so there is no chance of pulling the dog forward. With the slightest tug the dog will walk toward you and that is undesirable without a command. Keep the leash hand (the left) slightly above the waist for greater control of the dog.

The next thing to do is employ the voice command. It is

important that the tone of voice indicate to the dog that coming to you is one of the most exciting, fun things he could do. The dog should be happy coming to you because he's going to get a tremendous amount of praise. Because this is an action command, employ the dog's name as a prefix to the command "Come." However, use the expletive "Okay" before his name. The command, therefore, sounds like this: "*Okay,* Princess, come!" The "Okay" should be delivered in a very cheerful, upbeat tone of voice. Try to communicate your affection. Never sound harsh or stern. Accentuate the "Okay" and let the "Princess, come" trail along. The dog should start moving on the "Okay." It is quite possible that in the past, the traditional squeaking of the lips sound was made to get the dog to come. You know the sound, the one that's like a squeezed balloon. Lip squeaking and whistling are poor substitutes for a definite command. Very few of us can whistle or squeak loud enough if the dog is in the middle of the street with the distraction of traffic or other outdoor noises.

It is quite possible that the dog will come on the first try. If he does, be sure to reward him with lavish praise. It is not important, at this point, that he sit once he gets to you. If he jumps on you the first few times it's quite understandable. *Do not correct him when he is being taught a new thing.* He may always associate "coming" with the correction and the command is shot forever. He can always be corrected at another time, after he has learned the command properly.

Tugging the leash. Once little Kitszi starts coming to you freely, extend the leash hand and give a gentle tug on the word "Okay." Always tug the leash on the word "Okay." The sequence is: "Okay" (gently tug the leash) "Waldo, come." (He comes to you.) "That's a good fella!" As soon as he comes to you give him his praise. Make it very exciting for him. We emphasize the praise in this command because later you will be competing with very great distractions, and the only way to overcome them is to motivate the dog properly. That can only be done with praise.

The hand signal. The next step is to teach the dog the hand signal that accompanies the voice command. This is very useful if the dog is a great distance away. The hand signal is a natural, logical gesture that should feel very comfortable. It is simply a matter of moving your right hand upward from the side of your body and swinging it around toward your left shoulder. (See Fig. 20.) This gesture is used by humans for the same purpose. The sequence becomes: "Okay." (Tug the leash with your left hand. Swing your right hand around, making a complete gesture.) "Melba, come." Give her a lot of praise when she gets to you.

Going into the "Sit" position after "Coming When Called." After the command is given, pull in the leash—using both hands, one after another—until the entire leash is in and the dog has no choice but to sit when he gets to you. In order

FIGURE 20. *Proper hand signal for "Come When Called."*

to help it along, pull up on the leash once he is at your feet and give the command "Sit." This sequence is: "Okay." (Tug the leash with your left hand. Swing your right hand around, making a complete gesture, *but grab the leash this time.*) "Pete, come." (Pull in the leash, using both hands.) "Good boy, good boy." (By now you have pulled him gently to your feet. Raise the leash with your left hand.) "Sit. Good boy. That's a good boy."

The animal is taught to sit when he gets to you for a couple of very practical reasons. First of all, when he responds to the command "Come" he will start running to you. If he is some distance away it is quite possible that he will crash into you at about forty miles an hour, knocking you off your feet. Or he may shoot right by in his inability to stop. If he is conditioned to sit when he gets to you, he will automatically slow down as he approaches. Repeat these techniques ten or fifteen times or until he responds properly. Remember, all of this is done *on-leash.* At no time should you try it without the leash. The most important reason is safety. But another reason is for control so that he can be guided if he starts veering left or right. To increase the distance for him to come, simply back up as he approaches you. Give him encouragement as he walks toward you. It helps to hold his attention and also motivates him for future commands. "Okay, Pete, come. Pete, come. Okay. Good boy. Good fella." Once he gets to you, "Sit." "Good boy."

"COME WHEN CALLED"—OFF-LEASH

To teach this command off-leash, outdoors, one must be prepared to spend several months at it. It is not recommended for city dogs. But if you have lots of acreage or access to a fenced-off park or field, it can be done with no danger. You should be cautioned that in order to be successful with this off-leash command you must start with a young dog or puppy. Once a dog is six months or older it is almost impossible.

Start by teaching him to come from a ten-foot distance. Do not drop the leash and walk away thinking the dog will stay there until he is called. Obtain a fifty-foot clothesline and hook it to the loop of his leash. With the six-foot leash you had total control of the animal. At ten, fifteen, twenty, twenty-five feet, or more you are not going to have the same amount of control. Start off by using the same *on-leash* technique as before, but this time allow ten feet of leash. Once the dog has performed perfectly at ten feet, go back to the six-foot distance and then back to ten. The repetition reinforces the learning process so he'll never forget what he's been taught. Obviously it cannot be done in one session. It will take two, three, or four lessons for the six-foot technique alone.

Extending the length of the leash. If the dog is responding perfectly to the ten-foot distance, extend the leash to fifteen feet. At this distance you will not be able to reel in the leash as quickly as he can run to you. But if he comes to you at ten feet, then reeling it in hand over hand is no longer necessary. The theory is that if he'll come at ten feet perfectly, then he'll come at twenty or even forty feet. It's then a matter of practice. After the six-foot technique is perfect, go to ten feet, fifteen, twenty, twenty-five, thirty, thirty-five, etc.

Correction from a long distance. The purpose of always having the clothesline tied to the leash is to have some control of the dog, even if he cannot be reeled in as on the six-foot leash. Suppose you are training him at twenty feet and the dog is coming toward you. All of a sudden he spots another dog at fifteen feet and bolts. Without the line on him that would be the end of the session. But what can be done is to lift up the line and hold it tightly. When he reaches the end of the rope he will be stopped cold. At that instant yell "No!" The correction will be a shocking surprise, one that he will not forget. The point is that even at thirty or forty feet you still have the ability to correct him if he bolts. This, incidentally, is a common occurrence and will happen many times. Continue the technique until the dog is responding perfectly at fifty feet. At this point it is time to try him without the clothesline.

Without the clothesline. It is possible that the dog has, all along, recognized that the leash is on and he has to obey. But what happens once the leash is removed? He may recognize the difference. It is for this reason that you are working in an enclosed area. If he runs away, *do not panic. Do not run after him.* If you do, he'll dart away. The thing to do is run in the opposite direction saying, "Come on, boy." He'll follow because it will seem like a game. If that doesn't work, get down on your hands and knees and cheerfully entice him to come to you. Once he is back in your control do not reprimand him if he has responded to your entreaties. If you do he will never respond to them again. Once he comes to you, even if it took half an hour, praise him for it. Never correct a dog when he comes to you. That is why this command requires a great deal of patience.

If the dog does not come off-leash after having worked up to the fifty feet of clothesline, it means starting again at six feet. Of course you will be able to move from distance to distance at a much more rapid pace. It is safe to assume that the dog has learned the command but only associates it with the leash. At this juncture the formula: command, correction, praise is brought to bear. Give the command. "Okay, Pete, come." If the dog doesn't come when called, give him a correction, "No!" This should get him going. When he gets to you, give him his praise. In this manner proceed from distance to distance until you have reached fifty feet. When you try him off-leash this time make sure there are absolutely no distractions. Give him every opportunity to perform properly. He will always obey the command if it is enforced properly. Once he is coming when called off-leash, without distractions, try when there are distractions. You may be pleasantly surprised.

Never use the command "Come" in a harsh tone of voice and never reprimand the dog after he has obeyed the command. This carries over into the home as well as outdoors and during the training sessions. If the dog chews something in the living room and you call him in from the kitchen in order to scold or correct him, you will be destroying the value of this command. In your everyday usage of these commands you will reinforce the training if you execute these techniques properly.

12 / "Go to Your Place"

———◆———

Unlike humans, dogs do not feel insulted if you put them in their place. As a matter of fact, it is a blessing for them to know where to be in order to stay out from underfoot. Dogs are not immune to the frustrations of trying to please an indecisive and inconsistent colleague.

Although "Go to Your Place" is useful for people who live in a full-size house, it is manna from heaven for the city apartment dweller. The average apartment has a bedroom, living room, and kitchen. When the apartment dweller is trying to prepare dinner for a small dinner party, the dog is usually driven mad trying to keep out of the way. If he settles at your feet in the kitchen, he is scolded and told to go into the living room. Once he settles in the living room, he has to dodge the dust mop and avoid being sucked up by the vacuum cleaner. By this time he has been yelled at seventeen times and he's just about ready to steal several caviar canapes (dogs love caviar), which will evoke a shrill hysterical scream from the belabored epicure. The dog is then locked in the bathroom for the evening until a guest uses it and passes out in fright. In the meantime the dog is suffering from boredom and claustrophobia with a pinch of paranoia thrown in for good measure. Of course the hosts are nervous and on edge and ready to give the dog to the first farmer who says he can use him to bite cows. Thus ends another potentially happy relationship between dog and owner. It's too bad, because all this can so easily be avoided with the command "Go to Your Place."

DEFINITION OF "GO TO YOUR PLACE"

At your command the dog stops whatever he is doing and leaves wherever he is doing it, goes to a designated place, and stays there for an indefinite time.

BENEATH THE SURFACE
OF THE TRAINING

The dog should have an out-of-the-way area that is designated as his little corner of the world. The area should be carefully selected so that at no time is he in anyone's way or in danger of being forced to move once he's placed there. It is especially considerate if the area is not too removed from the activities of the family. Dogs get vicarious pleasure from merely watching the evening's entertainment. An added benefit from this command is that it ends begging for food once you have sat down to dinner.

One of the ways to enhance the training is to place his toys, playthings, and bones in his designated area. He will feel quite at home and much more secure. Give him a small piece of carpet or an old cushion in order to make his area cozy and comfortable. Once all this is established the dog will be in a much better frame of mind. Psychologically, it is very important for his well-being.

In a household where there is more than one animal, this designation of territory is very important. If there are two male dogs, for instance, there is a constant competition for territorial rights. In this situation, designate a place for each animal and never violate the established territorial rights of each respective dog. With a cat and a dog, never let the cat use the dog's area for anything. In the case of a male and a female dog when the latter goes in heat there is very little that territory can do to avoid contact. The dogs must be kept apart (assuming you don't want them to mate) in more practical ways. Outside of a mating situation, the animals will quickly learn to respect each other's territorial rights.

This command offers the owner a firm control over the animal's behavior at very important times. If a friend or neighbor enters the home and does not want to be annoyed with the dog's demand for attention, simply tell him to go to his place and that's the end of it. This goes back to the time of the caveman when the dog stayed outside as a guard. That was his place.

It is helpful to understand that the dog will always go to his place on command if it is not made to seem like a punishment. Even though your motive is to get the dog out of mischief, always give the command on an upbeat so that he does not feel that something bad is connected with going to his place.

It is not to be equated with "Go to your room," an expression that many a parent has used on an errant child.

PROCEDURE AND TECHNIQUE FOR "GO TO YOUR PLACE"

The first step in teaching this command is to select a permanent spot that will be used exclusively by the dog as the one place where he can go and never be in the way.

Starting at five feet. In teaching the lesson, use the standard six-foot leash and choke collar. Because this is an action command, always use his name first. Start out five feet away from the designated place and say, "Pete, go to your place." Then commence to walk the dog to the spot. Once you get him there, give the command "Sit." Praise him. Then give him the command "Down" and, finally, "Stay." Praise him. Leave him there as you walk six feet away. Do not leave his vision. He will probably stay, provided you're in the room. Assuming the dog has learned "Come When Called," call him to you. Repeat this procedure fifteen times.

The command "Go to Your Place" should be given in a pleasant and gentle tone of voice. Even though learning is hard work for a dog, make him feel that this is a pleasant command, one which he will enjoy. However, do not lose the firm, authoritative sound that you have developed. Add a happy quality to it.

Once the dog willingly accompanies you to his place from five feet, try it at ten feet. Again, get his attention with, "Pete, go to your place." Walk him to the spot. Place him in "Sit." Place him in "Down" and then "Stay." Walk six feet away and after a few seconds call him. Repeat the whole thing several times. Don't be surprised if he starts leading you to his place once he's been doing it a few times. This is a happy experience for him. He gets a lot of praise and affection for doing it properly. Do not, however, become too lax during the training period. If he starts sniffing something on the way to his place, exercise firm leash control. Direct him to the exact location of his place. Nothing must stand in the way once you have given the command.

Extending the distance. Take a twenty-foot clothesline and tie it to the loop of the dog's leash. Stand back the full distance of the line and give the command, "Pete, go to your place." Let him do it by himself. The reason for tying a line to him is control. If he veers away from his place, correct him, say "No" and then repeat the original command. If he gets confused or decides not to do it, walk him there as before. The command, unlike some of the others, involves more teaching than discipline.

Other rooms. The next step is to teach him this command from other rooms. Using the six-foot leash repeat the procedure, but this time from another room at a greater distance. Try it several times from every room in your apartment or house. You will actually be teaching him the path to his place from every part of your quarters and it will be permanently printed in his brain. The toughest room for him will probably be the bedroom because it is usually the farthest. But once he learns that, he will know the command perfectly. Once the dog knows this command on-leash it is guaranteed that he'll be able to do it off-leash.

A word of caution. Do not give this command promiscuously. Do not make it a family joke or something with which to impress friends and neighbors. Only use the command as it's needed. If he has to go to his place every five minutes it's going to make him crazy. Let him enjoy going to his place. Let him consider it his little haven when things get difficult. He will soon be going there without the command. He'll probably pick that area to stay for most of the day. That will be his little indoor doghouse. A home within a home.

Now that you have successfully completed the last twelve chapters, you may consider your dog obedience-trained. Congratulations! Both you and your dog deserve a biscuit.

The next part of the book is more or less graduate work. Now that your dog is obedience-trained, you may tackle his individual problems as outlined in "Puppy and Mature Problems," "Mature Problems Only," and "Problem Dogs." The first twelve chapters have given you a basis from which to work.

PART II

After The
Obedience Course

Fortunately for us, dogs do not respond to Freudian analysis, touch therapy, or any other form of psychotherapy. If they did there would probably be a stampede to dog "shrinks" and sniff-touch encounter-group studios. It would create a new set of economics in an already costly pet market.

In this chapter a great deal of territory is covered in an attempt to give some useful information concerning the dozens of behavioral problems that occur in dogs. Selected here are those that come up the most often, but no doubt others will be overlooked owing to the limitations of space or technical/medical information available. Many of these problems never arise because a successfully completed obedience course, such as the one outlined in this book, was initiated. Many of these problems can be diminished in degree simply by going over various aspects of the obedience course. A well-trained and disciplined dog will not eat up the carpet, bark excessively, bite, etc. However, inadvertent environmental factors sometimes play a destructive part in creating those annoying bad habits that dogs very often acquire. For example, a family that goes to work every day, leaving the dog alone, may come home to a destroyed couch, never knowing that the phone rang continuously, putting the dog into a mad frenzy. Incorrect discipline is the main cause of these problems and tends to worsen them as long as it is continued. Punishments, scoldings, temper tantrums, beatings all tend to create problems and worsen those that already exist.

Besides continuous brushups on the obedience course, we suggest that you try to think through a dog's situation from his perspective. Like a psychologist, one can often solve a problem by understanding its cause. You would then be in a position to change or remove those factors that are upsetting the dog and making him behave the way he does. Teasing, roughhouse play, abuse from children, chaining him down, overexcitement are but a few of those factors that may be at the root of the problem. Some dogs will not respond to the suggestions made in this chapter and will require the long, tedious kind of attention that only a professional trainer can provide. If you love your dog and want to keep him, it is best to take this final but effective step. A good trainer not only has the technical facility to handle most dog problems, but is emotionally uninvolved, thus giving him the needed patience that underlies all good animal handling. It is like the difference between an aspirin and a doctor's prescription.

The first two chapters in this part, "Puppy and Mature Problems" and "Mature Problems Only," describe problems and their solutions. These are all measures that any dog owner can take and experience good results with. The last chapter, "Problem Dogs," does not offer any such measures that the owner can take himself. These are problems that only a trainer can solve. What we do offer is an aid to recognition of these problems so that the owner can take the proper steps in obtaining professional assistance.

13 / Puppy and Mature Problems

BEGGING

This is a problem that starts out in puppyhood as a cute stunt and winds up as an obnoxious annoyance in mature life. There is nothing worse than a dog sitting next to you at the dinner table, looking up, and whining for food. Although barely tolerable when it's just a daily family dinner, it is completely unacceptable when you are entertaining guests. It can ruin an otherwise pleasant social occasion.

Obviously, this is a habit that is formed when the dog is very young, and once again the owner is to blame. When you give the dog snacks and between-meal treats, you are on the way to teaching him to beg. He begins to expect food at any time of the day or night and never learns that his feeding time is the main meal of the day. He has learned that his eating area is anywhere that you are dealing with food. As in the section "Taking Food from the Table," make it a firm rule never to feed him anywhere but in his bowl, in its regular place. Also, never give him anything except his own food, *at his regular feeding time only*.

In order to break him of his begging habit, start placing the leash and collar on him before dinner. Sit down to dinner and wait for him to make his move. The instant he starts begging from anyone, give him a hard corrective jerk accompanied by a loud "No." Tell everyone at the table what is about to happen so it doesn't upset them and ruin their meal. Alternatives to this method are: Use of the "throw can" accompanied with a firm "No"; the command "Down" and "Stay"; and the command "Go to Your Place." If you do it consistently he will stop this nasty little habit in short order.

CHEWING

Chewing is one of the most expensive and destructive problems that any dog owner faces. We are talking about chewing furniture, curtains, draperies, appliances, baseboards, shoes, clothing, etc. Owners have lost hundreds and sometimes thousands of dollars in damage. Very often chewing has been the cause of failure in owner-animal relations and has resulted in a parting of the ways. For the owner it ends in frustration, but for the dog, it means an uncertain future in terms of his mortality. It's sad because there is no excuse for the problem, inasmuch as it is readily solvable.

There are several solutions. Some dogs will respond favorably to any one of the many sprays on the market. You spray the items that the dog has chewed and tends to go back to. Some sprays are unpleasant to the dog's sense of smell while others are unpleasant to taste. An alternative is to use alum, a powder that can be purchased inexpensively in any drugstore. Mix it with a small amount of water, make it into a paste, and smear it on the dog's favorite chewing spots. The mixture tastes bitter and is extremely unpleasant for the animal. Although alum is not harmful if ingested, it should be used in small quantities. Alum is used medicinally as an astringent and a styptic and could upset the dog if he swallowed a large quantity. However, that is not likely to happen owing to its unpleasant taste. Tobasco or hot sauce is also effective.

Some people have had success merely by playing the radio during the time they are not at home (when most chewing takes place). Others have made one- or two-hour tape recordings of conversation, which tends to make the dog uncertain about the owner's presence. "His master's voice" can be effective because dogs rarely chew when the owner is home. Record one or two hours of conversation with an intermittent correction. In other words, yell "No" and shake a "throw can" every five minutes during the first twenty minutes of the tape recording.

If the dog's favorite chewing object is a couch cover or bolster or bed pillow, the mousetrap technique will certainly end the problem. (See "Jumping on Furniture.")

When the chewing problem pertains to a puppy, stay alert to which objects the animal is chewing and discourage it immediately before it develops into an adult habit. Discourage him from going after wooden objects or anything at all that might resemble furniture, clothing, carpeting, curtains, or anything you value. A rawhide toy that he can call his own is the safest preventative you can employ to avoid a destructive behavior problem. Do not wait until it is too late and you have lost your valuable carpeting. A puppy's chewing problem is usually because of teething. When you leave the house leave several ice cubes around for the dog. The coldness will numb his gums and ease the pain. An alternative is to soak a washcloth in cold water and freeze it. This will serve the same purpose as the ice cubes.

Many adult dogs chew when left alone because they are bored, frightened, nervous, or insecure about whether or not you will return. They do not do it as a spiteful act. Punishment is counterproductive and changes nothing except to add to the dog's insecurity. If you can make a determination as to why he chews, you might be able to change the conditions of his environment and correct the problem. For example: take the phone off the hook if the bell frightens him, do not leave him alone for too long a period of time (have a friend look in on him), get him a cat for a playmate, leave plenty of rawhide toys or bones, etc. With careful deliberation every problem can be solved.

EXCESSIVE BARKING

There are two aspects to the problem of excessive barking. The first is when the dog barks while the owner is home, and that is usually caused by a doorbell ringing, noise outside the door, a stranger at the door, a desire for food, a desire to go out, etc. The second aspect is when the owner is not home. The owner comes home from work or shopping and finds an angry note from a neighbor or landlord to stop the dog from barking or else face the legal consequences.

Solving the barking problem when the owner is home is much easier than when the owner is not at home. By leaving the leash and choke collar on the dog you are prepared to deliver a corrective jerk and a firm "No" when the dog barks. Even shaking the "throw can" and saying "No" often works. But the corrective jerk is the most effective method.

If the dog barks excessively when no one is home, the solution lies in the basic obedience course. There are many reasons why a dog will bark when he is left alone. He may be undisciplined; he may hear a lot of noises outside; he simply may want his own way, i.e., to have you walk through the door and play with him. Basic obedience lessons tend to calm him down, reassure him, make him responsive. The more responsive the dog is to you, the more eager he is to please. If the dog has had no basic obedience lessons this is the time to start. If he has had lessons then simply go over three or four commands as a refresher. Run him through his paces, so to speak, and remind him of his training. Don't forget to praise him every time he performs properly.

If that doesn't work, then try leaving the house and waiting outside. Do everything you normally do when you leave. Follow the established routine, such as putting out certain lights, closing the curtains, etc. Do not lock the door. Be sure to leave his leash and collar on. Pretend to leave the house and do not stand so close to the door that the dog can smell your presence. He must be convinced that you have really left the house. When he starts to bark, run in, grab his leash, and execute a hard corrective jerk accompanied by an angry "No!" If you do this three or four times with very firm corrections (jerking hard enough to lift him off the ground) he will understand exactly what you want him not to do. Praise him afterward for having stopped barking. This is a problem that must be solved, because it can result in having to get rid of the dog or finding yourself evicted from your house or apartment. A very hard corrective jerk is recommended if it's going to work. It's much more humane in the long run than having to surrender the dog to an unknown home or institution.

You may run into the problem of his not barking for an hour after you leave. One way to solve this is with the use of a one- or two-hour tape recording of family conversation with an intermittent correction. Yell "No" and shake a "throw can" every five minutes for the first twenty minutes of the recording. If he suspects that you are around, he will not bark. An alternative is to wait out the hour outside the house on a weekend when you can spare the time, and use the corrective jerk as outlined above. But in either case the problem must be dealt with before it is too late.

In all these suggested methods you must always accompany your action with a firm "No" and then praise after he responds properly. In a short while you will only have to use a firm "No."

EXCESSIVE WETTING

Holding his urine is one of the primary requisites for a domesticated pet. But many dogs tend to release it in small quantities at the most peculiar moments and sometimes trail it all over the house. There are several explanations. It can be a symptom of sickness, disease, or injury to the kidneys and bladder. It doesn't hurt to have your dog checked by a veterinarian. Assuming the dog is in good health, wetting can be an indication of a very shy or timid dog. A dog of this temperament will "piddle" when he is punished or yelled at. He wets from fear or perhaps excitement. Urinating is an instinctual act of submission to the domination of another animal and is a direct parallel to excessive authority from the dog's master. When a male puppy is confronted with a mature dog of the same gender a ritual takes place. They determine each other's sex by sniffing and then decide who will prevail in the situation. There is usually a brief, physical encounter with the puppy or young dog losing the battle and indicating his submission by rolling over on his back and urinating. It is his way of acknowledging the older male's superiority. The identical interaction occurs between you and your dog when you punish him or yell at him and he urinates.

One way to cope with it is to be much more gentle than usual and to eliminate punishments and scoldings. Do not use threatening gestures or sudden movements. A limited water intake can help reduce the problem. Weaning the dog away from his shy or timid temperament will eventually end the problem. (See "The Shy Dog.")

GOING INTO THE GARBAGE

Unless it has already happened to you, this problem seems to be one of those endearing little habits that make such good anecdote material for people who enjoy talking about their dogs. In our opinion this nasty little trait is not only disgusting but has all the potential for costing the owner a great deal of money. More than once a dog has ripped into the garbage sack and scattered it all over the house. In addition, the little devil chewed up much of it and ingested such savories as eggshells, coffee grounds, etc. The dog then moved into the living room and regurgitated all over the two-hundred-year-old Persian rug. To come home to that is to experience the first emotions of *dogicide*. Of course, if the dog happens to split a few hollow chicken bones with his teeth and then swallows the jagged ends you might come home to find a dead dog. Going into the garbage can be serious.

This problem arises whether you are home or away. Because of the powerful smell, animals are extremely attracted to this symphony of scents. Obviously, the easiest way to solve the problem is to simply not leave the garbage pail around, especially if you go out. But that doesn't really teach the dog anything. Set up a simulated situation. Place the leash and collar on the dog and purposely open the lid to the garbage pail. Walk away. The minute the dog sticks his nose in the pail give him a hard corrective jerk and a very loud "No." *Then praise him*. You may also try shaking the "throw can" if it's more convenient. You should get good results if you repeat this technique four or five times. In the event that you are leaving the house sprinkle Tabasco sauce or hot Chinese mustard on top of the garbage. This is an object lesson that really works.

JUMPING ON FURNITURE

This is another undesirable characteristic of many dogs, both young and old alike. It comes from poor discipline on the part of the owner who allows the habit to develop. If the dog is allowed to sleep with his owner in the bed, it is very logical for him to assume that the chairs and sofas are merely an extension of the bed. Furniture is furniture and the dog makes no distinctions. Therefore, the question must be asked: is the dog allowed to jump on the furniture or not?

There are several solutions to the problem. If the dog is still a puppy the "throw can" is very effective. Wait for the animal to jump on the furniture. The minute he does, you shake the can and say "No" in a firm voice. Do not throw the can as you might with an older dog. You do not want to scare the young puppy. As you are aware by now, the "throw can" solves a multitude of problems. Do not forget to praise the dog immediately after he responds to the correction.

In the case of an older dog, apply the same technique with this exception: *throw* the can. Of course it is not suggested that you throw the can directly at him. Throw it to the side. Because the dog is older, it takes a little more than shaking the can to startle him. Once again say "No" with a firm voice and then praise the animal after he responds.

In the event that the "throw can" method does not work, it is suggested you use the leash and choke collar. When you are home leave the leash on until he jumps on the furniture. As he does, give him a very firm corrective jerk accompanied by a stern "No." As soon as he stops jumping give him his praise. Remember, without the praise the correction is meaningless.

A very upsetting aspect to this problem is when the dog waits for you to leave the house before he jumps up on the sofa or whatever his favorite spot is. (You can be sure he has one.) Do you come home and discover fur, saliva, or worse on your expensive bedspread or brocade slipcover? If so, it indicates that the dog waits for you to leave, commits his crime, and scoots off the minute he hears you coming. One answer is to tape record one or two hours of conversation with an intermittent correction. Every five minutes yell "No" and shake a "throw can" for the first twenty minutes of the recording.

Another solution to this problem sounds awful, but in reality is painless and quite humane. Set ten or fifteen small mousetraps over the couch or bed and cover them with five or six thicknesses of newspaper. Tape the paper thoroughly so that the dog cannot hurt himself. When you leave, the dog is probably going to jump on the couch and set the traps off. The traps will hit the newspaper with a loud noise and startle him. This works almost every time. Repeat the technique until you come home to find that the traps have not been set off.

It is important to remember that dogs are taught to jump on furniture. If they are not allowed to do it at any time then they won't. Most people think it's cute to cradle a puppy in their arms and sit on the couch with it. There is no difference between a puppy sitting directly on the couch or sitting in your arms with you seated on the couch. That is the beginning of your problem and that's the time to nip it in the bud. Remember, it ceases to be cute when the dog is full grown and the habit firmly established. Allowing the dog to sleep in your bed is also an open invitation to jumping on the furniture. The choice is yours.

JUMPING ON PEOPLE

Almost any dog will jump up on people if he is excited, happy, and untrained. This happens on the street and in the house when someone comes to visit. The animal usually wants to play and get some attention. The biggest problem connected with it is the behavior of the owner. If the puppy or the dog is not supposed to jump up on people, then that rule must apply in every situation. You cannot have the dog jump up on you when you feel playful and then expect him not to do it when you are no longer in the mood. It is too confusing for him. Consistency is the only sure cure. In most cases where this problem exists you will find that the owner encourages the dog to jump up once or twice a week. The rest of the time the owner does not like it and yells at the dog when he jumps. It is precisely because of this inconsistency that the dog jumps on anyone who pays the slightest attention to him. One must answer the question: do you want him to jump on you or not?

If the answer is no, then a correction (the corrective jerk and a firm "No") will stop him in most cases, providing that you maintain that attitude. (See Fig. 21.) If you give in just once you will destroy the training. If you teach a puppy not to jump by correcting him when he tries it, he will never do it unless you permit him that one time.

Puppies can be taught with the use of a "throw can." (See "Equipment.") Whenever the puppy tries to jump or climb up on you or anyone else, shake the can vigorously and say "No" in a very firm tone of voice. Do not scare the little dog, simply command his attention and impress upon him that this behavior is displeasing. Once you have made the correction and he responds properly, then give him affectionate praise. Do not bend over and pet him or he'll jump again. Tell him he's a good dog in a friendly voice. He will soon understand that he doesn't have to jump to get your love.

In the case of a grown dog who has been indulging in this behavior for a while, use a different technique that's based on the same principle. Arrange for a relative to have the dog on leash and choke collar before you come home. When you walk in the door and the dog makes a jump, the person holding the leash gives him a corrective jerk and a very firm "No." Assuming the dog has been obedience-trained, he should be commanded to "Sit" immediately following the correction. Give him his praise after he obeys the command. If the dog

FIGURE 21.
Jumping on people. Employ the corrective jerk. Wait until the dog is standing on two legs before executing the correction.

has not yet been obedience-trained, then the corrective jerk must be done with vigor as you pull to the right side. He may still try to jump after the first jerk. Simply do it again until he stops. If this process is repeated several times in one evening you will be surprised at the results.

If the infraction occurs outside on a stranger or anyone else, do not merely pull him away. Give him a corrective jerk to the right and walk in the opposite direction. This jerk will cause the dog enough discomfort to discourage him from trying it again. Do it every time he jumps up and you will solve the problem. But remember, if you or anyone else encourages the dog to jump up this training will have no effect. You must inform everyone who comes in contact with the dog that they must not give the animal any invitations.

No cruel or excessively harsh techniques that have been used in the past are recommended, such as kneeing the dog in the chest or stepping on his toes. These painful techniques are not necessary if you remember to be consistent in your demands.

NIPPING

All puppies have a teething problem, as do all infants. Because teething is painful, puppies bite or nip to ease the pressure of the incoming teeth. They will bite hands, fingers, toys, and furniture. Sometimes they are encouraged to bite if the owner makes a habit of placing his hand in the animal's mouth when playing. This is like teaching the dog to bite. There are several ways to ease this situation. One method is to soak a washcloth in cold water and place it in the freezing unit of the refrigerator. When it is frozen give it to the dog to chew. The coldness will numb his gums and relieve the pain. Consequently, he will not bite as much as he did. Quite often this is done with babies by refrigerating their teething rings.

Another approach to the problem is to give the puppy a rawhide or synthetic toy. It is not suggested that the dog be given an old discarded shoe or sock. You will be sorry later. The dog will not be able to distinguish between an old shoe and a new one. The rawhide toys may be used in conjunction with the frozen washcloth.

It is important to solve the nipping problem early in the dog's life because it can lead to a serious biting problem later.

The puppy should always be discouraged from nipping at your fingers or anything else. It is better to substitute a rawhide toy for your fingers than to inflict a harsh punishment or scolding. All the yelling, hitting, or finger-pointing in the world is not going to stop the dog's teeth from growing and giving him pain. And if you scare the dog when he is a young puppy he may grow shy or aggressive and then you will have a biting problem that is much more difficult to solve.

RUNNING OUT OF THE HOUSE

This is a problem that could mean life or death for the dog. If he runs out the door and into the street he could be struck by a car, and good-bye dog. Most dog owners have either had this problem or are still experiencing it. Even though a dog has had some form of basic obedience course and has been taught the "Sit-Stay," he will still attempt to run out the front door if given half a chance. The reason is simple. Going through the front door represents a happy experience to the dog. It is through that door that he is taken outside to play, to relieve himself, to see children and other animals. Obviously, he is primed at a second's notice to go dashing out to the never-never land of fun and games. He must be taught that he can only go through the door when given permission.

In order to break him of this habit, set up an artificial situation so he can be corrected when he tries to run out. Put his choke collar and training leash on and keep it in hand. Prearrange to have someone ring the doorbell. Place the dog in "Sit-Stay." Tell the person to come in. The door should open and be left open. When the dog bolts for the door give him an extremely hard corrective jerk, shout "No," and turn around and walk the other way. Then place him in "Sit-Stay" again. Naturally, the dog must be taught "Sit-Stay" in order to do this. Every time the doorbell rings he should be placed in "Sit-Stay." Repeat the procedure several times a day until he no longer tries to run out. It may take a few days but it's well worth the effort.

In practicing make sure you maintain absolute control of the dog. He may not respond properly at first and if you do not keep a firm grip on the leash he will run out. Do not lose the dog in the process of teaching him. Any time he makes a lunge for the door give him a firm corrective jerk and walk the other way. Praise the dog after each and every correction. Maintain a good relationship with him so that he doesn't think he is being punished. Test the dog's level of training by placing him in "Sit-Stay." Open the door and see if he'll remain in position. At no time should you let go of the leash. Once the dog is responding well you can then answer the door yourself as the dog walks with you. Place him in "Sit-Stay" before opening the door and chances are he will no longer run out.

TAKING FOOD FROM THE TABLE*

Stealing food from a set table or kitchen counter is not considered one of the more serious pet problems. As a matter of fact, almost every dog owner has at least one such favorite story about his little Princess. However, the habit is annoying and can cause considerable expense in view of the high cost of sirloin or prime rib.

This problem is somewhat similar to that of begging, which is covered elsewhere in this chapter. There are two things necessary to cure the dog of this bad habit. First, never feed the dog anything from the table or food-preparation area of the kitchen. Make this a hard-and-fast rule and do not allow anyone to violate it. This alone, after a while, will end the habit of expecting a reward for "hanging around." Next, bait him. After placing the leash and collar on him let him roam around as he pleases. Take a small quantity of freshly cooked food or food that you know appeals to him and leave it on a table or counter top. Step back and wait. When the dog goes for it, as he surely will, grab the leash and administer a hard corrective jerk accompanied by a loud "No." Immediately afterward praise him for obeying. Repeat this several times until he no longer tries to steal the food.

The use of the "throw can" is also very effective. For a young dog or puppy, yell "No" and shake the can vigorously. With an older dog, yell "No" and throw the can to the floor (do not hit him with the can). This type of correction will startle him and help to end the annoying habit.

TALKING BACK

One of the cutest things a dog can do is bark at you after you give him a command. It is especially true in the case of a puppy. People fall to the ground in laughter and many an owner actually regards it as though it were a terrific trick that he has taught the dog. The problem is that it is all too often an expression of defiance and unwillingness to respond to commands. Experience has proven that it leads to aggressiveness, where the dog, in some cases, becomes a bully. Usually, when a dog is given a command it is for a good reason and therefore should not be disobeyed, ignored, or protested. As undemocratic as it sounds, it is the only correct relationship between a dog and his master. The dog-owner relationship is pure feudalism. Dogs are totally dependent on their masters for everything connected with their well-being. And very often a command is very much in the best interests of the dog. Therefore, he must obey, and talking back is an indication of disobedience.

If your dog barks or howls at you after you give him a command he should be corrected. The corrective jerk with the leash and collar accompanied by a firm "No" will end this behavior. Don't forget to praise him immediately after the correction.

AFRAID OF CARS

Many dogs are afraid to ride in cars and run away the minute the car door is opened. Once forced inside, they generally whine, bark, or howl to be let out. Why? Perhaps they've had an unhappy experience with a car, or they feel trapped inside, or because it's simply a new and strange experience.

A car may have caused your dog to have a trauma you know nothing about. One of the great causes of dog deaths is heat prostration. It usually happens when an owner, ignorant of the small lung capacity of a dog, locks the animal in a car while shopping. Even on the mildest day with the windows rolled down a few inches the sun will immediately turn the car into an oven. The dog feels the intense heat and resulting oxygen shortage and panics when he finds that he can't get out. Eventually he will claw, scratch, and even hurl his body against the windows to get out. Often the result is death. But it is possible that the owner appears in the very early stages of this nightmare and, without knowing it, rescues the dog. After an experience like that it will be almost impossible to get the dog back into a car and the owner will never understand why. (Obviously, the windows of a car should always be open wide enough for good ventilation when locking a dog inside.) Heat prostration is only one of many traumas that a dog may have experienced while in a car by himself. Auto backfires, dogs in heat, teasing children, gasoline fumes, etc., are but a few of the possibilities.

Patience is the only solution. To begin with, make auto riding sound like fun. Turn it into a game. Get him in a cheerful mood with statements like, "Who wants a ride in the car? Let's go in the car, boy." Make it seem like a treat. If he won't take the bait then try coaxing him with a gentle tone of voice. Open the door on both sides and let him investigate on his own before starting up the engine. Once you get him inside on his own let him sniff around and leave if he wishes. Do not force him to stay. It is important that the dog never feels trapped with no way out. A cornered animal soon panics and behaves irrationally. Once he sits down, close the doors gently and start up. Drive one block and stop and let him out. If he gets back in then drive another block. If he refuses to get back into the car then let it go for another day. Try it again and again until the dog is relaxed enough to drive several miles. Petting him, praising him, and sitting in the back seat with him for a few minutes will also help to reassure him that nothing bad is going to happen. Do this three or four times a day for a few days and the problem will be solved.

CAR SICKNESS

There is really only one undeniable symptom of car sickness and that's when the dog loses control of his orifices and either vomits, urinates, or defecates all over the seat. Certainly, one possible reason for car sickness is feeding and watering before a long trip. With stop-and-go traffic the dog gets nauseous and loses control one way or another. A good rule is never feed or water a dog immediately before taking him in an automobile. And don't let the dog get overexcited before a trip. His running around will sometimes lead to the unpleasant physical sensations that cause car sickness.

If a dog is not really relaxed about riding in a car, he is going to have intense emotions that will induce car sickness. Therefore, it would be desirable to allow him to slowly adjust to riding in gradual stages. Open the door to the car and allow him to walk in by his own choice. Let him smell around and walk outside the other door if he wishes. Let him sit in the car for a few minutes without actually starting the engine. Let him claim the car as part of his territory before driving off. Animals panic if they feel trapped in an unfamiliar situation. When you finally decide to give him his first ride, have him sit in the back seat and hold on to his leash from the front seat. Drive a block and stop. Get out for a minute or two and then try it again. Repeat this process until you feel the dog is relaxed enough to continue without stopping.

It is also useful to convince the dog that riding in a car is fun. Try relating to the dog with cheerful enthusiasm just before entering the car. "Want to go for a ride? Come on, boy.

Let's get in the car." This kind of entreaty does work in changing the dog's attitude about riding. If the dog is not emotionally upset, then chances are he will not get car sick.

On the other hand, you do not want him to be uncontrollable. Maintain a firm control of the leash so that he does not jump around. Give him the command "Sit" and correct him if he does something wrong. The commands "Down" and "Stay" before driving off will undoubtedly help. The idea is to get him to ride in the back quietly and be a good passenger. Sometimes opening the window three or four inches is enough to satisfy him. It makes him feel less trapped and allows him to enjoy the fresh air and scenery. However, it is not a good idea to allow him to keep his head outside the window while the car is in motion. It can create eye irritations.

CHASING CARS

When a dog chases after a car he creates a clear and present danger, not only to his own life but to the occupants of the car he is chasing. It is horrible enough to think about him getting under the wheels of the moving vehicle, but what if the car smashes into a pole or tree in an effort to avoid the offending animal? There have been situations where a driver was startled and was made victim of a head-on collision with another car. For these reasons car chasing must be taken very seriously.

There are many possible reasons for a dog behaving this way in the face of terrible danger. One explanation is the instinct of the dog to be a running hunter. In his wild state, the dog (or wolf) must outrun his prey if he is to eat. This instinct is clearly demonstrated in greyhound racing where a mechanical rabbit is used as bait. Another possible explanation is that the dog might have had a bad experience with a moving car, i.e., backfire, a near-miss by a passing vehicle, or something tossed at him from a car window. Motor noises, exhaust fumes, or any number of factors may have conspired to create this abnormal reaction to moving autos. It is one of those rare situations where a knowledge of the cause offers little help in ending the problem.

What is needed here is to communicate to the dog that chasing cars displeases you and offers nothing but intense discomfort for his efforts. A strong choke collar and training leash can be employed the next time the dog indulges his habit. Let him go to the end of his leash as he runs toward the moving vehicle. Then pull for all you're worth, yanking him off his feet. As he reaches the end of the leash shout "No." Then praise him. If the problem does not end, then use a long length of rope in the same manner. Make sure it is a double thickness of strong rope so that he doesn't break it when he reaches the end. The longer the distance, the harder the impact when he reaches the end of it. You cannot allow yourself to be squeamish and hold back on that hard yank. It is absolutely certain that it will give the dog a great discomfort. But compare that very temporary discomfort with getting entangled in the wheels of a moving car.

THE SENSUOUS DOG—MOUNTING, ETC.

Mature female dogs go into heat twice a year for a two-week period and have very little, if any, interest in sex at other times. However, mature male dogs can become sexually aroused at any time, depending on their degree of sexual frustration and pent-up energy. If the mature male has never been mated and has little opportunity for his daily exercise requirement, then chances are he will mount the leg of a child or adult whenever aroused. If he is constantly segregated from female dogs, he will probably develop strong human attachments which can, at times, be sexual in nature. The habit of mounting is more than just embarrassing. If a large dog attempts to mount a young child he can inflict mental and physical injury. It is, however, not a common occurrence. Most mounting problems consist of a sexually frustrated dog wrapping around the leg of his owner or friend and simulating the movements of coitus.

Any mounting behavior should be dealt with immediately. Mating the male dog is one answer. Another is to give him plenty of daily exercise and allow him to work off the sexual energy. It does help. But, finally, when all else fails the dog must be corrected. Put his choke collar and leash on him and wait for him to mount. The minute he tries it, administer a hard corrective jerk and say "No" in a firm voice. Make the correction a tough one and do not allow the dog to get very far before administering it. If the dog is allowed to get very intense in this activity he may snap when you try to stop him.

It is best to stop him as quickly as possible. A loud shaking of the "throw can" may be used effectively as an alternative to the corrective jerk. And this is one of the few circumstances where we recommend raising the knee to the dog's chest to knock him down. No matter which technique you use it should be made very clear, as soon as possible, that mounting humans is totally unacceptable behavior.

SNIFFING UNDER DRESSES

Without being too graphic, it is quite clear that this is an embarrassing, annoying, and definitely undesirable problem. It is hardly necessary to deal with why a dog develops the habit. What is important is that he be broken of it.

Once again use the choke collar and leash. When the dog begins to indulge his bad habit, grab the leash and execute a hard corrective jerk and a loud "No." If the dog is a small, fragile creature, shake the "throw can" vigorously and deliver a stern "No." It is important to communicate your displeasure strongly whenever the dog misbehaves.

15/ Problem Dogs

The following problems occur after the dog has matured completely. They are so difficult to solve that the aid of a professional trainer is suggested. What can be done to help is to clarify the problems. This will allow you to recognize them so that you do not aggravate the situation, thus making them more difficult to solve.

BITING

A biter is a dog who has been *allowed* to become a biter. It could be a result of the growling that was never dealt with or the overaggressiveness that was never stopped. If you hit a dog enough times he is going to bite you. With the exception of dogs with congenital damage, no puppy was ever born with a vicious desire to bite. Why does a dog who licked your face when he was seven weeks old become a biter or even a killer at one or two years old? Usually because he has been hit during the housebreaking period, has had his nose rubbed in his own mess, has been kicked, has had objects thrown at him or fingers pointed at him, or has been swacked with rolled newspapers. If punishment has been the keynote every day of the dog's life, as it has been for some dogs, then he probably is the terror of the neighborhood. The dog has been trapped and his only way out has been to bite—usually the hands that feed him. If you hit with your hands he's going to bite at your hands.

It is sometimes dangerous to give a corrective jerk to this type of dog. He may react by biting you. He will bite especially if he knows he can get away with it. There is little the average owner can do other than restrain the dog at all times and seek the services of a professional trainer. If you don't, then we suggest you take out a large personal liability insurance policy.

FEAR BITING

The fear biter is different from the usual biter. The biter is an aggressive dog who is not afraid of anything. The fear biter is just the opposite, even though he has been abused just like the aggressive dog. He has experienced all the punishments and assaults that the other one has, but he has reacted conversely. He is afraid. He bites out of fear. If you confront a fear biter, he will back away until you turn around, at which point he will bite you on the calf, the rump, the hand, or the arm. A fear biter is extremely aggressive when on-leash, but cowers when released and runs away. His bravado comes from the security of being with his master and he will bark menacingly when a stranger comes into the house. If you yell at him or confront him in any way he runs. The minute you turn your back on him he will nail you. This kind of dog also bites if he is cornered under a table or chair. If he feels trapped and has no escape he will become aggressive.

His problems could have been caused by a combination of factors such as poor breeding and harsh treatment as a puppy and young dog. Again, there is little an owner can do without expert assistance. Training techniques for these various problems are complex and difficult and require a skilled handler.

GROWLING

A growl is a menacing sound that comes from deep in the throat of a dog and should be taken as a warning to stop what you are doing or to come no closer. In most cases this warning should not be taken lightly. Growling very often is the result of hitting the dog when he was young or delivering excessive or abusive corrections. Using the hands for punishment (hitting, slapping, pointing, etc.) helps to create a growler.

Growling can be the beginning of a dog turning on his master. It is important to understand that dogs never turn on their masters unless they have been abused in some way, and this applies to Dobermans and Shepherds. All too often you never know the other side of the story when you hear about a Doberman who turned on his master and attacked him. A puppy comes into the house and the owners, in their ignorance or frustration, slap the dog for every false move. After ten or twelve weeks of being hit, a conditioned reflex is created in the dog's brain and he flinches at every sudden movement. The dog grows up in fear and finally starts to fight back.

If a dog has grown up thinking of the human hand as an instrument of punishment, he will growl the minute a hand is used for anything to do with him. Some dogs will growl if you try to take something from their mouths or if you try to pet them.

Growling is also the result of spoiling the dog and never correcting him (in the proper way, of course) for anything. If he is allowed to get away with all manner of bad behavior, he is likely to growl when he finally is disciplined. From his perspective his owner is turning on him, so he growls in anger or defense. If his behavior is effective in getting things his way, he continues until he becomes a bully.

If the dog were still a puppy he could be taught with a firm corrective jerk and a stern "No." It is not so simple with a fully grown dog, however. It is important to understand why the dog is growling. If it's caused by you for any reason, punishment will only make matters worse. As a matter of fact, you will probably get bitten. If this problem has gone on for a year or two and you are terrorized by the dog, you have only two alternatives: call a professional trainer . . . or get rid of the dog.

DOG FIGHTING

Fighting usually happens between male dogs. It is sometimes so unpleasant that the joys of owning a dog are completely obscured. For those who own dogs in the city it is especially trying due to the large dog population. You find yourself avoiding the dog's walk or avoiding his romp in the park, for fear of meeting up with another dog and witnessing another fight. Your dog may have started fighting because he was attacked by another dog when he was very small. If so he will never like other male dogs. The best you can hope to do is control him when he is around other dogs. Another source of the problem from puppyhood is if he was allowed to attack a larger dog in play. The larger dog may tolerate his impish behavior and everyone may think it's cute, but if he becomes accustomed to challenging another dog he soon will be doing so on a permanent basis.

If your dog does get into a fight, there are a couple of ways to stop it. (However, never place your hand near the dog's face. In the heat of battle a dog doesn't know whom he's biting.) If the dog is on-leash, turn around and walk the other way, giving the dog a very hard pull. If the dog is not a Toy or not too big, pick him up off the ground by the leash. If he is choking he cannot do much of anything. If the dog is off the leash pull him up by the tail. Again, do this if the dog is not too big. If he is a short-tailed dog pick him up by his back legs. Use the corrective jerk as effectively as you can. Maintain the collar high on the dog's neck so that he will feel the full impact of the jerk. When he is about to engage in a fight with another dog give him a very hard corrective jerk. When the collar is low on his neck he hardly feels the tug of a correction. When all else fails, seek the services of a professional trainer.

THE NERVOUS DOG

The nervous dog reacts to ordinary situations differently from the average dog. If he gets excited he will wet. He is afraid of traffic, afraid of going outdoors, afraid of strangers, and afraid of other dogs. These high-strung dogs are very often the result of poor commercial breeding. But there are environmental situations that could also have caused such abnormal behavior. For example, if the dog has had several owners and was commanded in different ways each time, he may have developed a nervous temperament. The confusion leads to insecurity and an inability to please the current master. The result is a nervous dog. Very often the dog will acquire the inconsistent tendencies of his owner. Sometimes a nervous or neurotic dog reflects a nervous or neurotic master. Dogs are sometimes made nervous from traumatic experiences such as being too close to an auto backfire or a gunshot. If a dog was not taken outside the house for the first six months of his life a bad first experience could severely frighten him. Pampering the dog and making him overly dependent upon the owner can make him run away at the sight of a stranger. The problem is prevalent among the Toy breeds. The minute they leave the protection of the human "mother" they get the shakes, start to whine, and wet on the floor. Sometimes dogs resent the introduction of children into "their" house and become nervous. A totally dependent dog gets upset and nervous when a new child intrudes into the routine of the dog's life.

There is no fun in owning a nervous dog. Much of the pleasure that one usually has with a dog is completely missing. Some of these nervous problems can be solved if the dog is treated like a dog rather than a human child. It does not necessarily mean less attention, but a different kind of attention. Let the dog go out for frequent walks and meet other dogs. Do not hold him too much as if he were an infant. In general, do not use the dog as a substitute for a baby. In most cases of nervous dogs one should see a professional trainer.

OVERAGGRESSIVENESS

An overaggressive dog is not merely an exuberant or playful animal. His behavior is characterized by his ability to demonstrate to children, adults, or other dogs that he does not like them. The overaggressive dog will lunge, chase, push, growl, bark, dog-fight, or even bite to prove his point. Any negative, abnormal behavior falls into this category. It does no good to indulge in rationalizations about it. To say that the dog is perfectly behaved except if you get too close, or any other excuse like that, is to leave yourself open to much trouble.

If the dog were still a puppy any of the above-mentioned traits could be eliminated with a corrective jerk and a firm "No." If the dog was not corrected for this symptomatic behavior as a puppy then the result is an aggressive dog and that is not easy to cure. There are many reasons for abnormal behavior, both known and unknown, and the average dog owner is simply not equipped to deal with the problem. Sometimes a change of environmental conditions offers the best cure. But one must understand the nature of the dog's specific problem to make the proper change. Professional help must be sought.

THE SHY DOG

A shy dog is a variation of the nervous dog. Again, it can be due to poor commercial breeding. Or he may have been the runt of the litter and was bullied by the others. It is often unknown factors that create the shy dog. But no matter what the reason, he should be handled with *tender loving care*. If the dog is frightened of most things it will take a great deal of patience to cope with him. Few demands should be made on the dog and he should be showered with love and affection. Many dogs with this problem have responded to love and kindness. The problem must be coped with because shyness leads to nervousness which can turn the dog into a fear biter. Consult a professional trainer.

PART III

The Breeds

A Dictionary of Training

If you have recently purchased a dog, or if you are *about* to purchase a dog, this section will be of considerable help. Here, the training problems unique to the specific breeds are explored. It is obvious that a German Shepherd will pose a different set of problems from a Toy Poodle. It is exactly those differences that are dealt with in this portion of the book.

This part is divided into the six breed groupings as defined by the American Kennel Club. They are: Sporting Dogs, Hounds, Working Dogs, Terriers, Toys, and Non-sporting Dogs. Within these groupings, each breed is listed alphabetically and is dealt with as extensively as possible. Part III of *Good Dog, Bad Dog* is a dictionary of training problems indicative of the sixty-six breeds that are listed.

Each breed is discussed in terms of its Positive Characteristics, Negative Characteristics, and Specific Training Problems as a mature animal. It is a fair assumption that all puppy problems and solutions apply to every breed. This information will offer some aid in knowing what to expect from the dog of your choice. It is important to understand why you prefer one breed over another. Some people want a dog for protection. Others want a family pet, a gift for children or an elderly couple, relief from loneliness, or a friend and companion. To anyone shopping for an animal, it is suggested that he familiarize himself with the many breeds available. Each breed fulfills many combinations of needs. To know about each breed and understand what you personally want from a dog helps you make the correct choice. For those who have already brought a dog into their homes, this section will give them a clear idea of what to expect from it.

The following dictionary of training is based on information learned the hard way. It represents a synthesis of the first-hand experience that coauthor Matthew Margolis has gained in his capacity as owner-operator of the National Institute of Dog Training, Inc. He has trained well over five thousand dogs representing every breed listed in this section. Where a breed has been omitted, it is simply because he has had too little experience with it. The dogs he has trained have come from every conceivable source. Many have been among the most expensive dogs from the most exclusive kennels. Others have come from pet shops, adoption agencies, the ASPCA, private kennels, commercial kennels, and even home litters.

It stands to reason that not all specimens of each breed will be alike. But when training hundreds of dogs from any one particular breed, certain behavioral patterns become apparent. These patterns formulate the basis for Mr. Margolis's evaluations.

While not attempting to upgrade one breed at the expense of another, it is all too clear that some breeds are more responsive to training than others; some are more willing to please; some are more independent. Mr. Margolis has attempted to give a fair appraisal of each dog's temperament. It is all based on his personal experience and may contradict the legitimate experiences of any number of individual dog owners. But it is asked that one consider the source of the dog. A specific dog may come from a superior bloodline, and that certainly would be a factor in any contradiction. The converse of this also holds true. Some dogs are the poor result of too much inbreeding, even though they are of a well-tempered breed. The appraisals offered here have been determined by experience with a cross-section of dogs from each breed. It is felt that this part can help the prospective dog owner anticipate what to expect from the breed of his choice.

Dogs differ in personality and behavior as do people. For every person there is a dog to match his personality, needs, and desires. What is a negative factor for one person could very well be a positive factor for another. Do not turn a jaundiced eye on a breed that has a long list of negative characteristics. Those traits that are considered negative may be the very traits that would endear the dog to you and thus afford fifteen years of pleasure and gratification. All dogs are good guys until proven otherwise.

Group I

Sporting Dogs

———◆———

POINTER, GERMAN SHORTHAIRED

Positive characteristics. Members of this breed are very lovable and capable of giving great warmth and affection. They are friendly and exceptionally good with children. Powerful dogs such as these are very good in the country because they have a great desire to run and need a great deal of exercise. If they are kept in the country and get the proper amount of exercise they will be very responsive to training. They make excellent companions.

bined with an accumulation of pent-up energy, results in total
Negative characteristics. German Shorthaired Pointers are very high-strung animals. They are nervous, excitable dogs. Unless they are given sufficient daily exercise, it is difficult to keep them in an apartment. Their desire to jump, com-

chaos. They will jump on furniture, jump on people, steal food from the table, get into the garbage, and chew anything, whether it's nailed down or not.

These are stubborn dogs with very strong wills. If the owner is not very firm, his animal will be a constant source of trouble. These dogs require a great deal of authority. If the owner spoils the dog he will regret it for the rest of the dog's life. These Pointers must be trained as soon as possible. If the owner waits the customary year to begin training it may be too late. Strict training should begin after the third month.

Specific training problems. Use a good strong choke collar and a six-foot leash. When executing a corrective jerk be certain the leash does not get caught in the dog's long, flapping ears. It can cause him great pain and make him aggressive.

Because these are hunting dogs, they are not as attentive as other breeds. They are constantly indulging their keen senses of smell and must be forced to pay attention to commands. After the dog obeys a command, wait four seconds to give him praise, and do not be too exuberant. In the "Heel," try to keep their attention by talking to them. The more you capture their attention the more responsive they will be.

These dogs should be worked exceptionally hard in the "Stay," since they are not too good at it and will remain in "Stay" for only a short time. It is especially important in the city where there are so many distractions to lead them into trouble or danger.

They should never be allowed off-leash in the city. Their greatest difficulty is in the command "Come When Called."

Because these are hunting dogs, they must be made to obey absolutely. The more obedience training they are given the more responsive they will be in the city. One of the best ways to keep them out of mischief indoors is to give them a place that is exclusively their own in the apartment or house. (See Chapter 12, "Go to Your Place.")

Hunting dogs must be obedience-trained more vigorously than other breeds if they are going to share a house or an apartment with a family. Vigorous obedience training at an early age is the key to enjoying the many pleasant aspects of this breed.

RETRIEVER, GOLDEN

Positive characteristics. Golden Retrievers are a very friendly breed. They are considered by many to be the most ideal pets because of their lovable behavior. They are affectionate, warm, and very good with children. These dogs have few grooming requirements and are good in either apartment or house. As a breed they are extremely responsive to training and execute commands with great ease. For this reason they are used frequently as Seeing Eye Dogs.

Negative characteristics. Because they are hunting dogs, their minds stray from time to time, making them inattentive. Occasionally they are nervous, but this can be caused by inbreeding. It is not true of the entire breed. If possible, the prospective owner should examine the dam and the sire for nervousness.

Although these are not stubborn dogs, they do take advantage of the owner when they can. They must be told what to do and made to obey each command.

Specific training problems. When you execute a corrective jerk, be certain that the leash does not get caught in the dog's long, flapping ears. It can cause him great pain and make him aggressive.

After the dog obeys a command, wait two seconds to give him praise and do not be too exuberant. In almost all the basic commands Golden Retrievers have a tendency to inch up after obeying. That is an infraction of the rules, and if they are allowed to get away with it they will become less and less responsive. When giving the "Sit" make sure they "Stay" for a short period of time without moving. When executing the "Heel" do not let them walk ahead. The same applies to the "Down" and the "Down-Stay." "Come When Called" may be a problem in the city. Remember, they are hunters. Do not give this command in the city without a leash. It is dangerous.

One of the best ways to keep these dogs out of mischief is to give them a place that is exclusively their own in the apartment or house. (See Chapter 12, "Go to Your Place.")

Hunting breeds are not usually considered city dogs. However, because of their beauty and many other attributes they are desired by many urban dwellers. It is therefore recommended in that case that an intense training program be initiated as soon as possible.

RETRIEVER, LABRADOR

Positive characteristics. Because of their keen hunting instincts, these dogs are generally considered better for the country. They adjust perfectly to family life and are very tolerant and patient with children. Labradors are being used more and more as Seeing Eye Dogs for the blind, and that speaks highly of their ability to be trained. That ability is good for all types of training, including basic obedience and guard work. Because they respond to human beings so well, they can be taught much more readily than many other breeds.

They are one of the most intelligent of the breeds and enjoy a long life span.

Negative characteristics. Dogs of this breed require a great deal of exercise, which can be a problem for the ones who live in apartments. They would have to be exercised at least two or three times a week to make up for the lack of country life. Like all hunting breeds, Labradors are not ideal for the elderly. They are too energetic and physically demanding and they require a firm, strong hand.

Specific training problems. When executing the corrective jerk, be certain the leash does not get caught in the dog's long, flapping ears. It can cause him great pain and make him aggressive.

Be certain your dog obeys all commands the first time with no delays, otherwise he will take advantage of you and only obey when he feels like it. Make great demands of the dog and enforce all commands. Give immediate praise after a command is obeyed. Be exuberant. Do not allow him off-leash in the city.

Obedience training must be initiated in puppyhood to avoid the characteristic mischief a Labrador Retriever can create in an apartment situation.

Labrador Retrievers are usually not aggressive. However, many become that way after being hit by their owners with either a hand or a rolled-up newspaper. The most good-natured dog has his turning point and will only take so much hitting. This breed is one of the most tolerant and your Labrador will remain so if he is not physically abused. One of the best ways to keep him out of mischief is to give him a place that is exclusively his own in the apartment or house. (See Chapter 12, "Go to Your Place.")

SETTER, ENGLISH

Positive characteristics. English Setters are easygoing to the point of lethargy. Unlike most other hunting breeds, they are ideally suited to elderly people because of their sedate temperaments. They adjust to apartment life very well. These dogs are wonderful with children. In fact they are so gentle they will let you do almost anything to them without ever complaining or acting aggressive.

Negative characteristics. They are very stubborn, strong-willed, and difficult to housebreak. And they can develop destructive chewing problems if left alone. But their stubbornness takes the form of resistance rather than uncontrollable obstinacy. Instead of pulling on a leash, they simply will not walk. Instead of going into "Sit," they will lie down. When called they will come slowly instead of the immediate response that a command demands.

Specific training problems. The basic obedience commands must be handled with great diligence, more so than with other breeds. Extra patience is required and also extra firmness. After a command is obeyed, give immediate praise and be very exuberant.

Setters must be made to obey each command. For example, if your dog refuses to "Heel," you might go so far as to get on the ground and call him to you, backing up a little as he comes, all the while praising him and giving him confidence. This gets the dog moving but at the same time gives him the opportunity to feel at ease about it. Strongarm tactics with this breed will bring nothing but disappointment.

The "Down" and "Down-Stay" will be very difficult to teach. The dog will fight you every inch of the way. In this case the training sessions should be broken up into shorter sessions and spread over a longer period of time.

They do not respond quickly to "Come When Called." With most Setters a slow response is to be expected. These dogs will rebel at browbeating. Therefore, they should be trained as puppies while they are still carefree, playful, and energetic. One of the best ways to keep them out of mischief is to give them a place that is exclusively their own in the apartment or house. (See Chapter 12, "Go to Your Place.")

There are many years of rewarding pleasure ahead if the city dweller begins an obedience program when this member of the hunting breeds is a puppy.

SETTER, GORDON

Positive characteristics. These gentle, friendly dogs are very good with children. Their need to run and exercise in open spaces makes them ideal country dogs. For the connoisseur or fancier, they are special, uncommon, stylish, almost regal-looking. This intelligent breed, with its handsome black and tan coat, has the bearing of strength and great dignity.

Negative characteristics. Gordon Setters are stubborn. One of the reasons they are not seen in the city very often is the difficulty they have adjusting to apartment life. Although they are not the largest breed, they behave as though they were and require a firm, strong hand from their masters.

Specific training problems. Exercise care in administering the corrective jerk. Their long ears can get caught in the choke collar and leash.

Housebreaking should begin immediately. Gordon Setters, like most other hunting breeds, have a hard time with housebreaking. Paper training should never be started and then abandoned for housebreaking. It is difficult for them to un-learn one thing and adjust to something new.

In administering corrections, the first jerk should be quite firm rather than wasting five or six easy jerks. The more you jerk the more they will rebel. One hard jerk will be enough to let them know who's boss. Give immediate praise after a command is obeyed and be very exuberant.

Do not let them off-leash in the city. Like other hunting dogs they become distracted with squirrels, pigeons, and other animals and refuse to "Come When Called." Their response to this command is unreliable even with a leash.

In an apartment, Gordons manifest many annoying problems such as chewing, jumping on furniture, going into garbage, etc., which is precisely why an early start with obedience training is important. Problems that arise in puppyhood are difficult to end as the dog matures. It is important to mention that this breed should never be fed from the table. Once you start you will have a canine dinner guest for the rest of his life and he can be a large nuisance. One of the best ways to keep him out of mischief is to give him a place that is exclusively his own in the apartment or house. (See Chapter 12, "Go to Your Place.")

If the Gordon Setter is to be enjoyed as a pet rather than as the hunter he was meant to be, then it is definitely advisable to begin obedience training at an early age. Three months old is not too soon.

SETTER, IRISH

Postive characteristics. Temperamentally, these dogs are affectionate and loving, gentle and sweet-natured. Excellent hunters, they are ideal country residents. Irish Setters are easy to groom, have good appetites, and adjust to family life very well.

Negative characteristics. They are very stubborn dogs. Their strong wills require firmness in all training matters. It is important to administer strong corrections when they ignore commands, otherwise they tend to do as they please. Obviously, they are not convenient for elderly people. Training must begin as early as possible to avoid adult problems that begin in puppyhood. If these dogs are not trained properly they can literally ruin an apartment. It starts with messing in the middle of a good carpet and ends with chewing expensive furniture to sawdust. However, they can adjust to apartment life if given an obedience course from the minute they first enter the household.

Specific training problems. Irish Setters have extremely long ears which can get caught in the leash and choke collar when a corrective jerk is administered. So be cautious. Wait three or four seconds after the dog obeys a command to give him praise and do not be too exuberant.

Setters have difficulty with housebreaking. This part of their training will not be easy. Every aspect outlined in the housebreaking chapter should be applied with diligence, i.e., diet, walks, etc. They must be watched carefully until the housebreaking is completed.

The correction "No" does not work effectively unless they have come to associate it with a firm corrective jerk. Throughout most of the training period the corrective jerk should be administered firmly but not excessively. Too many corrections will make the dog jerk shy. Next to housebreaking, walking in "Heel" is their biggest problem. One minute they will walk in perfect "Heel" and the next minute jerk your arm out running to play with another dog. They are very easily distracted and use force to get what they want. It is important that heeling be strictly enforced. Never allow one infraction of this rule without administering a corrective jerk.

Never allow this breed off-leash in the city. Irish Setters have been known to run off and never return. City life imposes a limitation on much-needed exercise and creates a great deal of pent-up energy that can be destructive. For this reason alone these dogs should not be allowed off-leash in the city. One of the best ways to keep them out of mischief indoors is to give them a place that is exclusively their own in the apartment or house (See Chapter 12, "Go to Your Place.")

SPANIEL, COCKER

Positive characteristics. Cocker Spaniels are sturdy animals, capable of taking strong correction. If trained at an early age, they will respond quickly to any command they have been taught. They will "Heel" perfectly and lie down on command almost the instant it is given. They are excellent with children and adapt to apartment life very well. Because they are not very large dogs they do not require too much exercise. Because they are not too active or rambunctious they can be handled easily by elderly people. They are ideal for people who want an in-between dog.

Negative characteristics. Due to excessive inbreeding many Cocker Spaniels have become aggressive. In addition, if they are hit they will become growlers, biters, dog fighters, and generally hostile. It is not because of the breed but rather the inbreeding. Spaniels have appeared in recorded English history as far back as the twelfth century and have developed a large popularity in the United States. The Cocker Spaniel is a subdivision of the land Spaniel and is identified as the smaller of the Spaniels, which accounts for its great popularity in this country. It is this popularity that has led to its massive inbreeding, much to the detriment of the breed. The best advice is to exercise caution and selectivity before purchasing one. Investigate the puppy's pedigree. If possible, examine his parents; ask a lot of questions. Try to evaluate the temperament of his progenitors. You should do all this because only a well-bred specimen will respond favorably to training.

Specific training problems. Cocker Spaniels are hunters and have the same problems as the other hunting breeds. Avoid entangling their long ears in the choke collar and leash when administering the corrective jerk.

These mischievous dogs will jump on furniture, take food from the table, jump on people, etc. These are problems that must be solved in puppyhood or they will remain throughout the life of the dog. If you allow the puppy to sit on your lap he will eventually jump up on people. If you let him sleep on the bed he will jump on the furniture.

When giving Cocker Spaniels commands, make sure they are forced to respond. If you give in at the beginning they can never be relied upon to obey. Wait two seconds after the dog obeys a command to give him praise, and be exuberant. "Go to Your Place" is very useful for Cockers because they tend to get into mischief, and this will give you a tool for control. "Down-Stay" is useful, too. "Down-Stay" will also help in the car. They don't travel well as a rule. Excitement or nervousness makes them jump from seat to seat; "Down-Stay" makes them stop.

Hitting this breed can cause more behavioral damage than with other breeds. The result will be a nasty animal. House-breaking is usually when hitting begins, and with Cocker Spaniels that's the beginning of an aggressive temperament. Most of the negative characteristics can be avoided if you exercise self-control and avoid hitting or terrorizing the dog in any way.

Cocker Spaniels are hunters and as such are best in the kennel of an estate. However, if yours is a house pet he must be obedience-trained as a puppy so that you may both enjoy fifteen years of pleasant relations.

SPANIEL, ENGLISH SPRINGER

Positive characteristics. Springer Spaniels are good city dogs and good country dogs. They make excellent pets for children and elderly people. They adjust well to apartment life, are easy to get along with, are well suited to training, and adapt easily to most situations. Beauty and utility are combined in this even-tempered breed.

Negative characteristics. Recently Springer Spaniels have developed medical problems such as eczema and general skin irritations. A close scrutiny of the individual dog's bloodlines should be made before purchase.

Specific training problems. Like all hunting dogs, they are difficult to housebreak. Housebreaking should begin as soon as possible.

Be careful of the dog's long ears when administering the corrective jerk. Do not catch them in the choke collar and leash. Give immediate praise after a command is obeyed and be exuberant.

During all training, but specifically the "Heel," be alert to their tendency to wander away and become distracted by other animals, as is characteristic of all hunting dogs. If you bear down on the "Heel," you will not have problems with the other commands. "Go to Your Place" is important for this breed. "Down-Stay" is another important command. These commands give you tools for greater control and make it easier for the dog to please you.

Vigorous obedience training at an early age is the key to enjoying the many pleasant aspects of this breed.

VIZSLA

Positive characteristics. These natives of Hungary are very good with children. They make wonderful house pets and are also good in the country. They adapt very well to apartment life. Appetite is never a problem (except during illness) and their life span is from twelve to fifteen years. This short-coated breed requires very little grooming. Because of their short coats they do not shed very much. Sweet-natured and affectionate, the Vizsla is well suited to training and responds without too much correction.

Negative characteristics. Like other hunting breeds, they are stubborn. Occasionally, due to poor breeding, they develop a problem of nervous wetting. Inbreeding has created many nervous Vizslas. Although they are good apartment dogs, there is one qualification. If training does not begin at a very young age they develop chewing problems and cause much destruction. Even a trained Vizsla will chew up an apartment if he is not exercised regularly. Chewing is caused by confinement. Exercise combined with obedience training is the only answer.

Specific training problems. Administering the corrective jerk is critical with this breed. Their ears are very long and get tangled in the choke collar and leash, which can be very painful for the animal. Be careful. Wait four seconds after the dog obeys a command to give him praise and do not be too exuberant.

Vizslas are difficult to housebreak. Never paper train them if you plan to switch to housebreaking later on. The change-over is almost impossible for them. Do not correct a puppy if he fails to use the paper when messing indoors. Simply confine him to one small area, as explained in the paper-training chapter.

These are very excitable animals and will cross in front of you or jump on you when learning to "Heel." Emphasize the "Heel" and do not let them pull you. They will respond to an authoritative voice. Because they crave affection in large doses, they will work very hard to please you. The trick is to know when to withhold the affection and when to give it as a reward for responding properly to a command.

With this breed emphasize the "Sit-Stay" and "Down-Stay." Vizslas tend to demand great attention from anyone who enters the house. They also like to run out the door the minute it is opened. By emphasizing the "Stay" command, you will be able to maintain a greater control over them. "Go to Your Place" is another important command.

The plains of Hungary are the natural habitat of this great hunting breed. Keeping one as a house pet demands that obedience training begin at a very early age if the dog is to live compatibly in a domestic situation.

WEIMARANER

Positive characteristics. There is a great ambivalence in most Weimaraner owners. They are stubbornly loyal and abso-

lutely devoted to these "Gray Ghosts," despite the many
difficulties involved in owning one.

Weimaraners are excellent companions for children. They
have a tremendous tolerance for the rough-and-tumble treatment usually meted out by small children. They will endure
a child's eye-gouging, ear-pulling, back-sitting, and tail-
yanking. Because of their need for exercise, they will run a
great deal and can be a joy to behold in the country. The more
exercise they get the better they are to live with.

These German hunting dogs are strong and lively and can
be used effectively for guard work. They can be trained to
growl, bark, or bite on command. Protective of their families
by nature, they adapt to this work very well. However, guard
work can only be accomplished with expert training. Because
of their even temperament, they can be trained to bite one
minute and lick the victim's face the next. A short-coated
breed, they require very little grooming and do not shed.

Negative characteristics. Weimaraners embody all the negative characteristics of the hunting breeds. They are stubborn
and self-willed and try to get away with everything possible.
At times they do not obey commands. They will wander off
if given the chance. If their pent-up energy is not released
in some positive form of exercise, they are capable of destroying entire apartments.

Once they understand that the master does not operate
with great authority, they will take large liberties such as
pulling him down the street. Such liberties are usually taken
with women owners. Because Weimaraners are so lovable,
women find it hard to avoid mothering them.

Weimaraners are dog fighters. They are not recommended
for elderly people. They require a firm, strong hand and will
respond to nothing else. Chewing problems are common in
this breed. They are notorious for destroying, in some instances, thousands of dollars' worth of furniture and personal
posessions. Their chewing will try every ounce of patience
you possess, and if one does not possess great patience it can
be a difficult struggle to train them. It is a situation with built-
in failure. Unless these dogs are forced to respond to obedience training through patience and authority, they will be
miserable to own.

Specific training problems. Their long ears get tangled in the
choke collar and leash. Be cautious when administering the

corrective jerk. It is critical, because they require a very firm correction. Without firm correction they will take advantage of the owner and make a simple walk a living nightmare. They need to be handled with authority. These dogs will always test their owners to determine how much they can get away with. When administering a firm corrective jerk, do not be frightened if they whine and scream like babies. Even though you are stared at by strangers and thought to be murdering your dog, do not be fooled by this ploy. They are not hurt. Continue to deliver firm corrections, especially when teaching the "Heel." The "Sit-Stay" and "Down-Stay" will be very useful commands when control is needed, as it often is. Wait five seconds after the dog obeys a command to give him praise, and praise him in a subdued tone of voice.

They can be pests, demanding attention and affection when the situation does not call for it. That's when the "Stay" commands are very handy. Weimaraners should never be taken off-leash in the city. They are completely untrustworthy and will chase the first animal they see, which could cause a bad accident.

Like other hunting breeds, they are difficult to housebreak. They must be watched carefully. The housebreaking should begin as soon as possible. One of the best ways to keep members of this breed out of mischief is to give them a place that is exclusively their own in the apartment or house. (See Chapter 12, "Go to Your Place.")

Owners of this breed are legion in declaring their great pleasure and love in living with them. Weimaraners can be tolerable house pets only if they are trained at a very early age.

AFGHAN HOUND

Positive characteristics. Many people consider these dogs beautiful in appearance and regal in manner. It is the quality of elegance that has made them so popular. There is great snob appeal connected with the Afghan. Their history is documented as far back as 3000 B.C., where they were seen on the Sinai Peninsula between Suez and Aqaba. Historically this breed has been identified with royalty, which would account for the ostentatious attitude of many Afghan owners. During the great days of the British Empire, Afghans were used for hunting the leopard. Despite their haughty, delicate look, they have been used for centuries as first-rate hunters in the mountainous regions of Afghanistan. In the United States these aristocratic hunters have been used primarily as ornamentation. If you enjoy fussing and primping, this is the breed for you. Their long, silken fur requires daily attention.

Negative characteristics. These are stubborn dogs and consequently offer much resistance to training. Although some *former* owners consider them stupid, it's not true. They merely lack a desire to please and manifest an unwillingness to learn. It is extremely hard to train them. Where most breeds can begin training after they reach twelve weeks, Afghans will not respond to training until they are at least six or seven months old. By that time, housebreaking becomes extremely difficult. Housebreaking should begin early. Many owners have experienced some degree of successful training.

The Afghan's tolerance for children is low and they are not ideally suited for apartment living. They can be aggressive bullies.

Specific training problems. Patience is absolutely essential. These dogs cannot be treated like any other breed. You must take your time throughout the training period. Give immediate praise after the dog obeys a command and be very exuberant.

Do not use a metal choke collar because it will ruin their silken fur. Either a leather or nylon choke collar is suggested. Do not work this breed for long periods, especially when teaching the "Heel" and the "Sit." Break up the training periods so there are more sessions for shorter periods of time.

Unless you are home a great deal and can walk them five or six times a day, you are going to have a terrible time housebreaking them. They must be caught in the act of messing indoors before they can be taught to understand what you expect.

Members of this breed do not want to be left alone. They can be very destructive and have been known to chew their way through large quantities of valuable furniture and personal possessions. Because of their stubbornness you will have to be extremely firm teaching the "Down" and "Down-Stay." Despite their great beauty and elegance, the training period will be a battle of wills between master and dog.

BASENJI

Positive characteristics. Basenjis are very well-tempered, loving, and affectionate animals. They are highly individualistic dogs who tend to attach themselves devotedly and loyally to one person. Adapting to city life very well, they make excellent apartment dogs. These are quiet dogs that never bark. Their short coats require very little grooming. They are responsive to training and indicate a willingness to please. Results are much greater if training begins at a young age. These enjoyable animals are distinguished by their almost human-looking faces. They are good with children and can take the rigors of a child's play. Because they are not a nervous breed, they can be left alone for many hours and still maintain their even temperaments.

Negative characteristics. Since they are stubborn dogs, we do not recommend them for elderly people. Once they decide to do something you will have to match their obstinacy with your firm authority every inch of the way. Because they are "barkless" they make poor guard dogs.

Specific training problems. Because of their stubbornness be sure to give each command properly. Be very firm and let them know who is boss. Give immediate praise after the dog obeys a command and be very exuberant. You should not have many training problems with this breed.

BASSET HOUND

Positive characteristics. Bassets are very good with children and make excellent house pets. Because they are not very active, they never run wild through the house. One could say there is an absence of overexcitement. Their lethargic demeanor joined with their droopy face are considered part of their charm. This breed has come into its own since advertising agencies discovered their amusing appeal and started making salesmen out of them on TV commercials. They are truly ideal apartment pets. They enjoy a normal life span (twelve to fifteen years) and have gentle, sweet temperaments. Bassets respond very well to training, even past the training period of the average dog.

Negative characteristics. They have very few negative traits. Housebreaking is sometimes a problem, but even that can be overcome if training begins early. Many Bassets are picky eaters.

Specific training problems. Pay attention to their long, floppy ears when administering the corrective jerk. They sometimes tangle in the choke collar and leash. It is very painful. In some cases the choke collar is not recommended. Whether or not to use it would be determined by the temperament of the dog.

In "Heel" your dog is going to have difficulty keeping up with you. Bassets walk much more slowly than other breeds and have trouble keeping up a brisk pace. It also takes them longer to go into the "Sit" than other breeds. You should make allowances. The "Stay" will be the easiest command for them. Maybe it's because they don't like getting up too often.

They respond more to praise and affection than correction. Give immediate praise when the dog obeys a command and be very exuberant. It is recommended that the corrective jerk be administered gently and not too often. You will get better results from a loving, gentle tone than from a firm discipline. The "Down" and "Come When Called" are good commands for them. These lovable animals are endearing and can make training sessions a delightful experience. Most professional trainers enjoy working with Basset Hounds.

BEAGLE

Positive characteristics. Beagles adjust well to apartment life or country life. These sweet little dogs look like stuffed toys and are very good with children. They are usually gentle, playful, and even tempered. They are hardy eaters with a good life span (twelve to fifteen years) and have a short coat that requires a minimum of grooming.

Negative characteristics. Because this is a stubborn breed, many owners try to use force to get their way. The consequences are many. Most important is that the dogs become aggressive and nasty if mistreated. They have been known to turn on their masters, bite children, growl, and get into dog fights. Much of this can be avoided if one exercises patience and a minimum of discipline. Force will only bring out the worst in them. The key to their training is to maintain an attitude of teaching as opposed to one of harsh discipline.

Specific training problems. Start training early to avoid the negative aspects described above. Even though they are stubborn, they are easy to teach at a young age. Watch their ears in administering the corrective jerk. A metal choke collar is not recommended if you are going to teach a puppy. Use nylon or leather. An older Beagle can tolerate a very fine metal choke collar.

Be firm but not harsh. Most of the basic commands will be relatively easy to teach. However, they offer resistance to the "Down." Give immediate praise when the dog obeys a command and be very exuberant.

When training these dogs, select a location that offers few,

if any, distractions. You must command their attention more
than the average breed.

BLACK AND TAN COONHOUND

Positive characteristics. Black and Tans are affectionate.
They enjoy the country much more than the city. They are
very responsive to training and have excellent appetites.

Negative characteristics. These dogs are not well suited to
city life. Like many of the hound breeds, they do not adapt
well to the restrictions of a small apartment. You must be
on top of them all the time. Their attention span in the city
is poor, owing to their inclination to wander, both mentally
and physically.

Specific training problems. As is true of many hounds, Black
and Tans abound in energy and require a great deal of exercise. There is nothing like a good long run to make them more
responsive to training. A good daily exercise program will
help them work off their nervous energy and make them
easier to live with in the city.

   Wait two seconds after the dog obeys a command to give
him praise, and do not be too exuberant.

BORZOI *(Russian Wolfhound)*

Positive characteristics. These are marvelous, elegant-looking
dogs. Thin and lanky, they move with great speed and dash.
Many city dwellers consider them status symbols and very
chic to own. Borzois are regal in stature and appeal to very
special types. In most instances, they are purchased for reasons of ornamentation or, perhaps, ostentation. These tall
beauties are easygoing, capable of sitting outside a fancy shop
for many hours, and staying put in the position in which they
were placed. Because they are not too active, they make excellent city pets. They are quiet, dignified animals who are
very willing to please. In their natural habitat Borzois are
hunters, and for that reason are very well suited to country
living like most of the sporting dogs.

Negative characteristics. Borzois are not especially suited to children. They do not respond well to rough treatment. Aloof animals, like cats, they neither ask for nor give much affection. People who own Borzois are often of the same temperament.

Specific training problems. One need not administer too many firm corrections. Give immediate praise when the dog obeys a command and be extremely exuberant. Giving them a great deal of praise whenever they respond properly will get better results than overcorrection.

Be gentle with the leash because they resist constant jerking. Show them what to do and they will do it.

DACHSHUND
(Smooth, Longhaired, Wirehaired)

Positive characteristics. These dogs are among the most even-tempered animals in existence. They are very good with children, and especially good with elderly people. Dachshunds, no matter what kind, are ideally suited to apartment living. Their eating habits are good and they live a long time. They require very little grooming. Very few people can resist their frisky, gentle manner.

Negative characteristics. Dachshunds are one of those breeds that have great difficulty making the transition from paper training to housebreaking. If you begin with paper training then you should stay with that technique. If, ultimately, you want the dog to go outside, then begin housebreaking from the start.

Specific training problems. Do not use any type of choke collar. Dachshunds have tender necks and can be hurt very easily, which is true of most small breeds. An ordinary leather collar will do the job.

If you begin training them as young as three months old, then work slowly. They need a lot of praise and affection. Wait one second after the dog obeys a command to give him praise and use an exuberant tone of voice. Do not use "No" too often. Small dogs can be frightened very easily, causing behavioral complications that are not inherent to their natures.

Exercise patience when teaching the "Sit." Because of the irregular shape of their bodies, it takes them longer to sit properly. They will be very slow getting into position. They also have trouble heeling properly. Their legs are very short, so they walk slower than the average dog. Consequently, they will not be able to keep up if you walk too quickly. You will probably have more problems with them lagging behind than pulling ahead.

Be patient reaching the "Stay" and the "Down." They are eager to please, but it takes them longer to respond to a new command than is usual with other dogs. They need a lot of praise. Dachshunds respond to "Come When Called" better than most commands, owing to their great desire for affection. Be sure to give them a lot of praise when they respond to this command.

GREYHOUND

Positive characteristics. It is the look and the elegance of the Greyhound that make them so appealing. Greyhound owners take great pleasure mentioning that this breed is the fastest in the world. Outside the racetrack they are not too common, which is another source of pride for the Greyhound owner. Their truly distinctive gait gives them an aristocratic air. They prance while they take their daily constitutional. That agility allows them to respond to commands very quickly. They adapt to country life best because there is an absence of noise and distraction. They are much more responsive when it's peaceful and quiet.

Negative characteristics. These timid, high-strung animals are not suitable for elderly people or children. They are a nervous breed and do not fare well in the city with its traffic noises, etc. Because of their high spirits, they do not make the ideal family dog. They are simply too nervous.

Specific training problems. Training should begin quite early in the dog's life. Gentleness is required. They cannot be jolted with too many firm corrections; they are too high strung for that. The best way to train this breed is to show them what to do and give them a good reason for doing it. They cannot take constant harassments such as "No," "Bad dog," and "Shame." Give immediate praise when the dog obeys a command and be exuberant. Do not expect the same kind of response that you would get from a German Shepherd or even a Beagle. They are highly excitable animals and require tender loving care.

IRISH WOLFHOUND

Positive characteristics. Rugged, playful, and protective, Irish Wolfhounds are very good with children and make ideal house pets. They are at their best in the country where they can run and play hard. It is difficult to resist their sweet, gentle natures and affectionate personalities. In the city they are lethargic for the most part and sleep a great deal, adjusting to apartment life quite easily. Their wiry coats require a minimum of grooming.

Negative characteristics. The very size of these dogs can discourage the city dweller from owning one. They are among the largest dogs in existence and require a great deal of food, so if economy is a consideration then you should think twice before buying one.

Specific training problems. Irish Wolfhounds require a very firm hand. Because they are so large, you cannot equivocate or back down from a command. If they get out of hand it could lead to serious problems. It would be impossible to handle a 34-inch, 175-pound Irish Wolfhound that suddenly became aggressive. That is why early training is absolutely necessary. Although this breed responds well to training, it does so at a slower pace than others. Irish Wolfhounds take a little longer to "Sit" and will lope to you on "Come When Called" rather than run swiftly.

If the dog is ever to be handled by a woman, it is essential that training take place while the dog is still small and manageable. Firmness is important. When using the corrective jerk, deliver it with great firmness. If you emphasize the "No" simultaneously, you will eventually be able to achieve the same corrective results without the jerk. The vocal correction will suffice.

Give immediate praise when the dog obeys a command and be exuberant.

NORWEGIAN ELKHOUND

Positive characteristics. Because they are inclined to bark a great deal, these animals are very good watchdogs. They love the roughhouse play of children and make excellent house pets in both city and country. They have good appetites, live between twelve and fifteen years, and are even tempered.

Negative characteristics. Norwegian Elkhounds shed profusely and must be brushed often to avoid clumps of fur on the furniture and floor. These excitable dogs run and play very hard and consequently are not recommended for elderly people. They are very stubborn and require a firm hand to control their tendency to take advantage of owners, especially those owners who allow them to get away with the slightest disobedience. If they are hit they will become aggressive.

Specific training problems. They respond very well to training. Housebreaking will offer few problems. However, if left alone, frequently they will develop chewing problems or will chase around the apartment doing damage. Strenuous exercise before leaving these high-spirited dogs alone may help.

Teaching them the proper commands will not be difficult. Authority and firmness should be the rule. Give immediate praise when the dog obeys a command and be exuberant.

RHODESIAN RIDGEBACK

Positive characteristics. Members of this large, powerful breed function very well in guard work. They are very tough and make excellent guard dogs. They are aggressive, but not in a vicious sense.

Ridgebacks are very intelligent dogs. They play and exercise hard, they are well suited to either the country or the city, and their short coats require minimal grooming.

Negative characteristics. These dogs are very self-willed and are definitely not for elderly people. It takes a very strong, firm individual to command them. Women, as a rule, have a difficult time handling these dogs. They take advantage of any owner who does not enforce discipline or allows poor response to each command. They can be very stubborn when they want to be.

Specific training problems. Because these are extremely stubborn dogs, you must exercise patience when teaching the basic obedience commands. However, you must make them obey every command given. Once they have been trained, do not allow them to disobey. Firm corrections are the only way to achieve success. They must be made to obey the first time, every time. Give immediate praise when the dog obeys a command and be exuberant.

When they walk, they must be made to walk by your side, rather than pull ahead as they tend to do. Ridgebacks are aggressive toward other dogs. This problem must be dealt with the minute it happens. (See Chapter 15, "Problem Dogs.") The basic obedience course will help. The key to their training is complete control at all times.

SALUKI

Positive characteristics. Considering their size, Salukis are good with elderly people. They are even-tempered animals and make excellent house pets in the city or country. These are very quiet, exotic dogs.

Negative characteristics. Because they are independent and aloof, they are not good family dogs. They usually appeal more to rugged individuals who lead rather singular lives. These dogs are not extroverted and, consequently, appeal to a few special types of people. It is hard for the average family to relate to this exclusive, private type of animal.

Specific training problems. Salukis respond to training, but not as well as other breeds because they are nervous and high strung. Noises make them skittish. It is not advisable to train them near busy streets or noisy environments. A peaceful country setting is the optimum training place. Because of

their nervousness, you must reassure them with affection and
praise whenever they respond properly. Give immediate
praise when the dog obeys a command and be exuberant.
Do not hold back.

WHIPPET

Positive characteristics. These truly are racing dogs much like
the Greyhound, only smaller. They are affectionate, intelligent animals capable of running thirty-five miles an hour.
Although they are geared for high-speed racing, they make
very good house pets. They will sit indoors in a quiet, graceful
manner and add dignity and decor to any room. Because they
bark at strangers, they make good watchdogs. However, they
are gentle in nature.

Negative characteristics. Whippets are fragile. They are very
sensitive to loud noises and get skittish on the street. They
are not recommended for children. These delicate creatures
are not outgoing and are not demonstrative in a family
situation.

Specific training problems. It is almost impossible to teach
them commands while outdoors. The outdoor noises are too
frightening for them. They must be trained indoors, with
no distraction. Be sure these dogs have been taught to obey
each command before trying them outside.
   Do not use a metal choke collar. We suggest a nylon or
leather choke, and at that you should not be too hard with
your corrections. Give immediate praise when the dog obeys
a command and be exuberant. Training will require patience.
If you are too hard on this breed they will not trust you and
will become very nervous. Their problem is that they are
babied too much and often not allowed outside, which results
in a very nervous, frightened dog. It is advisable to take them
outside as small puppies and get them used to strange noises.

Group III
Working Dogs

———◆———

ALASKAN MALAMUTE

Positive characteristics. These dogs are like teddy bears. They are large, furry playmates and enjoy the roughhouse treatment of children. Children have been known to ride them like horses. Although it is not recommended, the breed can take a lot of punishment. These are cold-weather dogs, and can stand being outside the house for many hours during the winter months. Their fur is so thick that they are capable of enduring the coldest temperature without feeling it. However, these big dogs adapt to apartment life very well. They do not require too much exercise and behave lethargically when indoors.

train. Many of them become aggressive. These dogs need the *Negative characteristics.* Malamutes are long-coated and shed a great deal. They are very stubborn and difficult to

firm hand of a strong man. They tend to become dog fighters.

Specific training problems. Although a metal choke collar is required for a firm correction, do not leave it on all the time. It will wear away the fur around the animal's neck.

Malamutes will housebreak satisfactorily if they are walked often and watched carefully during the training period. Obedience training must begin at an early age. These are stubborn dogs and not inclined to please their masters. They will constantly test you to see how much they can get away with. Give immediate praise when a command is obeyed and be exuberant.

If they are not trained properly they will become aggressive. They must not be hit, punished, or bombarded with "No."

There have been several cases where Malamutes have turned on their masters. It is not because they are a vicious breed, but rather because their owners believed a large dog requires harsh punishments.

"Heeling" is one of the most important lessons for these dogs. They grow to ninety or one hundred pounds and can pull you down the street. Be firm and demanding with them at an early age. "Come When Called" off-leash presents a problem. At times they refuse to respond. This command should be emphasized at all times.

Be very firm with them and make them obey as quickly as possible. Do not tolerate a refusal to respond to any command. Firm corrections are needed. The key to training these dogs is to start when they are very young.

BERNESE MOUNTAIN DOG

Positive characteristics. These are wonderful house and apartment dogs. They are very good with children. They have no special medical problems. They have excellent appetites, and live long, normal lives. These ancient Swiss aristocrats are extremely gentle and have even temperaments. Bernese Mountain Dogs are all-weather animals and require a minimum of grooming care. They are very loyal and focus their affections exclusively on their own families.

Negative characteristics. None.

Specific training problems. This is a very sensitive breed. Be patient and gentle in all training commands. Too many hard corrections will make the dog jerk shy.

When using a metal choke collar, do not leave it on the animal for long periods of time. It can wear away the long fur around the neck.

Give immediate praise when a command is obeyed and be exuberant.

BOUVIER DES FLANDRES

Positive characteristics. These large, shaggy animals are fine guard dogs and make excellent house pets. They are open with children and adore family life. Bouviers des Flandres are eager to please and learn quickly. They respond to training better than most breeds. They are in a class with the German Shepherd and the Standard Poodle as ideal domestic pets. They have even temperaments and are exceptionally gentle and loving.

Negative characteristics. The only negative factor is that their long-haired coats require a great deal of grooming which must not be put off. There was a case where a dog had to have his entire coat shaved because of the owner's neglect.

Specific training problems. None. If you show this dog what to do, he will do it. Give immediate praise when he obeys a command and be exuberant.

BOXER

Positive characteristics. Part of the great appeal of this breed is its wonderful facial formation. The sloping jowls and wrinkled cheeks create the most fascinating and heart-warming expressions. These dogs have such open, expressive features that you can tell what they are about to do before they do it. They are excellent dogs for children. They are powerful and can survive a child's play with great ease. Once they have been trained they respond very quickly when a command is given. There is very little grooming required for their short coats. They are sturdy and hearty and have good appetites.

Negative characteristics. The temperaments of Boxers vary from gentle to nervous to aggressive. It all depends on the bloodlines of the individual animal. Be sure of the breeder and the progenitors of the dog before making a purchase. This is one of the breeds that has been hurt by commercialization and inbreeding. Don't be afraid to ask questions or to ask to meet the puppy's dam and sire.

Specific training problems. Boxers are sensitive to corrections. They are also stubborn, which makes training difficult. The younger the dog, the better he will respond to obedience training. Once they reach six months or more, they are going to be set in their ways and offer great resistance to training. Teaching "Down" will be the most difficult command. They do not want to respond to it. Take your time with this command and spread it out over a long period.

Housebreaking will not be a difficult problem if it is started at a very early age.

Wait two seconds after the dog obeys a command to give him praise and be exuberant.

BULLMASTIFF

Positive characteristics. Bullmastiffs are solid-looking brutes that combine size, strength, and even temperaments. They are, in their own way, beautiful dogs. They were originally bred in England as a nonvicious attack dog for controlling poachers on large estates.

However, these are easygoing dogs and make excellent pets for elderly people. Regardless of their size, they are easy to handle. They are good with children and adapt to apartment life very well. They are also very good in the country. Members of this breed make fine guard dogs. They are gentle, alert, and very responsive to training. When kept indoors they are lethargic and sleep much of the time.

Negative characteristics. Because they are so large, they can be a problem if they become too protective as guard dogs. If economy is a consideration, then you must understand the expense involved in feeding these large, hungry animals.

Specific training problems. Training should begin when the dog is very young. Some of them can be stubborn, but this can be overcome in early training before it develops into a mature characteristic. The hardest command will be "Down." But here, too, if the training begins early in the dog's life it will not be a major problem.

Give immediate praise when a command is obeyed and be exuberant.

COLLIE

Positive characteristics. Most Collies live up to their reputation for beautiful temperaments. Naturally, the Collie's public image comes from the many many years of television's favorite dog, Lassie. Because of the Lassie TV series we tend to think of the Collie as a free spirit, roaming the countryside, running and walking great distances. That image is true if the animal is a country dog and allowed to roam around without being kept on-leash. However, the Collie is an excellent city dog, adaptable to apartment living, and not in dire need of much exercise.

Collies are easygoing and get comfortable in one area and stay there. They respond to training very well, obviously. They are wonderful with children and develop lasting relationships. So far, the breeding of Collies has been very responsible, producing a stable, even-tempered, responsive animal. Because they are not too high spirited and are not hard to handle, they make excellent pets for elderly people.

Negative characteristics. Collies are stubborn dogs to train. This opinion, however, is based on experience in training older Collies. They are more willing students when they are puppies. If training is put off they tend to develop aggressive traits (especially if they were ever hit) such as growling, nipping, or even biting. Some of them have turned on their masters.

Specific training problems. You must not leave a metal choke collar on the dog for any great length of time. It will wear away the fur around his neck. A leather choke collar is preferable.

Some Collies develop bad chewing habits when they are left alone. Make sure you are very patient with these dogs and never abuse them. You will create complex behavioral problems if you are too harsh or if you overjerk them. If the dog is too frisky and outgoing before a training session, simply calm him down in a soothing manner. You must use a soft touch. Give immediate praise when the dog obeys a command and be exuberant.

DOBERMAN PINSCHER

Positive characteristics. This breed is endowed with a tremendous willingness to please. Dobermans make formidable adversaries as guard dogs but are also fine companions who do very well with children. Contrary to their bad press, it is not true that they are vicious curs who will turn on their masters. It is only when beaten or abused that members of this breed have used their strength and biting power on their owners.

These dogs have never endeared themselves to anyone who has met them in the execution of their watchdog duties. These unusual animals offer the unique combination of love and protection for their families. In training they will respond to a basic obedience course better, quicker, and with more grace than any other breed. Dobermans have been bred and trained in several ways for various purposes. For example, the companion Doberman is ideal as a house pet and as a psychological deterrent against would-be assailants. There are also protective Dobermans, guard Dobermans, and attack Dobermans. As a unique member of the dog world, the Doberman has proven himself to be a loyal, faithful, and affectionate companion.

Negative characteristics. The negative aspects of these animals result from the breeding of each individual dog. Negative traits are common in Dobermans that have been bred from a line of high-strung and nervous dogs. It is important to examine a Doberman's pedigree before making a purchase. Seeing the dam and sire will help. If the dog is extremely sensitive he will require extra handling around strangers, in cars, and in new environments. Because of his protective nature, he can be regarded as vicious if he senses an impending attack on either himself or any member of his family. This, however, is often regarded as a positive trait.

Dobermans have a very low tolerance for overly strict discipline or abusive treatment. No one other than the immediate family can handle them. In many cases the master is the only one who can give a command. Unless the dog has been bred as a moderate-tempered animal, he must be introduced to strangers, and he will have nothing to do with them in any case. He will merely accept those strangers his master accepts. Often the dog's sensitivity causes nervousness and out of this can come shyness or over-aggressiveness.

It is very important to know why you want this breed. Be absolutely clear about the dog's tasks. They will greatly affect the kind of Doberman to purchase.

Specific training problems. It is important to know your Doberman's temperament. Is he easygoing, friendly, unafraid of noises, crowded areas, other people? If so, he can be trained in exactly the same way you would train most other breeds. A highly sensitive Doberman should be in the hands of a professional dog trainer.

The only difference in technique for the even-tempered Doberman is that the corrective jerk should not be too firm. These dogs are quick to learn and will understand in five minutes what it may take thirty minutes for other breeds to learn. Give immediate praise when a command is obeyed and be exuberant. This is important if they are to keep their good temperaments. They must never be made to feel that they are being punished. The keynote here is to maintain a light touch. Because of their extreme sensitivity they must not be shouted at or handled with abusive authority.

These dogs will not want to "Stay" in the "Sit" position for too long. Use a longer leash and keep praising the dog every moment he stays in position.

The "Down" and "Down-Stay" will require a little more time than usual for this breed. They must be introduced to these commands very gently.

With this breed conduct shorter but more frequent training sessions—two or three times a day are ideal. Dobermans must not be rushed into each command. If this time span is observed the results will be truly rewarding. It must be emphasized that affection and praise are quite necessary. However, a firm "No" must always be applied with each correction. Dobermans will respond to it better than most dogs. They must be taught that you are the boss and totally in control of the situation. If you are afraid of them they will know it immediately and use it as an advantage against you.

The guidelines for Dobermans are:

1. Do not abuse them.
2. Do not pamper them.
3. Make them feel that they are part of the family.

    4. Do not display fear because they will react to it.
    5. Treat them with kindness, praise, and affection.

GERMAN SHEPHERD DOG

Positive characteristics: This is the smartest breed of dog ever
trained by Matthew Margolis. There is no dog more willing
to learn and to respond to all phases of training. They represent everything a good, all-around dog should be. They are
used for the blind, for guard work, for narcotic detection,
and, at the same time, make a truly great house pet. Anyone
can own a German Shepherd Dog. They are wonderful with
children and elderly people. They are good in the city and
the country. They are healthy eaters and live to a ripe old
age. They can adapt to any environment.

Negative characteristics. These dogs are inordinate shedders.
They shed their coats continuously.

    Because they are so popular, an inbreeding problem has
developed over the years. Hip Dysplasia, a hereditary disease,
seems to attack Shepherds more than other large breeds.
This disease, in oversimplified terms, is a congenital dislo-
cation of the hip socket and often cannot be detected until
the animal is past eight months. Recent medical studies
have indicated that overfeeding a Shepherd puppy can be a
cause of Hip Dysplasia. Before purchasing a German Shepherd Dog it is important to discuss the animal's bloodlines
with the breeder. If there is any evidence of Hip Dysplasia
in the animal's background *do not buy it*. There is nothing
more heartbreaking than living with a dog, any dog, for eight
or ten months only to have him destroyed or undergo major
surgery because of this painfully mortal illness. This is a grim
consideration in choosing a German Shepherd Dog. Otherwise, there are no other negative aspects to the breed.

    There are many stories about Shepherds turning on their
masters. Any dog that can be trained to lead the blind cannot
be born with a vicious trait. No animal will remain even tempered if he is yelled at, hit, or beaten, which remains true for
Shepherds, Dobermans, Collies, or Dachshunds. It is important to note that some animals have been purposely made
vicious by their foolish owners.

Specific training problems. Give these animals every chance to learn, reward them with praise, make training a lot of fun, and you will have no problems with the obedience course in the first part of this book. Give immediate praise when the dog obeys a command and be exuberant.

GREAT DANE

Positive characteristics. There are many positive features attributable to the Great Dane. These are fine city and country dogs. Despite their size, they adapt very well to apartment living. Because of their size, they are very lethargic. Consequently, a small apartment does not represent a stifling existence. It is not cruel or unjust to keep a Dane in the city. They are wonderful with children. Their largeness is often overwhelming when they run and jump but their bounciness is always in the spirit of play. They are easygoing dogs with gentle natures. Because of their short coats they are easy to groom. Danes can be used in guard work.

Negative characteristics. There are some medical problems with this breed. Some specimens develop a swelling or soreness around the knees. These swellings are usually filled with water and other fluids. Because they are big-boned animals, they sometimes develop bone disorders and severe callouses. Consult a veterinarian for more details.

The medical history of the animal and his progenitors should be investigated before making a purchase. They are large eaters; one cannot be economy-minded and own a Great Dane.

Specific training problems. Great Danes should be housebroken at three months and obedience-trained at four months.

They are very sensitive dogs and require gentle handling. Too much jerking will make them shy and skittish. Give immediate praise when they obey a command and be exuberant. They should be exposed to traffic, noise, and strangers as young puppies.

These dogs are leaners. For whatever the reason, they like to lean on those closest to them. This can be a problem when they weigh 250 pounds. Decide early whether they are to be allowed this habit or not. Once you indulge it, they are going to be stubborn about breaking the habit. The same applies to jumping on the furniture. It's cute when they are puppies but very disturbing when they reach full size. These are wonderful dogs to own and offer very few training problems.

NEWFOUNDLAND

Positive characteristics. These outgoing dogs are among the finest-tempered, most responsive dogs in existence. They are lovable, affectionate, and very good with children. They will tolerate the abuse that children notoriously dish out. Newfoundlands love to play. They will never react with anger or snappishness to overexuberant children. They are wonderful family dogs and they thrive in the country. Their coats are very thick so they can take the coldest weather with ease and pleasure. In the city they adjust to apartment life with no difficulty because they are lethargic indoors. Most oversized dogs would rather spend the day sleeping or staying put in one place than running and jumping like many of the smaller, restless breeds. For this reason they make excellent pets for elderly people. They are companion, guard, playmate, and loyal friend combined in one magnificent dog.

Negative characteristics. These are very large dogs and require large amounts of food. They are not for the economy-minded. Although well suited for city living, they are not practical in a tiny apartment.

Specific training problems. You cannot be hard on Newfoundlands when training them. They are very sensitive and will become shy and skittish if jerked excessively. Although their great size demands a metal choke collar for training, it should be removed immediately after each session. The metal choke collar will wear the fur away from long-haired dogs.

When teaching the "Heel" or any basic command, take the time to show this breed what to do even if it takes a lot of repetition. It is better to repeat the teaching process than administer too many corrective jerks. Because they are so large does not necessarily mean they require hard correction. Easy correction is suggested because of their great sensitivity. However, this breed is very willing to please and will make hard corrections unnecessary. Give immediate praise when they obey a command and be exuberant.

Commands such as "Sit" and "Down" will take longer to teach. Eventually, they will respond properly. Be patient. Give them time to respond and then lavish a great deal of praise on them. The keynote to training this breed is to give them a lot of love and affection.

OLD ENGLISH SHEEPDOG

Positive characteristics. This breed has become popular because of its unique, furry appearance. These dogs seem to be stuffed animals come to life. The American Kennel Club standard indicates that their coats should be profuse but not excessive. However, it has become fashionable to promote the excessive coat look. Television advertising has, of late, recognized the visual appeal of the breed and uses it in many dog food commercials.

Sheepdogs have good temperaments and are ideal with children. Although they are irresistible as puppies, they become even more appealing as adults and add a woolly beauty to any household. Like many other breeds, they adjust well to city and country life. Because they are so strong, they can take the roughhouse play of children without getting hurt. These sturdy dogs can take a good strong correction and will offer few problems in an apartment.

Negative characteristics. Because of inbreeding, Old English Sheepdogs are sometimes nervous, aggressive, and stubborn. If they have been hit they are capable of having bad tempers and might even be vicious. In some cases both bad breeding and bad handling have conspired to create a very bad specimen. Because these dogs have become so commercialized, the breeding selection has been poor. Many specimens are bred without regard to weeding out the temperamentally unfit. The only safeguard is to become familiar with the animal's progenitors. Do not hesitate to ask questions about the dog's bloodline.

In reference to the animal's handling, it is common sense that an abused dog is eventually going to strike back out of fear and distrust. The answer is obvious. Never hit your dog.

Another negative factor is the required grooming, especially if you maintain that excessive, shaggy look. They do not have that marvelous look after one week of neglect. The fur becomes matted, soiled, dried, and hopelessly tangled. If they are not kept up every day they will eventually have to be completely shaved so that the fur will get another chance. It is costly to have these dogs groomed by professionals. Unless you can afford the cost of a professional groomer, you must be prepared to take on this daily task yourself. These excitable dogs are too difficult for elderly people to handle.

Specific training problems. This is a very stubborn breed and requires great firmness. Training should not begin until they are at least five or six months old. They do not mature until they are at least sixteen months old, thus making early training pointless. This only applies to obedience training. Housebreaking should begin at a very young age.

Do not use a metal choke collar at any time. The heavy metal will wear away the fur around the neck.

Almost every command in the obedience course will result in a struggle between you and the dog. This is especially true of "Down" and "Heel." These two commands should be emphasized. Give immediate praise when a command is obeyed but use a subdued tone of voice.

Sheepdogs should never be allowed off-leash; off-leash training is not recommended for this breed. When purchasing a Sheepdog, understand that it is going to take a lot of work to train him.

PULI

Positive characteristics. Sometimes known as the Hungarian Sheepdog, this breed offers an unusual feature. There are many persons who desire a dog that can tolerate a lot of roughhouse play, but at the same time do not want an oversized animal. These dogs fill that need. They are medium-sized dogs and are not fragile. Both dog and child can play for hours without hurting each other. They are also very responsive to training. Pulis make wonderful watchdogs. They are very protective of their families and demonstrate proper aggressiveness when necessary. Apartment life offers no hardship or difficulty for the Puli. They do not run around wildly or need excessive exercise.

Negative characteristics. Pulis can be too aggressive, almost to the point of viciousness. They are nervous and high-strung animals and are not recommended for elderly people. Occasionally you will find a specimen that is not good with children at all. The best way to purchase one is to deal with a reputable breeder and investigate the animal's bloodline for behavioral traits. When not from good bloodlines, Pulis are difficult dogs to own.

Specific training problems. Even a well-bred Puli is going to be stubborn. If the animal comes from poor bloodlines he may prove to be too nasty to live with. Training must start early in life, and the techniques of fear and punishment will irreparably damage their personalities. If they are hit they will become aggressive and, perhaps, biters as well. Give immediate praise when they obey a command but use a subdued tone of voice.

ROTTWEILER

Positive characteristics. These animals are among the finest guard dogs in the world. They have been bred especially for this work and have proven to be extremely effective. Family life suits them. They have even temperaments and are excellent with children. Because great care has been exercised in their breeding, they are capable of tolerating the rough play of children and even adults. These dogs are very responsive to training and highly tolerant of correction. If you need a very obedient dog and a good protector, then this is definitely the breed to buy. These powerful animals are majestic in carriage and beautiful in appearance.

Negative characteristics. Rottweilers are stubborn dogs. They require a very strong, dominant man's hand to maintain control. The stubbornness is the same as that of some of the hunting breeds.

Specific training problems. Because of their stubbornness, you are going to have to work very hard teaching each command. But the end result is well worth the trouble. They are very responsive to learning and ultimately obey perfectly. Getting through their stubbornness is the problem. They will fight you on each command. When being taught to "Heel," they will try to pull your arm out of its socket. The only answer is a very firm correction each time the dog fails to respond to your command. When practicing the "Heel" place the choke collar high on the animal's neck so that he will feel your corrections. Give immediate praise when they obey a command and be exuberant.

ST. BERNARD

Positive characteristics. The St. Bernard is the greatest bundle of fun in the world. They are phenomenal with children. These gentle dogs are very good in the country. They can endure the coldest temperatures for many hours. However, despite their size they are very good in the city and in an apartment. They are very responsive to obedience training. They want to please and can take a firm correction with no negative reaction. St. Bernards are loving, affectionate, and passive enough for elderly people to handle. They are not nervous or high strung, and because of their lethargic manner are well suited to small apartments.

Negative characteristics. St. Bernards slobber; saliva constantly foams at the corners of their mouths. It can be unappealing, depending on your tolerance for the more earthy qualities of animals. It could also be costly if you have fine furniture and carpeting. St. Bernards shed fur constantly and in large quantities. These huge dogs eat a great quantity of food daily so you should be aware of the cost.

Specific training problems. None. Teach them each command as outlined and they will respond very well. Some St. Bernards are more outgoing than others. The more lethargic the animal is the less willing he will be to please. The reverse is also true. When selecting a puppy try to choose the most outgoing of the litter. He will respond best to obedience training. No matter which puppy you get you will find him easy to housebreak. These are very clean animals. Do not overjerk them in your corrections. One firm correction should suffice for these willing pupils. Give immediate praise when they obey a command and be exuberant.

SAMOYED

Positive characteristics. Samoyeds are among the most beautiful dogs in the world. They have a pure, regal white fur broken only by a black nose and dark, almond-shaped eyes. They are good country dogs, especially in the winter. Their thick fur coats allow them to endure the coldest of climates. They respond well to training and are excellent with children. These rugged dogs weigh between fifty and sixty pounds and easily take the punishment of a child's play. They are easygoing dogs and respond well to the city because they do not require too much exercise.

Negative characteristics. These are very stubborn animals. They completely rebel against being left alone. This may account for their chewing problems. Housebreaking is difficult. As a matter of fact, teaching every command will be a battle between you and the dog. Eventually they will do what you want them to, but it will be a fight to reach that level of training.

Samoyeds require a great deal of grooming. They shed profusely and if their white fur is not cared for the beauty of the animal is lost.

Specific training problems. You must use a metal choke collar because of the need for firm correction. However, remove it immediately after each training session. The metal collar can wear the fur away. A leather choke collar is a good alternative.

The main training problems will be housebreaking and destructive chewing. If you are very patient with them, Samoyeds will ultimately respond well to training. You must be very firm if you are ever to get to that point. These dogs require the authority of a strong man during the training process. They are extremely stubborn. Punishment is no answer to their chewing problems. (See Chapters 13 and 14, "Puppy and Mature Problems" and "Mature Problems Only.")

Give immediate praise when they obey a command but use a subdued tone of voice.

SCHNAUZER, GIANT

Positive characteristics. Giant Schnauzers are one of the three types of Schnauzers. The Standard and Miniature are almost identical to the Giant except, of course, in size. Giant Schnauzers originated in Bavaria, where they were developed from the Standard to work with cattle. Since then they have been highly successful as guard dogs in Germany.

These are large, powerful dogs, and if they are going to be with elderly people, and they can, training is essential. These are good guard dogs and are great with children. They adjust well to country and city life and are not overexuberant. Giant Schnauzers have gentle natures and good, even temperaments. Because they are short-coated, little grooming is required.

Negative characteristics. The Giant Schnauzer is a very independent dog and is sometimes regarded as stubborn. For many owners this is the attraction and would, therefore, be discounted as a negative trait. It depends on one's personal attitude and taste.

Specific training problems. Adjust your teaching efforts to the temperament of your dog. If he is hypersensitive, then you must not be as hard on him as you normally would. If he is extra stubborn, then you must be extra firm. If he is typical of Giant Schnauzers, you need only show him what to do and he will do it with a minimum of correction. Give immediate praise when the dog obeys a command and be exuberant. These are beautiful animals to work with and they will respond very well to training.

SCHNAUZER (Standard and Miniature)

Positive characteristics. Both Standard and Miniature Schnauzers respond very well to training. Except for size, there is little difference between the two. They take corrections very well. Schnauzers are marvelous family dogs. They are very outgoing and affectionate and have a high tolerance for the rigors of a child's play.

These rugged animals are wonderful in the city. They are endowed with a positive kind of aggressiveness. They can be left alone for many hours without becoming lonely or bored. They are very responsive to affection and are eager to please. The more affection you give these dogs the more they will respond to you. Stemming from a work-dog tradition, Schnauzers are fearless and perceptive guard dogs.

Negative characteristics. Schnauzers have a stubborn streak. When they make up their minds to do something it is difficult to stop them. They are very strong-willed animals.

Specific training problems. For some unexplainable reason many Schnauzers have little desire to walk. They stubbornly stand fast and the more you pull the more they fight you. When you pull a dog you are actually choking him. Consequently, the more you choke him the more he's going to fight. If this happens, it is best to drop to your knees and coax the dog along, using playful entreaties and lavish praise. It will make a difference. Schnauzers require patience. Too much authority works against the training. You must show them what to do with patience and affection.

The toughest command to teach this breed will be "Down." Make sure they know "Sit," "Stay," and "Heel" before you teach "Down." However, they do respond to the other commands very well with no hesitation. Be firm with your corrections, but add a lot of praise immediately afterward. Give immediate praise when the dog obeys a command and be exuberant.

SHETLAND SHEEPDOG (*Sheltie*)

Positive characteristics. These miniature Collies are very loving, affectionate animals. They are excellent with elderly people because they are neither excitable nor aggressive. Quite the opposite, they are extremely gentle dogs. We suggest this breed for older children because Shelties are fragile and can be hurt by rambunctious six-year-olds. Shelties are ideal for small apartments. They take up very little space and are fairly docile. These dogs are also very good in the country. The peace and quiet of a rural environmint suit their sensitive temperaments.

Negative characteristics. Shetland Sheepdogs are nervous, hypertense animals, and tend toward shyness. They require extra loving and extra affection. These are not dogs that one can roughhouse with or even pat very hard. They are extremely sensitive. We do not recommend them as a family dog.

Specific training problems. Because of their extreme sensitivity they require tender loving care, especially during the training period. Do not use any form of a choke collar. Be gentle in all corrections; this applies to every command you teach them. This does not mean you shouldn't be firm when giving commands. Simply use a soft touch when making corrections and be sure to lavish them with praise. Give immediate priase when they obey a command and be very exuberant.

Shelties should be trained slowly. Take more time in teaching each command than in looking for immediate results. Otherwise, the result will be a very shy animal.

SIBERIAN HUSKY (*Siberian Chuchi*)

Positive characteristics. Increasing in popularity in the United States and Canada, these remarkably intelligent and gentle animals have the unique ability to adjust to any climate, any set of living circumstances. Siberians are dense-coated dogs capable of enduring the severest cold weather or the hottest temperature. They are a joy to behold in the country, especially in the snow, and yet live remarkably happy lives in the city. These beautiful dogs are usually silver and black (sometimes silver and red) and seem to wear a constant smile on their faces, owing to the unique shape of their lips which curve upward at the back of the mouth.

They are naturally gentle and friendly, rendering them useless as watchdogs but distinctive as warm, loving companions. Most silver- and black-colored Siberians have a black "mask" of fur around their eyes, which, when contrasted with the white fur of the head, gives them a menacing look that has often scared away a potential troublemaker. These North Country beauties are almost human in personality and engage in deep, meaningful relationships. They are the all-time pet for children. Sturdy and playful, they not only endure the rough play of children, they demand it. These dogs will go out of their way to sniff around a child, even a stranger, and entice him into playing. To hear the wolf-howl, or "singing," of a Siberian Husky is to be irresistibly drawn to him for life.

Negative characteristics. Siberians shed their thick coats several times a year and make a mess of expensive carpeting. It is impossible to brush up against one when you are in a dark suit without walking away with pounds of white fur on it.

These dogs sometimes develop into very picky eaters. If they do not have the company of another animal to eat with, or do not like what they are being served, they will go without food to the point of near-starvation. Huskies are extremely stubborn and hardheaded about having things their own way. For this reason they are not recommended for elderly people or for permissive men and women.

If not trained with great firmness and discipline, Huskies will pull your arm from its socket to get to another animal on the street or perhaps to some prospective playmate. They also do not tolerate being left alone for long periods of time. When this condition exists they will chew anything they can get to, including baseboards, curtains, and any number of household appliances. They are very high spirited and easily bored. Sometimes another animal is the only way to prevent their destructive behavior. Another dog or even a cat may do the trick.

Specific training problems. A metal choke collar is the only effective equipment for administering a correction. Bred for pulling heavy sleds, their collar and neck muscles are well developed and they will feel only the firmest correction. However, the metal collar must be removed immediately after each session as it tends to wear away the fur around the neck.

Occasionally an individual Husky has a hard time being housebroken. Huskies demand constant attention and many walks during the housebreaking period.

These dogs learn quickly and respond beautifully to training. However, they retain their self-willed independence and cannot be relied upon to obey every command even after the most arduous training program. They require frequent brush-up lessons to remind them who is boss and what is expected of them. They will test your authority every chance they can. Because they are so lovable and endearing, they will use all the wiles at their disposal to avoid obeying a command and to get their own way. Firmness and authority are the keynotes for controlling these dogs.

You must not allow yourself to indulge them when they violate their training. This will be the hardest thing about owning these magnificent childlike creatures. They will run, jump, or sing to distract you, and they too often succeed.

Wait one second after the dog obeys a command to give him praise and be exuberant.

———————◆———————

AIREDALE TERRIER

Positive characteristics. In a physical sense, these are probably the best of the Terriers. They are tall, dignified animals with a rugged, beautiful stance. Airedales make excellent guard dogs. They are very protective of their homes and families and make a lot of noise whenever an intruder crosses the family threshold. They are fearless in any confrontation. They never back down. An almost perfect family dog, Airedales respond to training very well because of their even temperaments and quick responses. These remarkable dogs are wonderful in the country mostly because of their keen hunting abilities. On the other hand, they adapt well to city life and get along with children. To groom their rough wire coats, simply brush daily.

Negative characteristics. Like all Terrier breeds they are very stubborn, strong-willed, and independent. Unless they are taught obedience with a firm hand, they are not very enjoyable to have around. They get spoiled and try to dominate their households. Some are very finicky eaters.

Specific training problems. Airedales are very good house pets. They are always responsive during training and are very alert. They are willing to please. Most problems can be avoided if training begins early, if they are taught what to do, and if they are made to obey and not allowed to ignore any commands. Give immediate praise when they obey a command and be exuberant. If you allow a year or a year and a half to go by before training, you will have many difficult problems ahead of you.

BEDLINGTON TERRIER

Positive characteristics. This uncommon breed has a very unusual appearance. Its blue-gray coat (sometimes liver color) is curly on the head and face and forms a topknot which is indicative of the breed. To the novice, this dog might look like a lamb. These very lovable dogs are rarely seen outside the home of a true fancier or the show ring.

Bedlingtons afford their owners the opportunity to answer all manner of questions from many uninitiated admirers. Unlike other Terriers, Bedlingtons are not terribly aggressive or high spirited. They are very easygoing and ideal for city life. They are also well suited for elderly people and children.

Negative characteristics. Like all Terriers, the Bedlington has a stubborn quality. Whether this is negative depends on each owner's respective point of view.

Specific training problems. Because these dogs are stubborn and strong-willed, you must be firm in all corrections. However, exercise patience during the training period. Give the dog plenty of time to learn each command before initiating any corrections. Wait two seconds after the dog obeys a command to give him praise and be exuberant.

Bedlingtons will test you quite often, so you mustn't be afraid to correct them. They are very sturdy little dogs and can take any reasonable correction. The trick is not to over-jerk them.

BULL TERRIER

Positive characteristics. It is accepted as fact that the Bull Terrier was created by mating a Bulldog with the now-extinct White English Terrier. The Spanish Pointer was later introduced to the line, as was the all-white specimen, to create the breed as we see it today. There are those who compare this dog with figures on an Egyptian wall carving and others who liken it to a carved face on a white squash. (What's so lovable about a white squash?)

To those who really know the breed, these animals are

friendly, affectionate, and good-natured. And certainly to those who own them or have owned them, they are beautiful brutes. These lively dogs are marvelous with children and are well suited to apartment life. Because they are so frisky, they also make excellent country dogs. They are gentle dogs who have short coats and require very little grooming.

Negative characteristics. Not everyone is suited to owning a Bull Terrier. It is suggested that you learn more about the breed on a first-hand basis before deciding this is the dog for you. (General George Patton took a fancy to this breed during World War II.) They are stubborn, like all Terriers, but for many fanciers that is interpreted as independence and is therefore considered a positive characteristic.

Bull Terriers were originally bred for pit fighting when it was a gentleman's sport in nineteenth-century England. The instinct to fight still remains, even though the sport does not. These animals make excellent guard dogs. However, once they are trained for that purpose they become very deadly weapons, and that's something to consider before going into it.

Specific training problems. Although these dogs are willing to learn, they still have the stubborn streak that is indicative of all the Terriers. They will resist each command you try to teach. This stubbornness can only be overcome by patience and firmness. Take each command slowly, but let the dog know who is boss in the situation. Give immediate praise when they obey a command and be exuberant.

CAIRN TERRIER

Positive characteristics. These mighty little dogs were developed in Scotland and, despite their small size, were bred as fine hunters. Cairns have sporting instincts with a good ability for vermin killing. It was a Cairn Terrier that appeared in the motion picture *The Wizard of Oz* as Judy Garland's dog. They are lovable and very devoted animals. They relate well to children and elderly people. Cairn Terriers adapt well to both country and city life and make excellent house pets. Their wiry coats require very little grooming.

Negative characteristics. None.

Specific training problems. As with almost all Terrier breeds, they have that aggressive, stubborn quality that makes them tough, scrappy little animals. You must be firm. Four months old is not too early to start their training. Do not overjerk any dog that is very young. Be gentle and patient. Give immediate praise when they obey a command and be exuberant.

DANDIE DINMONT TERRIER

Positive characteristics. This unusual Terrier breed was given its name by Sir Walter Scott. In *Guy Mannering,* one of his romantic novels about Scotland, the character Dandie Dinmont kept six of these small Terriers. The novel's success in 1815 immortalized the breed as Dandie Dinmont's Terriers. The breed itself was first immortalized by Gainsborough in 1770 when he painted a beautiful specimen in his portrait of Henry, third Duke of Buccleuch. Once a favorite hunting dog in Scotland and England, Dandie Dinmonts retain all the qualities of an excellent family dog. Very yappy, they make good watchdogs. They are wonderful for children and elderly people, and are truly the perfect apartment-size dog.

Negative characteristics. None.

Specific training problems. These dogs can become stubborn if they are not trained at an early age. Four months old is not too early to start their training. Do not overjerk any dog that is very young. Be gentle and patient. Give immediate praise when they obey a command and be exuberant.

FOX TERRIER *(Wire and Smooth)*

Positive characteristics. These small dogs, among the most popular in the world, are very sturdy and respond to training very well. They are capable of accepting a correction without being ruffled. Fox Terriers are adaptable to the city and are very well suited for long walks. Once they have been trained they do not pull on the leash, are easy to control, and do not get skittish. Although they are spirited animals, they are very good for children and elderly people. They are compact and travel easily. Their outstanding characteristic is their outgoingness, their desire for love and affection. They require very little grooming.

Negative characteristics. Fox Terriers are constantly yapping. They are nervous, high strung, and at times aggressive. Almost a reflection of our time, they do not know how to relax. They seem to suffer from hypertension.

Specific training problems. Because these dogs are so small and affectionate, they become spoiled by being overindulged. Owners tend to pamper them to the point where training is useless. Once they are spoiled they become stubborn and strong-willed. You must maintain self-control with this breed. You must maintain discipline, especially during the training period. Do not use a choke collar. Either a leather or nylon collar will suffice. Corrections must be firm but not severe. A strong vocal correction with a gentle corrective jerk will do the job. Wait four or five seconds after the dog obeys a command to give him praise and use a subdued tone of voice. Chewing and housebreaking are the most difficult problems to solve. Begin training at an early age; three months is suggested.

KERRY BLUE TERRIER

Positive characteristics. Kerry Blue Terriers represent the paradox that exists in the world of purebred dogs. These rare and elegantly groomed creatures, seldom seen out of the show ring, come from circumstances far less chic than the dog arena. Originating from the mountainous regions of County Kerry, Ireland, Kerry Blues were used for sheep and cattle herding, retrieving, and for killing rats, badgers, and rabbits. And yet, today they are true expressions of status and elegance when seen in a large city.

Despite that, they make excellent companions and house pets. They take to elderly people very well and enjoy all the roughhouse play of children. Strong and protective, they make fine guard dogs. Kerry Blue Terriers possess matchless beauty in their blue-black, curly coats. Many women compare their fur to Persian lamb. They never shed.

Negative characteristics. They are one of the most stubborn of all the Terriers. Kerry Blues are also very aggressive toward other dogs. They are constant dog fighters and require a very strong hand. Only women who are willing to be firm at all times should consider this animal. Under no circumstances should this breed be indulged. They take great advantage of those who spoil them.

Specific training problems. This is one of those breeds that absolutely requires a choke collar. You must use the choke collar firmly on every command. They can take firm corrections and must be made to understand that you mean business. Give immediate praise when they obey a command and be exuberant.

Teaching "Down" will present the biggest problem. They do not want to respond to this command. Extra patience and extra time will be required. Spread the lessons out for this command. Two a day for a week are not excessive. Give as many lessons as necessary for the dog to learn the command and to respond to it properly. Be patient and firm. It is also suggested that you select a training site that has no distractions. It will make the task that much easier for you and the dog.

SCOTTISH TERRIER

Positive characteristics. Legend has it that the Scottish Terrier is the original breed from which all the Scottish and English Terriers descend. Although it cannot be proven conclusively, many owners of the breed will swear it is true. These staunch little dogs are very popular in the United States. One was seen in the White House during the long administration of Franklin Delano Roosevelt.

They are very affectionate and make excellent companions and house pets. They are good in the city and the country. Their compact size and even temperaments make them ideal for children and elderly people.

Negative characteristics. Scottish Terriers do not like being left alone, which can create problems for those who must go to work every day, leaving their dogs to their own devices. They also have a difficult time being housebroken. These dogs manifest the traditional Terrier stubbornness.

Specific training problems. Extra time and patience will be required during the housebreaking period. Scottish Terriers have to be watched constantly for indiscretions. The minute the dog begins to mess, you must startle him with the "throw can," say "No" in a firm voice, and take him outside immediately. Other than that, they are very responsive to training and have no special problems. Give immediate praise when they obey a command and be exuberant.

SEALYHAM TERRIER

Positive characteristics. It is hard to believe that the elegant dog we see in the show ring, the one with the long, silky white fur was originally bred to kill vermin. The Sealyham originated in Wales and is named after the estate of its first breeder. Developed from an obscure ancestry, Sealyhams became proficient at exterminating badgers, otters, and foxes. It is, no doubt, these beginnings that created the Sealyham's instinct for guard work. They are excellent watchdogs and very perceptive at determining friend from foe.

In the home they are second to none as loving, loyal pets. They respond to training very well and have a great willingness to please. Sealyhams make excellent pets for children. They have a great propensity for play and a physical stamina for the rough treatment of children. The Sealyham is a unique breed and not too commonly seen.

Negative characteristics. The only negative aspect of this breed is the one that is characteristic of all Terriers: stubbornness.

Specific training problems. The most difficult command to teach them is "Down." It will require extra effort, patience, and much praise. Reinforce every command you teach with great affection. If you merely apply the corrective jerk when things do not go well, you are going to have a terrible fight on your hands. Like most Terrier breeds, Sealyhams will test to see how much they can get away with. Be firm. Use a choke collar. However, remove the collar immediately after training sessions, otherwise their fur will wear away at the neck. Give immediate praise when they obey a command and be exuberant.

WEST HIGHLAND WHITE TERRIER

Positive characteristics. Many dog fanciers consider the West Highland the best of all the Terrier breeds. These little dogs are surely the model for those fancy stuffed dogs sold at exclusive toy stores. They are among the best dogs for apartment living. They are compact, yet rugged, high in intelligence, and faithful to the end. West Highlands, with their marvelous temperaments, are ideal for children and elderly people. They are gentle, responsive, and beautiful.

Negative characteristics. None.

Specific training problems. They do not have the typical stubborn quality indicative of most Terriers. You merely have to show them what to do and they will do it. Give immediate praise when they obey a command and be exuberant.

Group V

Toys

CHIHUAHUA

Positive characteristics. The most obvious fact about this very special breed is its size. These dogs are ideal for those who want as little dog as possible in their lives without giving up the notion entirely. They are tiny creatures with "apple-domed" heads, and they range from one to six pounds.

The smaller Chihuahuas will fit into a jacket pocket or a woman's handbag. These frail creatures were introduced to nondog fanciers in the United States by Xavier Cugat and his Latin American orchestra. In most of his films the popular band leader held the dog in his arms during his musical numbers. This helped make the breed fashionable. They may be the best house pets for elderly people owing to their size and ability to be easily controlled.

Negative characteristics. Probably the most negative aspect of this breed is learning to spell Chihuahua. Although they are affectionate, they do not warm up to more than one or two people. Because these tiny animals are so pampered and spoiled (they are carried everywhere), they become insecure and frightened of anything unfamiliar. This causes them to withdraw from everyone but their owners. Dogs very often express their fears through aggressiveness, and that sometimes is the case with Chihuahuas.

Specific training problems. They are very difficult to train. They are trainable up to five or six months old. After that it is not really worth the trouble. However, they rarely have need for some of the obedience commands such as "Heel."

Give immediate praise when they obey a command and be exuberant.

MALTESE

Positive characteristics. Of all the Toy breeds, the Maltese is probably the brightest, the most responsive, and the most beautiful. Originating on the Island of Malta, this breed has been known as the aristocrat of the canine world for twenty-eight centuries. Through ancient and modern history, the Maltese has been associated with the cultured, wealthy, and powerful. They are truly the princes and princesses of the dog world.

Their long silken coats are of the purest white fluffy fur. Although they are officially classified as Spaniels, they may have a touch of Terrier, judging from their instinct for hunting. Looking like delicate porcelain figurines, these graceful dogs prance from room to room with mercurial speed. Their tiny appearance is misleading, however. They are sturdy dogs with great stamina and hearty appetites. They are clean, refined, and faithful. They are wonderful for elderly people and ideally suited to apartment life. Known to the Phoenicians, the Greeks, and the Romans, these beautiful creatures are historically famous for their sweet temperaments.

Negative characteristics. Of all the breeds this one tends to be pampered and spoiled the most. Consequently, they become insecure and totally dependent on their masters. Grooming them is a big job. Their long white fur can be a nightmare to deal with if neglected for even the shortest period of time. Their coats get matted and their eyes stain the white face fur. There is a great deal of daily work involved in keeping this dog beautiful.

Specific training problems. Never use a choke collar with this breed. They are too delicate.

Housebreaking will be the biggest training problem. Because they are so small they are usually paper-trained. However, after a while they tend to have many indiscretions. If you change to housebreaking once the dog has been paper-trained, you will experience great difficulty. The only answer is to keep a watchful eye on the animal no matter which technique you use, and continue to implement the training until the problem is resolved. The best answer would be to select one kind of training and remain consistent to it.

Give immediate praise when they obey a command and be exuberant.

PEKINGESE

Positive characteristics. Like collectors of rare, Oriental art objects, the Pekingese owners love to expound on the many esoteric facts and fantasies surrounding this breed. For example, the oldest strains—which were bred by the Imperial Family of China, dating back to the Tang Dynasty—were kept pure, and the theft of one of the "sacred dogs" was punishable by death. The Pekingese of today, though descendants of Oriental royalty, are more common among American dog fanciers and pet owners than their progenitors were among Chinese peasants. These unusual-looking dogs make excellent house pets, and are very well suited to apartment living. They are good with children, though they are best for elderly people.

Negative characteristics. Their long, silky coats require a great deal of grooming. Be prepared to spend a lot of time with a brush in your hand. They have a strong stubborn streak and can be very noisy when a doorbell rings.

Specific training problems. Gentleness is the keynote to training this breed. You must never use a choke collar for them. Pekingese are very willing to learn, but they are sensitive and should not be jerked too hard. Give immediate praise when they obey a command and be exuberant. If you take the time to teach them the basic commands, you will always have a responsive, disciplined pet.

Because of their size, paper training is suggested rather than housebreaking.

POODLE (*Toy*)

Positive characteristics. The most obvious factor here is size. The Toy Poodle is the smallest of all the various Poodles. For many potential dog owners, size is the most importa) consideration. As the name implies, these are tiny animals and measure under ten inches at the shoulder. It is important to note that all Poodles are similar in every way, except size. (See "Poodle [Standard and Miniature]" listed in *Group VI: Nonsporting Dogs*.)

Poodles are very affectionate dogs and are excellent with elderly people. They are also good with children, but perhaps the larger ones are more capable of enduring the rough-house play. Poodles are the only dogs that do not affect those who have various allergies. These dogs are very gentle, loving animals and set the standard for all house pets. They are among the best dogs.

Negative characteristics. They are usually spoiled by their owners and become stubborn and yappy. They will bark at the least bit of disturbance and insist that things be done the way they want them. This only happens when they are treated like human babies.

Specific training problems. These animals require discipline and the obligation to obey all commands. If they are indulged like spoiled children they will never be trainable. The key-note to training Poodles is to treat them like animals, not children. However, you must not use a choke collar on Toy Poodles. They are simply too delicate. Give immediate praise when they obey a command and be exuberant.

PUG

Positive characteristics. Can a dog with a pushed-in face, small brutish body, and loose lines of flesh around the shoulders be considered beautiful? Ask any Pug owner. Pugs do not need coddling and have adapted to various working tasks not expected of a Toy breed. These dogs are affectionate in a quiet, dignified way. They are good in a brace because the tend to get along with other dogs. Many owners keep two. They adapt very well to the city and make wonderful family pets. They are short-coated and require very little ⁀ming.

⌐ ‑aracteristics. They suffer from a shortness of ⁐en sounds like asthma. Because of their breathing difficulties, Pugs cannot be left alone in a closed car, even with the windows slightly open. They will suffocate. If you have occasion to travel frequently, this is not the dog for you.

Specific training problems. Never use a choke collar with this breed. Because of their breathing problem the training sessions must be very short. No lesson should last longer than five minutes and the dog must not be jerked very much. You may give two five-minute lessons within a one-hour period.

Do not train these dogs where there are distractions. The objective is to try to avoid as many corrections as possible. Be gentle and patient. Wait three seconds after the dog obeys a command to give him praise and use a subdued tone of voice.

SILKY TERRIER

Positive characteristics. The Silkys are very loving, affectionate, and outgoing dogs. They are true lap dogs, even though they have been used in their native Australia as workers, hunting rats and snakes. These compact animals are completely portable and travel well. They are also wonderful pets for small apartments. Silkys are small but very sturdy and capable of taking a great deal of abuse from children. They are ideal as an all-around family pet.

Negative characteristics. Like most Terriers, they have a stubborn streak. Housebreaking will be problematic. Their long silken coats bear constant care and grooming. Keeping the dog indoors is often the only solution to excessive grooming.

Specific training problems. Do not use a choke collar; use a leather or nylon collar and leash. These dogs can be excitable and consequently will be distracted very easily. Try to keep their attention. In the early phase of training use a quiet street or the privacy of your home. Once they learn the commands, you can work them outside where there are noises and strange people. Their stubborn quality must be met with firmness when they disobey. Wait two seconds after the dog obeys a command to give him praise and use a subdued tone of voice. Train them at an early age.

YORKSHIRE TERRIER

Positive characteristics. These diminutive aristocrats were developed as a breed late in the nineteenth century, but won early acceptance among the wealthy families of the Victorian era. Even today these spirited sprites appeal to the more fashion-minded pet owners and dog fanciers. "Yorkys" are very often kept as decorative lap dogs with no function other than raising the status of their owners. Nevertheless, Yorkshire Terriers are wonderful pets for children and elderly people. Because they are of the Terrier bloodlines, they are sturdy and have lots of spunk. They are equally at home in the country and the city. These dogs are extremely intelligent.

Negative characteristics. Yorkshire Terriers are difficult to housebreak. They manifest the same stubborn streak prevalent in most Terrier breeds. Because they have such long, silky coats, they require a great deal of grooming and constant watching. Many owners keep their "Yorkys" indoors to avoid extra grooming.

Specific training problems. They are aggressive and yappy. Their most difficult command is to "Heel." They dart from side to side and back and forth when being walked. You must be firm, demanding, and patient when teaching this command. Wait two seconds after the dog obeys a command to give him praise and use a subdued tone of voice.

It is recommended that you housebreak these dogs right at the start. Although they have difficulty being housebroken, they are even less reliable if paper-trained. They still have mishaps long after the training has ceased. During the housebreaking period they bear constant watching and many walks.

Do not use a choke collar; they are too delicate. Because they are stubborn, begin training at an early age. Be firm and patient. Most corrections should be vocal. Do not overjerk them. Because these dogs are so small and precocious, owners tend to spoil them. Once you do, they will never be trainable.

Nonsporting Dogs

———◆———

BOSTON TERRIER

Positive characteristics. The Boston Terrier is one of the very few purebred dogs developed in the United States. Like most original Yankees, they were developed from English stock. They are a cross between the Bulldog and the English Terrier. In existence only since the Civil War, they have firmly secured a place for themselves in the world of purebred dogs. Though very powerful, Boston Terriers are small in size. They range from fifteen to twenty-five pounds.

These unusual-looking animals were used for many many years as the advertising symbol for Buster Brown Shoes. *"I'm Buster Brown, I live in a shoe. This is my dog Tige, he lives there, too."* Many children grew up with the Boston Terrier in mind as the ideal child's dog because of this ad slogan. Despite the slogan, it happens to be a fact. They are lovable animals and are wonderful for children. They are gentle but rugged dogs. They make excellent pets for elderly people, too. For those who are looking for a small, lively dog who does not require too much exercise, this is it.

Negative characteristics. Like most Terrier breeds, the Boston manifests that stubborn, aggressive streak. They are also extremely sensitive.

Specific training problems. These dogs have a difficult time being housebroken. They must be watched carefully and walked frequently. Because of their stubbornness, you must be firm and constant in making them obey. Take your time with each command and give them lavish praise whenever they respond correctly. Wait two seconds after the dog obeys a command to give him praise but be exuberant.

BULLDOG

Positive characteristics. Until 1835 this breed, like so many others in England, was used in cruel sports—in particular, bull baiting—and it created a tough, vicious animal. However, since their sporting days ended, Bulldogs have been bred for their stately physiques and sweet natures. There is probably not a gentler and more even-tempered dog in existence. Although the current specimens look nothing like their athletic progenitors, the original stamina, intelligence, and courage remain. These stocky brutes with their pushed-in faces, flapping jowls, and barrel-shaped bodies snort out their love and affection as they scare the pants off any potential attacker. Bulldogs are wonderful with children because of their very playful spirits. They can take all the punishment a child can dish out. Although they are delightful to watch in the country, they also make wonderful apartment dogs. They respond to training very well.

Negative characteristics. Most people pass up this breed because they do not like their physical appearance. The Bulldog looks mean (even though he isn't) and difficult to manage (which he is not). They do slobber, and for the fastidious housekeeper they are problematic. They also have a bit of a breathing problem.

Although this breed is the national dog of England, it does not possess the table manners of the very proper English people. Bulldogs are sloppy eaters and make the most intriguing sounds at dinnertime. If not trained early they can become unmanageable and problematic.

Specific training problems. Because of their great physical strength they are capable of taking the firmest correction. However, they are sensitive in nature and should not be overjerked. Bulldogs can be very stubborn and must be dealt with in a firm manner. Training should begin early. When it does, you will find them very willing students who will respond to vocal corrections and praise. Wait two seconds after the dog obeys a command to give him praise and do not be over-exuberant. They respond so well to training that it is almost effortless to teach them a new command. Once they understand that they must respond to you they will, and then training is a pleasurable occasion.

CHOW CHOW

Positive characteristics. These dogs were given their name in a very undignified manner. When trade was first opened with China, the term "Chow Chow" was pidgin English for any sort of gewgaw or bric-a-brac that filled the British ships' holds on their return to England. Among the imports were these rare and magnificent dogs that date back two thousand years in recorded Chinese history. They were lumped in with all the porcelain figurines and bamboo back-scratchers; the entire cargo was called "Chow Chow." Today the pidgin English term also graces the label of certain pickle jars, denoting a mixed assortment of sweet and sour dills.

Despite these indignities, the Chow has gained wide appeal throughout the Western world and is universally accepted as a fine watchdog. Faithful to Chinese traditions, these dogs quickly develop deep-rooted loyalties and strong protective emotions about their families. Because of this quality they make the ideal guard and companion dog. When groomed properly they are among the most striking and beautiful creatures in the dog world. Chows also respond very well to training. After you've owned one, fifteen years later you will want another.

Negative characteristics. Because these dogs are very aggressive, they are not ideal for everyone. Unless you match their aggressiveness with equal firmness they will end up dominating the household. These are remote and aloof animals who do not need or desire any undue expressions of emotion or play. Their blue-black tongues and set scowls do not always endear them to the average pet owner. They are not ideal for those who are purchasing their first dog. They require a true "dog person" to own them. By that is

meant a strong, firm individual who has owned several dogs
before.

Specific training problems. Chows require training at a young
age, when you have complete control of them. They are very
responsive dogs and learn anything you teach them. However,
they are stubborn and require a strong, firm hand. Give immediate praise when they obey a command and be exuberant.

DALMATION

Positive characteristics. Named after a province in Austria,
these dogs may represent the oldest unchanged breed in dog
history. Although many areas of the world claim these dogs
as an indigenous breed, they are generally accepted as Aus-
trian. This firehouse mascot has been nicknamed the English
Coach Dog, the Carriage Dog, the Plum Pudding Dog, and
the Spotted Dick. In the United States he is known as the
Firehouse Dog. These nicknames usually indicate the various
jobs and activities the dogs have been involved in.
    These spotted beauties make ideal pets in the city and the
country. They are obedient, responsive to training, and wonderful with children. They are capable of taking the pounding
of a child's play. They possess keen memories and are endowed with a willingness to please.

Negative characteristics. Dalmations shed a great deal and
are very stubborn dogs. One of the physical defects of the
breed is deafness. For some genetic reason many of them are
born this way. Before purchasing a puppy it is a good idea
to check for deafness. Because of so much inbreeding they
can be nasty, aggressive animals. Some poor specimens have
been known to bite children. Before making a purchase investigate the qualities of the prospective dog's dam and sire.

Specific training problems. Despite their stubbornness, they
are responsive and desire to please. They will require a slow,
firm approach to training. You will have to be a little more
forceful because of their excitability and nervousness. These
dogs require a strong, firm hand. Wait three seconds after
the dog obeys a command to give him praise and use a subdued tone of voice.

KEESHOND

Positive characteristics. Native to Holland, these "barge dogs" were largely unknown as a breed until the Dutch political leader of the nineteenth century Kees de Gyselaer used his own Keeshond as a political symbol of the lower and middle classes. The breed then went into obscurity for over a century, as did the party represented by Kees de Gyselaer. Keeshonds made their comeback in the early part of the twentieth century and were accepted as a pure breed in 1933.

These lively and intelligent animals make ideal companions in that they have no desire to leave their master's side. They are very furry in appearance and have wolflike coats. Keeshonds are very loving and affectionate. They are even tempered and responsive to training. They are not nervous or distracted by traffic and fare very well in city life. These rugged dogs get along very well with children and make ideal family pets.

Negative characteristics. They are stubborn, but not excessively so.

Specific training problems. Remove the choke collar immediately after each training session. It will wear away the fur around their necks.

Apply the basic training techniques, give them a lot of praise and affection, show them what to do, and they will respond beautifully to the training. Wait two seconds after the dog obeys a command to give him praise and do not be overexuberant.

LHASA APSO

Positive characteristics. The Lhasa Apso presents a rare combination of good qualities in a dog. They are small, hardy, rugged, frisky, intelligent, and very very beautiful. They are not lap dogs, even though they have become extremely fashionable in big-city apartments. They are ultra-elegant animals found among the chic and the wealthy.

These Tibetan dogs are loving and affectionate. Despite their small size, they are not fragile like so many of the Toy breeds. They can take a great deal of roughhouse play and for that reason are wonderful for children. These versatile dogs are very responsive to training and are completely portable. They can be taken anywhere on long trips with a minimum of inconvenience. Lhasa Apsos are very even tempered and fare well in the city.

Negative characteristics. If they are hit or overjerked when corrected, they will become aggressive and growl, snarl, or even bite. If they are hit they will bite whenever anyone tries to touch them. Grooming requires a very gentle hand or else the dog will get pinched when the brush is run through his long hard hair. Anything that pains the dog will make him aggressive. There is a great deal of grooming involved in keeping up this breed's appearance.

Specific training problems. If training begins at a young age and with a good deal of love and affection, you will have no problems. They must never be hit or corrected severely. If you are going to train a Lhasa Apso that is one year old or over, you must exercise great patience and take your time in teaching each command. Give immediate praise when they obey a command and be exuberant.

POODLE *(Standard and Miniature)*

Positive characteristics. Although this breed originated in Germany, it is considered the national dog of France. In France it is called *caniche*. There is little difference between the Standard and the Miniature Poodle except size. The Standard Poodle is fifteen inches or more at the shoulder and the Miniature is between ten and fifteen inches at the shoulder. The oversized Standard is informally called the Royal Standard.

These dogs are intelligent, frisky, dignified, and very elegant-looking. Some owners prefer their coats grown out, despite the fact that most adhere to show requirements which insist on the "Continental" clip or the "English Saddle" clip. Poodle fur does not affect a person with allergies.

In sheer numbers, the Poodle is probably the most popular breed in America. They are extremely intelligent, brilliant in training, and very desirous to please their masters.

Poodles are good family dogs. They get along very well both with children and with other animals. Many people own more than one. City life appeals to this breed. In major urban areas such as New York and Chicago, they represent status. There is no dog more cosmopolitan-looking than a poodle. They bring the boulevards of Paris with them no matter where they go.

Negative characteristics. Because they are so primped and pampered, they get spoiled by many of their owners. Otherwise, there are no negatives.

Specific training problems. None. These dogs are brilliant. Show them what to do and they will do it. Give immediate praise when they obey a command and be exuberant.

SHIH TZU

Positive characteristics. The exotic Chinese name Shih Tzu means lion dog. Certainly a cousin to the Tibetan Lhasa Apso, these long-haired Toys have only recently come into their own in the United States. They can quite literally serve as toys for careful, well-behaved children. They are excellent for elderly people. The Shih Tzu is a very fashionable dog appearing in the most expensive homes and apartments. Despite their size they can be enjoyed in the country where they will run and play vigorously. These warm and even-tempered animals are very responsive to training and are completely portable. Shih Tzus are the perfect traveling companion since they cause no traveling inconvenience.

Negative characteristics. They are difficult to housebreak.

Specific training problems. Never use a choke collar on these delicate animals.

Housebreaking is problematic. You must choose whether to housebreak or paper train them and then stick with your choice. During paper training you will find that from time to time they forget to use the paper. When that happens you must go back over the training and reinforce what they have already been taught.

Give immediate praise when they obey a command and be exuberant.

Index

SIGNET Books for Your Reference Shelf

☐ **THE DOG FOR YOU: America's Most Popular Breeds by Bob Bartos.** No matter what kind of dog you are looking for, renowned dog expert Bob Bartos provides you with all the information you need about 50 of the top American breeds to help you choose *The Dog For You*. Illustrated.

(#J9130—$1.95)*

☐ **KING SOLOMON'S RING by Konrad Z. Lorenz.** A modern classic on animal behavior by a scientist whose gifts for storytelling and communicating with animals have made him famous. "Charm . . . lightness . . . carries the reader along with sustained and fascinated attention."—*The New York Times* (#J9052—$1.95)

☐ **HOW TO TALK TO YOUR CAT by Patricia Moyes.** Interpret the meaning behind the sounds and body movements your cat makes and learn to respond in ways your cat understands. . . . "Charming . . . for cat lovers of all ages."— *Library Journal* With delightful illustrations by Nancy Lou Gahan. (#W8560—$1.50)*

☐ **HOW TO KNOW THE AMERICAN MARINE SHELLS by R. Tucker Abbott.** Revised edition. A definitive guide to the shells of our Atlantic and Pacific coasts—featuring a digest of shell-fishery laws, a list of shells by location, full-color photographs, and black and white drawings. (#W6528—$1.50)

☐ **THE SIGNET/HAMMOND WORLD ATLAS.** See the world at a glance! Includes full-page, full-color maps of every country and continent; maps of all fifty states, plus the Canadian provinces; and special maps indicating world distribution of population, occupations, languages, religions, climates, and natural vegetation. (#E8150—$2.95)

* Price slightly higher in Canada

Buy them at your local

bookstore or use coupon

on next page for ordering.

SIGNET Gardening Books

☐ **THE WEEKEND GARDENER by D. X. Fenten.** Based on the series published by Newsday, the Long Island Newspaper. In this year-round guide for the part-time gardener are 25 fascinating projects of interest and challenge—each of which takes no more than a weekend to launch. For both the beginning and the experienced gardener, the complete guide to growing healthy trees, flowers, fruits and vegetables. Complete with how-to illustrations. (#W6953—$1.50)

☐ **THE ROCKWELL'S COMPLETE GUIDE TO SUCCESSFUL GARDENING by F. F. Rockwell and Esther Grayson.** Complete with illustrative photographs and line drawings, here is the book that busy homeowners have been waiting for. Now at last, whatever your project or problem, you can quickly flip the pages to find the specific information you need without laborious hunting. (#E7780—$2.25)

☐ **HOUSE PLANTS FOR FIVE EXPOSURES by George Taloumis.** The complete guide to lighting—and living with—your plants. Illustrated with many photographs, this book offers hundreds of ways to make your indoor greenery flourish like the great outdoors. A Selection of the American Garden Guild and the Woman Today Book Club. (#W6374—$1.50)

☐ **THE APARTMENT GARDENER by Stan and Floss Dworkin.** The total guide to indoor planting that will tell you how to pick plants that grow beautifully indoors, when water is your plant's worst enemy, all about those plants that love to hide in dimly lit corners, raising plants from pits and seeds, and hundreds of other plant-growing and protecting tips that can put a little bit of the country into apartment living. (#E8414—$1.75)